The Dominicans

The Dominicans

by

Benedict M. Ashley, O.P.

A Michael Glazier Book
THE LITURGICAL PRESS
Collegeville, Minnesota

The cover and illustrations in this volume are the work of Brother Placid
Stuckenschneider, O.S.B.

Religious Order Series

Volume 3

The Dominicans

A Michael Glazier Book

published by

THE LITURGICAL PRESS

Typography by Phyllis Boyd LeVane and Mary Brown.

1	2	3	4	5	6	7	8	9

Library of Congress Cataloging-in-Publication Data

Ashley, Benedict M.
    The Dominicans / by Benedict M. Ashley.
        p.   cm. — (Religious order series ; vol. 3)
    "A Michael Glazier book."
    Includes bibliographical references and index.
    ISBN 0-8146-5723-0
    1. Dominicans—History. I. Title. II. Series.
BX3506.2.A84   1990
271'.2—dc20   90-62034
                                                                  CIP

271.2
Aut

Contents

ST.
DOMINIC

Foreword

In our pluralistic age we recognize many traditions have special gifts to make to a rich, well-balanced spirituality for our time. My own life has shown me the spiritual tradition stemming from St. Dominic, like that from his contemporary St. Francis, provides ever fresh insights. No tradition, however, can be understood merely by looking at its origins. We must see it unfold historically in those who have been formed by that tradition in many times and situations and have furthered its development. To know its essential strength, we need to see it tested, undergoing deformations yet recovering and growing.

Therefore, I have tried to survey its eight centuries to give some sense of its chronology and its individual personalities, and of the inclusive Dominican Family. I have aimed only to provide a sketch to encourage readers to use the bibliography to explore further, but with regret I have omitted all documentation except to indicate the source of quotations. Translated quotations are mine.

I thank Sister Susan Noffke, O.P., Fr. Thomas Donlan, O.P., for encouraging this project and my Provincial, Fr. Donald Goergen, O.P., and my Prior, Joseph Gillespie, O.P., along with my brothers of St. Louis Bertrand Priory, St. Louis, especially Benjamin Russell, O.P., and also William Conlan, O.P., for reading the manuscript, and the faculty and staff of Aquinas Institute of Theology and PARABLE for supporting its completion.

1

Founder's Spirit

Blessed Cecilia Caesarini, who was received by St. Dominic into his new order, in her old age described him thus:

> He was thin and of middle height. His face was handsome and somewhat fair. He had reddish hair and beard and beautiful eyes. From his forehead and eyes shown a sort of radiance which drew everyone to respect and love him. He was always cheerful and alert, except when he was moved to compassion at the sight of someone's troubles. His hands were long and fine and his voice pleasingly resonant. He never got bald, though he wore the full tonsure, which was mingled with a few grey hairs.

Our knowledge of Dominic de Guzman's life is chiefly based on the *Libellus* of Jordan of Saxony, his successor as head of the Order of Preachers which Dominic founded. Jordan knew Dominic personally and wrote only about twelve years after his death, but had not been one of his close companions. The *Libellus*, although written to promote Dominic's canonization in 1234 is disappointingly sketchy. It tells us more about the origins of the Order than the personality of the founder. Unlike the Franciscans, the early followers of St. Dominic never showed much interest in their founder's cult and seemed to have feared that too much popular devotion to him might hinder the mission he had entrusted to them.

Dominic was born between 1171 and 1173 in the Castilian village of Caleruega, son of Felix de Guzman and Jane of Aza of the Spanish nobility. Christian Spain was still struggling to free itself from Moorish occupation and, even for a knightly family, life was austere in that stark, dry region where Felix as local lord owned little more than range land, a few flocks of sheep, and the manor house and tower (still standing) which served to guard the land. Jane of Aza was noted for her concern for the poor and was regarded by the local people as a saint. When Dominic was seven his education was put in charge of Jane's brother, a priest, and when he was fourteen he entered the school at Palencia, one of the few higher schools in Spain at that time and soon to become a university, where he studied liberal arts and theology for ten years. He lived a rather bookish life but during a time of famine sold his books to assist the poor. In 1196, when he was about 24, he joined the cathedral chapter of Osma.

The canons of the Cathedral were priests associated with the bishop who had recently reformed their community life to live strictly in poverty according to the Rule of St. Augustine. The prior and reformer of this chapter was the remarkable Diego de Azevedo who in 1201 became bishop of the diocese. It was he who had noticed Dominic the student and obtained permission of the former bishop, Martin Bazan, for him to enter the chapter and in a few months to be ordained priest. Soon Dominic was appointed sacristan, then sub-prior, thus gaining useful experience in administration and the work of reform. In 1203 when Alfonso VIII of Castile requested Bishop Diego to travel to Denmark to arrange the marriage of his son to a Danish princess, the bishop naturally chose the young priest to be his companion on the long, dangerous journey.

The journey proved the turning point in Dominic's life, opening his eyes to a wider world and its problems. As they passed through southern France they encountered a shocking situation. While Dominic knew of the Moors and Jews in Spain, here he met former Christians who had become alienated from the Church and converted to the religion of the

Cathari (Pure Ones), often called Albigensians from their stronghold at Albi.

This strange cult had its remote origins in the Gnosticism over which the Church had triumphed in the second century but had then passed through the Manichaeism of Persia to the Paulicians of Armenia, then in the ninth century to the Bogomils of Bulgaria, in the tenth to Constantinople, then in the twelfth with the Second Crusaders to northern Italy, France, and the Rhineland, and finally was achieving its greatest success among the nobility of southern France. There it took the form of a radical dualism according to which the visible creation was attributed to an evil god.

Salvation for an elite of the "Perfect" or "Pure" was to be achieved by an extreme asceticism and poverty, but for the majority, who lacked the courage for such a life, by receiving in the hour of death a special sacrament, the *consolamentum*, administered by the Perfect. This doctrine permitted most of its adherents to live much as they pleased until death, while pointing to their Perfect as exemplifying a holiness which utterly discredited the worldly clergy of the Catholic Church.

One night at an inn in Toulouse, Dominic engaged in a discussion about these doctrines with an innkeeper (who was probably a deacon of the Catharist church). Dominic was so moved by meeting this man deluded by the myth of two gods, one good but remote and hidden, and the other evil but creative, that, weary as he must have been after hours on horseback, he sat up all night talking with him and by dawn had won him back to the true God revealed in Jesus Christ.

From Denmark, Diego and Dominic returned to Spain with news of their mission accomplished, only to be sent back two years later to fetch the princess, and then to find that she would not return. Their time in Scandanavia, however, taught them that to the east there were vast pagan territories waiting for the Gospel. Consequently, on their return journey they went first to Rome to beg the great Pope Innocent III to let them go on the missions together, but he refused, saying the bishop was needed back home. Diego, however, decided to return by way of the famous abbey at Citeaux in France and there received the Cistercian habit, probably in order to induce some of the monks to work in his diocese.

St. Dominic

On the way back to Osma at the city of Montpellier in June 1206, Diego and Dominic met the Abbot of Citeaux and two of his monks who had been sent by Innocent to preach against Albigensianism. These three complained to Diego that they had no success in their preaching, chiefly because of the great reputation for holiness which the Perfect enjoyed among the people. Diego gave them a straight answer. They must not abandon their mission but must counter the Catholic clergy's bad example, by preaching as the Apostles had done, barefoot and begging. The Cistercians replied that they did not have the courage for this unless Diego would show them how—which he, with Dominic, proceeded to do.

For four years the band of preachers traveled about southern France preaching and holding public disputes with the Perfect. It was said that on one occasion the judges for one of the disputes threw the books in which Dominic and his opponents had written their briefs into a fire, and only Dominic's survived the test. In 1207 the preachers were joined by no less than twelve other Cistercian abbots and they separated into smaller bands, and Diego and Dominic, along with a companion, William of Claret, centered their preaching on the town of Prouille. Here Dominic soon gathered a group of about twelve ladies converted from the cult who wished to continue their ascetic life as Catholic nuns, but needed protection from their families. In the same year Diego finally returned to Spain, probably with hopes of returning with new recruits, but died there December 30, 1207.

Three weeks later one of the Cistercians, Peter of Castelnau, was assassinated at the behest of the Count of Toulouse whom he had tried to persuade to oppose the heresy. As a result Innocent III in 1209 launched a crusade against the noble supporters of the heretics under the leadership of Count Simon de Montfort, Earl of Leicester, a hero of the Fourth Crusade. De Montfort took up residence in the hilltop town of Fanjeaux near Prouille where he met and admired Dominic, who became a spiritual adviser of two of his daughters, one a nun. He baptized another daughter and married the Count's son to a royal princess of France. In gratitude the Count gave land and gifts to the convent at Prouille. Unfortunately, Simon, who was on the outlook for an estate, because his mother's lands in England had been withheld from him, soon turned the Crusade into one of conquest rather than conversion. It became a terrible bloody and exhausting civil war which was to last for many years.

In these troubled times, even after the Cistercians had finally returned home, Dominic went on preaching. Sometimes he stayed at the convent in Prouille which in 1213 he rebuilt and where William Claret was his companion. But most of the time he was on the road. At the canonization process at Toulouse three women, Guillelmine Martini, Noguera of Toulouse, and a nun of Saint Croix named Beceda, testified to having given him hospitality many times (probably during 1210-11) and observed his extreme poverty and rigor of life and his frequent exhaustion. He was often threatened with death and was reputed to have performed miracles and successful exorcisms.

Dominic had won the confidence of the local bishops (who were Cistercians) and during 1213 he was made vicar of Carcasonne and in 1214 parish priest of Fanjeaux. By this time he was beginning to see he needed a regular group of helpers and planned to locate them at Fanjeaux, but in 1215 he was called to Toulouse by the Cardinal Legate to preach. Here a certain Peter Seila invited Dominic and several companions Dominic had managed to gather one by one to live in his own house (still standing) which thus became "the cradle of the Order."

In this same year, 1215, Dominic accompanied Bishop Fulk of Toulouse to the IV Lateran Council in Rome and with the help of Cardinal Ugolino (the future Gregory IX, who also sponsored St. Francis of Assisi), gained permission to found an Order of Preachers, provided they would conform to the decree of the Council against new orders by accepting one of the traditional rules. Innocent III, one of the most far-sighted of the Popes, saw in Francis (to whose order he had given oral approval in 1209) and Dominic, whose fidelity to the Holy See he recognized, the solution to the problem of the itinerant preachers over which he had long pondered. Dominic himself seems finally in Rome to have seen (it is said by a vision of St. Peter and St. Paul he experienced in the Old St. Peter's) the universal meaning of the Order for which he had so long served an apprenticeship.

On returning to Toulouse he held a meeting of his companions who now numbered about 16 and announced to them (perhaps at Pentecost) an astonishing decision, which brought protests from the bishop and even from Simon de Montfort. Dominic had been warned in a vision that the Count would soon be killed and the work of preaching in the region stopped by civil war. Moreover, his new concept of the Order gained in Rome determined him to make a daring move—to disperse his brethren so recently formed into an Order, throughout Europe. The Spaniards included his brother Mannes who joined him before the end of 1207; Dominic the Little of Segovia; Miguel de Ucero, a native of Osma; Miguel de Fabra, a noble, learned enough to be later the first teacher in Paris; Pedro of Madrid; John of Navarre. Sueiro Gomez was a Portuguese knight who had come to France as a crusader. From the south of France were the saintly Bertrand Garrigue who was already a preacher against heresy when Dominic arrived on the scene; William of Claret of Pamier who had been with Dominic from the beginning of his preaching; Peter of Seila of Toulouse who had received the Order into his house; Matthew of France, a canon from the University of Paris who had come with De Montfort; Thomas of Toulouse, an especially gifted preacher; Noel of Repouille, prior at Prouille, who drowned the next year; Vitalis of Prouille, Stephen of Metz, and William Raymond. There were also Lawrence of England, far from home, and the first lay brother, Odier of Normandy, who had been a crusader.

Of these, Dominic kept William Claret and Noel at Prouille, Peter Seila, Thomas of Toulouse and perhaps William Raymond at St. Romaine's; but he sent Pedro of Madrid and Sueiro Gomez as a pair, and Miguel de Ucero and Dominic the Little as another to Spain. To Paris he sent Matthew of France (who had the title of "Abbot" of St. Romaine) and Bertrand Garrigue, and with them as students Lawrence and John of Navarre. John refused to go without money, much to Dominic's distress. In another party he sent Mannes, Miguel de Fabra, and Odier.

Dominic then set out on foot to Rome to obtain further papal privileges to make the work of the Order more effective and to overcome the opposition that had immediately appeared in Paris to the coming of the friars to the University. Successful in this, in 1218 he began a visitation of his dispersed men. Dominic the Little and Miguel de Ucero had already returned from Spain. Bertrand Garrigues and John of Navarre had come from Paris to report on the situation and Dominic then sent them to Bologna thus beginning a center at the second great university in Europe. Dominic, after visiting Bologna, and Prouille, went on to Spain where he set up a house of friars and another of nuns, and in Segovia, Palencia, and San Esteban de Gormaz more houses of friars. To the nuns of Madrid he wrote a short letter, the only writing, other than legal documents, which we have of his, urging them to a strict cloistered, contemplative life and protecting their control of their monastery. He had gathered a group of friars at Guadalajara but they quickly fell away, although through his prayers most returned.

From Spain he returned to Toulouse from which houses at Lyon, Montpellier, and Bayonne were soon to develop. Here he met Bertrand again and traveled with him to Paris, on the way somehow preaching to German pilgrims, although he did not know their language. In Paris under Matthew he found no fewer than thirty brethren, including Henry of Marburg, the first German friar, and Guerric, who was to found a house at Metz, Peter of Rheims, a future Provincial of France, Étienne de Bourbon, to be a famous preacher, and William of Monferrato, a theologian with whom Dominic two years before had discussed going on the missions. While Dominic encouraged study he also sent some of the brothers on missions from which new houses were soon to arise.

Dominic in August 1219 went to Bologna which would remain his home for the rest of his life. Here he found a large community including no less than four Masters from the University. This growth was due to Master Reginald, a teacher of canon law in Paris whom Dominic had previously met at Rome where Reginald had come on pilgrimage to the Holy Land. Reginald had later fallen sick, but in a vision was healed by the Virgin who showed him the habit of the Order which Dominic therefore adopted. Reginald had gone on to Jerusalem but then returned to Bologna where his preaching drew many vocations. Dominic immediately sent him back to Paris to deal with the difficulties in the university.

The community in Bologna had its troubles, including demonic incidents which, after Dominic's death, led to the establishment of the Salve Regina procession. Several of the brethren got the idea they should become Cistercians but were dissuaded by Reginald and Roland of Cremona who was to become the Order's first Master of Theology at Paris. Here Dominic also met a rich young lady, Diana d'Andalo who obtained a grant of land from her father for a monastery of nuns of the Order which she wished to enter in spite of much opposition from her family.

Dominic soon went to see the Pope at Viterbo for more letters of recommendation for his brethren now so widely scattered. The Pope sent him to Rome to reform a convent of nuns at San Sisto Vecchio in Rome and with the assistance of some nuns from Prouille he made this his third foundation of Dominican women. By this time his health was beginning to show signs of decline, worsened by grief over news of

Reginald's death in Paris, but the Pope made him head of a preaching mission composed of men from several religious orders.

Before starting this mission, Dominic had to return to Bologna for the First General Chapter of the Order with about thirty delegates, already including two from Scandinavia, which met on Pentecost 1220. Dominic first attempted to resign and was refused, but a system of four "definitors" was set up to assist him. At this Chapter it was established that the *Rule* and *Constitutions* were not to bind under sin and that all provisions were dispensable for the sake of the preaching mission. The *Constitutions* was written in two parts: the first covering liturgy and asceticism borrowed from the Premonstratensians but with appropriate modifications; the second, very original, covering the government of the Order. The supreme power of the General Chapter to legislate and the office of the Master of the Order were established. Strict mendicancy was adopted and immediately put into practice by giving up all revenue-producing properties. The studies at Paris were also regulated.

Dominic then proceeded to the preaching mission of the Pope in Lombardy which was also a territory where the Waldensians (an evangelical sect) and Albigensians were powerful, but found the country involved in war and in preparation for a crusade to the Holy Land. His work was cut short by his third illness in a year, and in 1221 he returned to Rome to report to the Pope and to finish the work of establishing the nuns at San Sisto, a community which included Sisters Blanche, Constance, Nubia, Theodora, Thedrana, Nympha, Maximilla, and Sabina.

Dominic was also seeking assistance to found more houses throughout Italy and dealing with a problem of brethren deserting the Order. It was probably at this time that he met St. Francis of Assisi, who was also a friend of Cardinal Ugolino, the future Gregory IX, who had assisted in getting papal approval for both mendicant Orders. After Easter the friars took up residence at the wonderful fifth-century church of Santa Sabina, on the family property of Honorius III, where they built a cloistered convent in which the cell of Dominic is still preserved. In front of San Sisto, Dominic miraculously raised from death or near death a young man, Napoleon, hurt in a horse race.

In May 1221 Dominic returned to Bologna for the Second General Chapter of the Order which set up eight provinces: Spain, Provence, France, Lombardy, Rome, and probably Hungary, Teutonia, and England. This Chapter missioned Master Paul of Hungary, prior of Bologna and canonist who at the request of Dominic had compiled a *Summa de Penitentia* for the education of the brethren, along with Blessed Sadoc, to Hungary, Solomon of Aarhus with some German brothers to Denmark, Gilbert Ash with companions to England, and Jacek of Opole (St. Hyacinth) and his brother Ceslaus and Henry of Moravia to Poland. By the sixth Chapter there were added the "minor" provinces of Jerusalem, Greece, Poland and Dacia and so the twelve remained to the end of the century.

After the Chapter Dominic continued to travel and preach and had the joy of receiving Diana d'Andalo into the Order and founding her convent of St. Agnes in Bologna. On July 28 he again fell sick and was confined to bed on August 1. Because of the intense heat in the city the brethren moved him to the Benedictine priory of Monte-Mario. On August 6 he called Prior Ventura, confessed, spoke to the brethren, asked to die at home, and was carried to the convent of St. Nicholas, where he again promised the brethren he would intercede to God for them and then died on the evening of the August 6, not yet fifty years old. Jordan of Saxony was elected as his successor, and at the initiative of Gregory IX Dominic was soon canonized in 1234. At the moving of his body a very well attested miracle occurred in the sweet odor of sanctity which filled the entire church and lingered for days.

Besides Dominic's predominant trait of compassion of which I have already written, what was his personality? He left us no writings, except the letter already mentioned to the nuns of Madrid and some letters of penance to heretics he had converted. Moreover, he seems to have been reticent to speak of his spiritual experiences. But his character is clearly manifest in the *Constitutions* which I will describe in more detail later and in testimonies of the witnesses at the process of canonization, as well as in the life by Jordan of Saxony, who, although he had not known Dominic long, carefully reported what he had heard from those who knew him well.

From these sources we gather that what was most evident to others was that Dominic's compassion for people in their spiritual needs fired him with a consuming desire to preach. To his last days he was constantly on the road, often walking barefoot as much as 35 miles a day, taking the frequent hardships cheerfully, and ready to be martyred for the Gospel. We do not know what his preaching was like except that it moved his audience and himself to tears. Yet it was often rejected by the heretics. He constantly urged his brethren to share in this same mission, even sending out novices to preach, but at the same time very much concerned to have them educated and to encourage them to study that they might preach well. At the end of his life his vision had grown to lead others not of his Order to preach and to extend this to the missions of the pagan east. He wanted nothing to get in the way of this task and therefore tried to turn the administration of the Order over to lay brothers and to resign as Master, and he repeatedly refused offers of the episcopate.

The second mark of his life was his prayer. He was convinced that preaching without prayer would not be effective. An early work called the *Nine Ways*, which is supported by the other evidence, shows that he loved to pray with his whole body, kneeling, prostrating himself, holding up his hands in various gestures. He prayed on his journey, sang hymns, and at night, even after a long day's journey spent hours in the church in prayer, and even slept there. He sang Mass frequently, often with tears, and he loved the Hours to be sung with spirit. His devotion to the Blessed Virgin established in the Order the tradition that eventually took a popular form in the holy rosary. He loved to keep silence and urged this on his brethren. Several witnesses repeated in the *Acts of Canonization* that "he spoke only of God or to God." Yet it is also clear from these testimonies that he was always approachable, friendly, and ready to encourage and console.

The third mark was the penitential character of his life, which also was associated with preaching, since he believed it was necessary as a witness to the truth of the Gospel. In addition to the hardships of his traveling and its dangers, he was merciless on himself with regard to fasting (in Lent on bread and water), and even when sick never ate meat. He wore a hair shirt, a chain, and frequently used the discipline to blood when praying at night for those he hoped to convert. His confessor testified that he was a virgin, but he admitted on his death bed that he had perhaps been more pleased to talk to young women than to old. Then he regretted that in thus trying to warn his brethren of the need to guard chastity he had seemed to boast.

Linked to his asceticism was his insistence on poverty. He himself had begged from the beginning of his mission in France, but only gradually came to insist on it for his Order. He wanted the friars to be poor in clothing, housing, food, and even their churches and liturgical vestments. On these points of ascetic observance he was very strict, although gentle in his corrections, and ready to dispense, but only in view of the preaching mission or the actual weakness of the brethren. On his death bed he promised to be of more use to his brethren than in life, but left them as his legacy, "Cherish love, preserve humility, possess only the poverty you have freely chosen."

After his death the early brethren understood very well that Dominic desired no cult of personality in his Order, since the real way to honor his memory was to carry on the "holy preaching."

Spirituality of the Order

Numerous attempts have been made to characterize the spirituality of St. Dominic and his Order. The noted theologian Reginald Garrigou-Lagrange interpreted it by St. Thomas Aquinas' formula, *Contemplata aliis tradere*, "To give to others what one has contemplated," and emphasized its metaphysical foundation in the love of truth and of St. Thomas' profound insight into the difference between Creator and creature, the supernatural and natural orders, and the growth in holiness through the Gifts of the Holy Spirit. Similarly others have taken as their key St. Catherine of Siena's report that God said to her, "I am He who is, and you are you who are not." Père Régamey, summing up the noted historian Père Mandonnet's thought, says that "Dominican spirituality is enlightened, theological, contemplative, personalistic, supernatural, apostolic, liturgical, and ascetic." More recently, Fr. Edward Schillebeeckx says that the "golden thread" which runs through Dominican history is:

(a) Trust in God not self.
(b) Evangelical living which proclaims the Gospel.
(c) Spirituality directed toward Jesus, especially in his humanity.
(d) Presence to the world, contemporaneity.
(e) Respect for created reality in its own right.
(f) Respect for individual gifts (hence dispensation).
(g) Religious observances and community life common to all religious orders but in a Dominican mode.

These characterizations seem too much colored by the preoccupations of the various writers. Fr. M.-H. Vicaire takes a very objective, historical approach based on Dominic's life and the *Primitive Constitutions* and groups these traits under the motto "To speak with God and of God":

1) With God
   a) Conversion.
   b) Penance.
   c) Common life (poverty).
   d) Study.
   e) Contemplation.

2) Of God
   a) Love for souls.
   b) Mendicant preachers.
   c) Mobile soldiers of the Church (clerics).
   d) Shepherds of the hungry.
   e) Identification with Jesus, the goal of life.

After Vatican II in the Chapter of River Forest, (Chicago, 1968), the Order revised its Constitutions (with the advice of Vicaire) on the following very significant plan:

Book I: Life of the Brethren
 Section I: The Following of Christ
         Chapter II: Liturgy and Prayer
         Chapter III: Study

Chapter IV: Ministry of the Word
Chapter V: Relation to the Dominican Family
Section II: Formation of the Brethren

Book II: Government of the Order

This raises an important question, discussed in recent years also by the Franciscans. In past reforms of religious orders "reform" always meant a return to "the primitive observance." But Vatican II instead spoke of "renewal" as a "return to the spirit (charism) of the founder." The reason clearly is that Vatican II theology has followed the lines of Cardinal Newman's theory of "the development of doctrine" and emphasized the necessary historical development of spirituality. We cannot simply return to "primitive observance" in a literal fashion because we cannot simply isolate ourselves from the changing world. To attempt to live literally like Dominicans or Franciscans of the thirteenth century would mean becoming museum pieces. In fact it is impossible, because novices today have never had the experiences of those times, and we cannot remake them from infancy. The spirit of the founder, however, remains alive today and must be expressed in appropriate forms.

Renewal of course does not mean simply jettisoning all traditions, because historicity itself demands that the present Order retain its identity not only in spirit but materially by incorporating elements of the past. Thus the Franciscans discuss whether St. Francis' emphasis on poverty is more fundamental, or whether deeper still is his Christocentricity which was made theologically explicit after his death by St. Bonaventure and Bl. Duns Scotus, while the effort to cling literally to this poverty seems to have produced serious aberrations. The same question has been raised whether the Order of Preachers is best characterized by St. Dominic himself or by St. Thomas Aquinas!

The writers of the 1968 *Constitutions* struggled with this question and finally stated their views in what they called the "Fundamental Constitution" of which the first four paragraphs must be quoted as the most authoritative present statement of the essence of the Dominican Order:

1. The purpose of the Order was described by Pope Honorius III in writing to St. Dominic and his brethren in these words: "God, who continually makes his Church fruitful in new children, wishing to bring our times into conformity with earlier days and spread the Catholic faith, has inspired you to embrace a life of poverty and regular observance and to devote yourselves to preaching the Word of God and proclaiming the name of our Lord Jesus Christ throughout the world."

2. The Order of preaching friars founded by St. Dominic "was recognized from the beginning as having been established particularly for preaching and the salvation of souls" (*Primitive Constitutions*). So, according to the bidding of their founder, our brethren "live everywhere like upright religious men who seek their own salvation and that of others and, like the men of the gospels, following in the footsteps of our Lord, speak to God or about God among themselves and with others" (*ibid.*).

3. To perfect our love and neighbor in the following of Christ by religious profession we are enrolled in the Order, completely consecrated to God, in a new way dedicated to the whole Church and "totally engaged in spreading the word of God" (Honorius III).

4. Because we share in the mission of Apostles, we also follow their way of life as St. Dominic conceived it: with one mind leading a common life; faithful to the evangelical counsels; fervent in the common celebration of the liturgy, especially the Eucharist and the Divine Office, and in prayer; committed to a life of study and constant in religious observance. All these practices contribute not only to the glory of God and our own sanctification, but are of direct assistance in the salvation of others, since they prepare and impel us to preach, they inform our preaching and are informed by it. These elements are all inter-connected; they modify and enliven one another and in their total harmony are the life of the Order. In the fullest sense this is an apostolic life in which teaching and preaching ought to spring from the fullness of contemplation. . . .

9. The Dominican family is composed of clerical and cooperator brothers, nuns, sisters, members of secular institutes and lay and priestly fraternities [although the *Constitutions* legislate only for the religious brethren and are intended to give] "unity to the Order without denying appropriate diversity."

This unity is preserved through the office of the Master of the Order (paragraph 6) and a communitarian form of government (paragraph 7). Paragraph 6 also states that religious brethren are constituted of ordained priests who share in the "prophetic function of the episcopacy" by their preaching and administration of the sacraments and cooperator brothers who through their baptismal priesthood also share in Christ's preaching mission. Hence, the talents of all the brethren are to be developed and used in the Order's mission. The *Constitutions* do not bind under sin and may be dispensed or changed in view of the preaching mission, provided the features stated in the *Fundamental Constitutions* are retained (paragraph 8).

As this *Fundamental Constitution* and the life of St. Dominic make clear, the "spirit of the founder" was the great desire to identify with Jesus Christ and his Apostles in the mission of preaching the Gospel. Fr. Vicaire in his book *The Apostolic Life* has shown that a return to this life has been the constant theme of every Church renewal and in a particularly literal way of the rise of the mendicant orders in the thirteenth century. St. Francis and his followers were shining examples of this renewal and in the Franciscan Orders, St. Francis, marked by the stigmata, is seen as the eschatological image of Jesus in His naked poverty, humility, and abasement, in which image the Risen Christ is joyously glorified as the very center and goal of all creation. St. Francis was not a priest, nor originally were most of his followers, but they sought to witness to God by presence to the world, carrying on whatever work they were occupied in before their conversion. Some like St. Francis himself preferred the contemplative, eremitic life. On the contrary, Dominic was from the beginning a priest called to ministry. He was not seen as a symbol, but simply as the leading member of a band called all of them to share in the common imitation of Jesus in his preaching activity. For St. Francis preaching was limited to a simple exhortation to conversion, but for Dominic it was a share in the whole prophetic range of the office of the apostles and bishops.

The Ministry of the Word

Historically, however, there has been no little discussion about the meaning of preaching. After the time of St. Thomas Aquinas, as we shall see later, the emphasis tended to shift to the notion that the purpose of the Order was "preaching *and* teaching," and that the nobler element was teaching in the sense of lecturing and writing on philosophical and theological topics. Often, "preaching" came to be conceived quite narrowly as preaching in church during the liturgy and it was urged that specifically Dominican preaching is "doctrinal," i.e., directed to the intellect and to intellectuals. Moreover, some were puzzled that this one Order could be specified by its activity of preaching, when most religious orders of men and all the secular clergy are supposed to preach. Others distinguished "preaching" from "teaching" by saying that teaching appeals only to the intellect, preaching principally to the heart. Others pointed out that in time the Order took up many kinds of work, including parochial care and the conduct of schools, and asked, therefore, whether in fact "Dominican work is what Dominicans do."

These confusions not only trouble the Dominican Order but they confuse what type of spirituality it can contribute to the whole Church. To clear them up we must first remember the teaching of Vatican II that all Christians by reason of baptism and confirmation share in the universal priesthood of Christ, the one true priest. As High Priest the services of Jesus and therefore of all Christians are threefold: to proclaim the Gospel (the prophetic office); to build the Christian community (the kingly or shepherdly office which includes all the corporal works of mercy); to praise God and sanctify humanity (the priestly office as such). Of these the third is the ultimate and highest, but the first is the most necessary, since without preaching there can be no faith, and faith is the foundation rock of all Christian activity. This is why Jesus, as founder of the Church, chose the office of preaching as his own principal task.

What preaching proclaims is not any human truth, not even that of theology, but is the Word of God. This Word is the Good News (Gospel) of the coming of the Reign of God, a Reign which is already realized in Jesus Christ, the Word made flesh in order to manifest the Father in our world in His life, death on the Cross, and rising to everlasting life. "We preach Christ crucified," as St. Paul said (1 Cor 1:23). Consequently, "preaching" in St. Dominic's sense must never be understood either vaguely or narrowly. It includes whatever truth reveals God through Jesus. Since Jesus came to bring the Good News even to the poor, Dominican preaching must extend to every class of human beings, rich and poor, learned and ignorant, young and old, according to their needs and capacities.

Nor is Dominican preaching in any way restricted in time, place, or mode. "I charge you to preach the word, to stay with this task whether convenient or inconvenient—correcting, reproving, appealing—constantly teaching and never losing patience" (2 Tm 4:2). St. Dominic preached not only in church or at Mass, but in private homes, open air, everywhere. Nor did he confine himself to one mode of communication. He conversed, debated, orated. And in time Dominicans were to use every available medium to communicate the Word and every opportunity. What counts is not that the Gospel should be shared by word, writing, picture, whatever, but that it should be communicated in a way that can be understood and change the receiver.

Yet this does not mean that St. Dominic regarded any useful ministry as preaching. He refused to be a bishop, and he constantly strove to keep his men single-mindedly at the task of communicating the Word. Any other activity for him was a waste of time unless it contributed significantly to this one purpose. As we shall see, the Order has always struggled to be true to this single purpose, broad as it is, and not lose its energies in other activities, however noble or necessary. Yet for this same reason there was never any thought preaching should be a *monopoly* of the Dominican Order. Dominic first preached with the Cistercians and others and at the end of his life was the leader of a band made up of men of many orders. Preaching is a duty of every bishop and priest; the Order of

Preachers cannot monopolize it, but seeks to give an example, to train others, and to stir up others to preach, even to the least members of the Church according to their gifts and calling. The Order arose because this fundamental task of the Church was being neglected and it strives to waken all to do their part.

Thus what Dominican spirituality can contribute to the spirituality of the whole Church is an understanding that to be a Christian is to be evangelical, to live in the Word and by the Word and to speak the Word to a world that longs for Good News. It is the spirituality of the *Gospel of St. Matthew* and the *Epistles of St. Paul*, Dominic's favorite reading.

The second element of Dominican spirituality which is very evident in all its sources, is that preaching, as the *Constitutions* say, "is a communitarian work and hence primarily the responsibility of the whole community." St. Dominic learned from his own experience that preaching cannot be done successfully by isolated individuals for two reasons. First, it is difficult and those who preach must have the support of others in their training, their temptations to preach not Christ but themselves, their weariness and discouragement, because it is a frustrating and thankless task. It requires the contribution of many talents and the individual speaker or writer is only the voice of a much larger activity. Secondly, and more profoundly, because the preaching of the Reign of God becomes credible only when the persons who speak have themselves experienced that life of love in a community. Jesus preached to the crowds out of the love he shared with his apostles. Hence not every Dominican must preach directly. In fact in the early days not only the cooperator brothers but many of the priests did not preach. What was important was not "What am *I* doing?," but "Is the Gospel being preached and am I contributing *something* to getting this job done."

Community in the mendicant orders meant something different from that in the earlier monasteries. The monks (as the name *monachos*, solitary, shows) were originally hermits who came together only to support one another in their contemplative life, which remained always centered in silence and solitude. The abbot was the spiritual father who guided his children to the perfection which he in a degree had already attained. In the modern congregations of which the Society of Jesus is the leading example the primarily active character of the life tends to subordinate the life within the community to the tasks at hand, so that each member executes the work assigned him with the guidance and support of the community through its superiors with fraternal assistance when needed but without dependence on living together.

The medieval mendicant brotherhoods, on the other hand, conceived of community in a way intermediate to these extremes. They retained the monastic choral liturgy, the chapter at which community affairs are aired, common recreation, a degree of community study, and a centering in contemplative quietude, while at the same time engaging in a very active ministry. This rhythm of contemplation and action tended to produce a *horizontal* network of relations different from the vertical relation of abbot to monk, or officer to soldier. In a healthy Dominican community (and they are not always so) there is a *conviviality* of prayer, of study, and of mission which we see reflected in the atmosphere of early Dominican life and which was evidently created by Dominic himself, in spite of his personal love of silent vigils.

The third characteristic of this life which Dominic so clearly exemplified was dedication to *prayer*. Dominic retained the monastic liturgy of the Hours and community Eucharist (which modern communities were to privatize in order to free themselves more for their work), although he was willing to dispense brethren from attendance at every service in view of study or preaching. Preaching must flow from contemplation of the Divine Word to be preached and this is most perfectly expressed in community worship based as it is on meditation on the Bible and the commemoration of the great saving events of Christ's life and their imitation by the saints. In addition Dominic spent long hours in private prayer, praying, as I have said, with his whole body and deep emotion, and he established the custom of prolonging Matins (today's "Office of Readings") with a period of private prayer in the Church.

Although there is no historic proof of the story that he received the rosary from Our Lady, it is certainly true that he loved to recite the Hail Mary as he genuflected in her honor and to sing her hymns, and the rosary as a meditation on the mysteries of Jesus' life like that of Our Lady who "treasured all these things and reflected on them in her heart" (Lk 2:19) has found its natural home in the Dominican tradition. Out of such meditation preaching naturally flows as "from an abundant spring." This life of personal prayer is also shared with the community. It is true Dominic seldom spoke of his interior experiences, yet since he "spoke only to or of God," he could not have been reluctant to share his faith with his brethren and the whole atmosphere of early Dominican life is one of great openness about spiritual experiences. Dominic did not hesitate to weep, groan, sing to show his feelings and he urged his brethren to sing the Office with spirit.

Closely connected with prayer, so closely that I believe it should not be numbered as a distinct element, is the life of *penance* which is so prominent in Dominic's life. Today we puzzle over this. We do not read in the Gospels that Jesus undertook special penances with the exception of his fast in the desert at the beginning of his ministry. Is there not something neurotic, masochistic, or at least destructive in the way Dominic and many of his followers abused their bodies by lack of proper food and rest, with painful clothing, flagellations, and overwork? We are used to comfort and give great attention to the proper care of the body as a real duty. I think we must admit that some of these practices in the light of modern medicine and mental hygiene seem harmful and we are not surprised that Dominic wore himself out before he was fifty. Granted all this we cannot help but also admit that these practices were inspired by three motives which have permanent value, nay, are essential to Christian life.

The first of these, common to all religions that emphasize contemplation, is the conviction that our love of pleasure and comfort must be tamed if real serenity of mind is to be achieved. Second is the Christian conviction that original and actual sin are facts of the human condition. We cannot achieve freedom from sin without a discipline that subjects inordinate appetites to the governance of reason enlightened by faith. We have only to think of the ravages of alcoholism and drugs to be convinced of this. Third is the Christian hunger for identification with Christ crucified and with suffering humanity. How can we learn to love as Jesus loved or to find solidarity with those who suffer if we are slaves of pleasure and comfort?

Necessarily, therefore, those who want to learn to pray well must fast, learn to keep silence, learn to keep vigil, and practice poverty and simplicity of life. All these disciplines are especially needed in our day and country which has perhaps the most consumption-minded culture in history. The manner in which we use these disciplines must be regulated no doubt by our modern knowledge of physical and mental hygiene, but we cannot neglect them. For Dominic it was all summed up in his desire to be one with Christ in offering himself for the sinners to whom he preached.

An essential element of asceticism is poverty. Some have said that Dominic copied the poverty of St. Francis, but as we have seen, Dominic's poverty had a different origin and motivation. He wanted to be poor to make his preaching credible to the poor who saw in the poverty of the Albigensian Perfect a holiness superior to that of the worldly Catholic clergy. The longer he lived the more convinced he became of its importance and he insisted on it ever more radically. He wanted his brethren to live a "common life" in which they possessed nothing but lived day to day in dependence on God's care. Only in this way could they be entirely free, he believed, to preach. We will see that this ideal, like that of St. Francis, eventually proved impractical and even seemed to get in the way of the Order's work, and required the moderating interpretation of St. Thomas Aquinas. Nevertheless, it remains essential to Dominican asceticism and therefore to Dominican prayer. Dominicans cannot be free to contemplate and preach the Word if they are occupied with temporal cares and they cannot make that Word credible if they seem to grow rich by their work.

The fourth note of Dominican life is very specific: *study* as a means of sanctification. For the monks, life was divided between manual work and prayer. When study was not engaged in, it was for the sake of feeding prayer, but was not conceived as itself sanctifying. St. Francis respected learned men and was content to have them remain students and teachers after they joined his Order just as he was content to have manual workers continue as they were, but he was very well aware that study and especially academic honors and competition can chill the heart and blind the intellect to pure faith and so he did not encourage his followers to study. Dominic, who certainly must have been aware of these dangers, nevertheless saw that study was not only necessary to the range of preaching which he had undertaken but could contribute to the sanctification of his brethren. It could be a salutary penitential discipline, and it could lead one to a deeper knowledge of the Scriptures and to a true humility of self-understanding.

The early *Constitutions* provided that not only should select students be sent to the great university centers but every priory should have a brother appointed as house professor (lector) to continue the education of the brethren throughout their lives. The novices were instructed never to be idle even when traveling, but to be learning and meditating what they had learned. From this arose that "intellectualism" which characterizes Dominican spirituality. This is not to be understood in the academic sense, but in the sense that the life of faith is a life which searches for Divine Truth, Truth which is not just a list of doctrines, but the Person of the Word of God, Jesus Christ. Christian perfection consists, as all agree, in love of God and neighbor, but how can we love God and neighbor if we have a distorted vision of them? If we love them, do we not long to know God and neighbor more truly as they are?

These four elements, therefore, (it seems to me) sum up Dominican spirituality: (1) *Dominican spirituality is a share in Jesus Christ the Word in his mission of announcing the Good News of salvation which he himself is*: (2) *This calling is fulfilled by a community out of its experience of living for God and for neighbors*: (3) *The source of its light is prayer, especially liturgical prayer, for which one is freed by ascetic discipline and simplicity of life*: (4) *This prayer is fed by assiduous study of the Scriptures and of all sources of truth that help us to understand the Word of God.*

2

Professors (1200s)

Community

In its first century the Order burgeoned in a Europe where feudal life was yielding to the development of great urban centers. Great popes like Innocent III (d. 1216) held three ecumenical councils for Church renewal, attempted to reunite the Eastern Church, and promoted crusades to save France from the Albigensians and Spain and Byzantium from Islam. They also replaced the Hohenstaufen dynasty of Emperor Frederick II with Hapsburgs. But at the century's end this climax of papal power was challenged by the French King Philip the Fair. The richly varied culture of the century was unified by the work of its greatest creation, the medieval university. In university cities throughout Europe Dominican communities contributed significantly to this cultural synthesis.

The life of these communities received its shape from the *Rule of St. Augustine* applied to the Preachers by the *Constitutions* written by the first two General Chapters of 1220 and 1221 under Dominic's presidency, completed in 1228, and revised by the great canonist St. Raymond of Pennafort in 1241. The first "Distinction" of these *Constitutions*, based on those of the Canons of Prémontré with important modifications, dealt with the friars' daily life. The second, marked by

St. Dominic's gift for organization, fixed the Order's government, which Sir Ernest Barker says influenced the English constitution and all subsequent democracies.

Supreme legislative and executive power was vested in a General Chapter meeting annually under the presidency of the Master of the Order whom it elected for life. It was composed of delegates elected by Provincial Chapters or in alternate years of Provincials, or of both when a Master was to be elected. Similarly each Province elected a Chapter and Prior Provincial. Each Province was composed of Priories headed by a Conventual Chapter and a Prior directly elected by the professed brethren, which sent its Prior and an elected delegate to the Provincial Chapter. Except the Master, these officers had brief terms.

Although great stress was placed on obedience to the superior, not only was he elected, but his power was limited by the *Constitutions* and his Chapter, and every priest-friar could speak and vote at least in his Priory Chapter. All friars could also make complaints directly to the Provincial or the Master of the Order when these periodically "visited" each of the convents. Finally there was a system of recall to remove incompetent or negligent superiors.

The first six Masters were remarkable men. Jordan of Saxony (d. 1237) attracted many candidates from the universities. The Spaniard Raymond of Pennafort (resigned 1240) is a major figure in the history of canon law. John of Wildeshausen (the Teutonic, d. 1252), once an imperial diplomat, protected mendicant preaching from the secular clergy, extended the missions to the near East, assumed the burden of the Inquisition, promoted the liturgy and university teaching. Next was Humbert of Romans (resigned 1263) whose writings are so informative for this century. Bl. John of Vercelli (d. 1283), an Italian from Lombardy, in spite of a crippled leg tirelessly visited the Order and guided it by some 22 pastoral letters which indicate that by this time the charity of the Order was growing cold. This decline became a scandal in the time of the Spaniard Munio of Zamora who was deposed by Pope Nicholas IV in 1291 because of his political support of his native country. Étienne de Besançon (1292–94) tried unsuccessfully to check this decline by severity, and Nicholas Boccasini

(Bl. Benedict XI) was elected Pope before he could act effectively. Munio's six and Étienne's three encyclicals denounce internal factions, ambition, private life and quarrels with other orders.

From the eight provinces, twenty priories and about 300 friars when Dominic died, the Order grew by 1228 to twelve provinces (Spain, Provence, France, Lombardy, Rome, Hungary, Germany, England, Poland, Scandinavia, Greece and the Holy Land). No new provinces were added before 1300, but some were divided into vicariates. By 1250 there were about 13,000 friars (10,000 priests), but not much growth the rest of the century. The growth of the Second and Third Order will be discussed in Chapter 4. Since the Order was essentially clerical and thus required literacy for all but the lay (cooperator) brothers, it probably recruited principally from the urban middle class. Many of its leaders, however, were university men and not a few of the nobility chose to be mendicant preachers. The Second Order nuns were even more likely to be middle class or nobility because of the requirement of a dowry.

The trend of religious orders today to promote close personal relationships by keeping communities small yielded to other Dominican goals. While Franciscans favored small priories, Dominicans preferred larger ones. Their typical convent had 30 to 50 members and some 100 to 300 in order that the whole pattern of Dominican life be observed, since it required enough to be able to send out preaching bands, while maintaining the contemplative life of study and liturgy at home, along with the necessary tasks of begging and household chores. Moreover, each convent included novices, students, and lay brothers (cooperators).

The writings of Bl. Humbert of Romans provide a vivid picture of thirteenth-century Dominican life. His writings include commentaries on the *Constitutions*, the *Rule*, a letter on the vows, and instructions on the offices of the Order. An *Instruction of Novices* is not his but dates from his time. Into the daily liturgical schedule of the friars were fitted necessary chores, begging, and study. The preachers (always at least by twos) traveled with breviaries and kept up this round of prayer as best they could. Time for moderate recreation, usually after dinner, came to be permitted. Every convent had a church or chapel in severe Gothic style with the choir shielded by a screen, a chapter room for community business and confession of faults, a refectory, and a common dormitory. The dormitory often had study cells on three sides with the library on the other.

Humbert tells us what a Preacher's community should be in his commentary on the very first precept of the *Rule of St. Augustine*: "Live together in unity and be of one mind and one heart in God, remembering this is the end for which you are gathered." This unity must be in work, word, and heart like that of the early Christians for whom Jesus (John 17) and Paul (Phil 1:3-11) prayed, a unity possible only if the community is one body with one spirit tending to a single goal. Community enables its members to be heard in prayer, to win the good fight, and to grow in every good. Disunity breeds bitterness, waste of energies and spiritual death. Unity is injured by fondness for one's own ideas, by pursuing other than Gospel values, by exclusive friendships, by love of one's own convenience, by stubborn willfulness, by resistance to God's will.

Yet there is also false community based on the world, the flesh, and the devil, which breeds refusal of correction, boldness in evil, and persecution of the good, as among those who conspired to kill Jesus. And there are some who although they do not consort with evil-doers, resist the good and oppose all efforts at reform and even good changes in the *Constitutions*. Finally, there are those who for the sake of friendship agree with others both in good deeds and bad. True unity is found only in God's will, which preachers to preach peace must themselves follow in peace (xiii-xviiii). This community, however, is not mere external conformity it must be based on the love of true *friendship*.

Why did this ascetic, dedicated, love-inspired community life begin to decline in the last quarter of the century? Perhaps in striving to meet this ideal the superiors made insufficient use of St. Dominic's moderation and principle of dispensation to make it practical for the weaker brethren, although Humbert's writings indicate a spirit of sober common sense and realism on his part, but this may not everywhere have been the case. From his writings, the encyclical letters of the later Masters,

St. Thomas
Aquinas

and the enactments of General Chapters, the chief factor seems to have been the decline of common economic life. Many friars found ways around strict poverty by retaining gifts, or obtaining special privileges and dispensations that gave them greater freedom to live their lives beyond community limits.

Study

As soon as Dominic had papal approval of his Order in 1216 he enrolled his friars at the cathedral school of Toulouse under the English master Alexander Stavensby. He then sent some to study theology, but not secular subjects, at Paris and made foundations in other university centers: Bologna (1218), Palencia (1220), and in the year of his death (1221), Montpellier and Oxford. Yet few Dominicans attended universities; a province could send only three to Paris or two to the other houses of study. Most *fratres communi* studied in their own priories under a house *lector* (or later, in a provincial house of studies) where everyone, even the prior, had to attend his lectures. Humbert of Romans in his *Offices of the Order* (c. xi) says of him:

> The job of a good lector is to adapt himself to his students' abilities and teach them whatever is useful and helpful easily and understandably; to avoid novel opinions and hold to established, solid views; ... and always to beware of that hair-splitting wordiness which often results from excessive repetition or from complicated language, etc. He should take pains to help his hearers profit from his lectures, either from the truth of the texts or in understanding useful questions, or through improvement of their lives. He should stick to the letter of the text and avoid digressions. ...

Nor should a lector permit others to call him "Master" but only "Brother," nor care for his room, make his bed, take off his boots, or carry his books, though he may have a teaching assistant. He should be willing to admit ignorance and to learn from others. Above all he should not be ambitious to teach in a more prestigious school. After Honorius III in 1221 gave the friars faculties to hear confessions everywhere, the *fratres communi* chiefly studied not dogmatics nor liturgy (in those days learned by doing) but moral cases. To help them, Paul of Hungary, a canonist Bl. Reginald of Orleans had won to the Order in Bologna, wrote a *Summary of Penance* and Raymond of Pennafort soon outdid Paul with a *Summary of Cases* (1224, revised 1235) which made him the patron saint of confessors and canonists. Born near Barcelona, he became a Master of Canon Law at Bologna in 1218, and in 1221 when almost fifty a Dominican in Barcelona. Gregory IX called him to Rome as his confessor, put him in charge of the Church's ministry of reconciliation, and set him to write the *Decretals*, a major canon law collection. Raymond refused an archbishopric, but was elected third Master of the Order in 1238, resigning after two years when he had revised the Order's *Constitutions* in correct canonical form. The rest of his long life in Spain he struggled with heresy and evangelized Jews and Moors. His *Summary of Cases* (still in print in 1744), unlike previous manuals, did not just list sins and penances, but systematically analyzed offenses against God (Book I) and neighbor (II), Church penalties (III), and marriage law (IV). He also wrote a handy summary of this great work and other canonical aids. Though the *Summary* is the work of a lawyer, it distills the heritage of Christian values. For example:

> Priests should be hospitable, because (1) as St. Jerome says, the houses of the clergy should be common to all; (2) the piety of hospitality is rewarded both temporally and eternally . . . ; (3) Abraham and Lot by hospitality entertained angels (Gn 18:1-15). Yet moderation and discretion should be used in how this hospitality is dispensed, since some guests such as preachers and prelates request hospitality as if it were their due.

Equally influential was the *Summary of Vices and Virtues* (1236-50) of Guillaume Peyraut (c. 1200-1271) who probably studied at Paris but was a preacher not an academic. The Franciscan chronicler Salimbene calls him "a humble but distinguished and courteous man, though of small stature." He also wrote *Sermons, On the Benedictine Profession Formula, On the Education of Religious* (often attributed to Humbert of Romans), and *On the Education of Princes*. His *Summa* (which reflects the Preachers' fight against Albigensianism) treats the seven sins (gluttony, lust, avarice, sloth, envy, vanity, anger) and the seven virtues (faith, hope, charity, temperance, fortitude, justice, prudence) along with the eight beatitudes and the seven gifts of the Holy Spirit. He compiled this chiefly from Augustine and Bernard and somewhat from John Damascene, but also from such pagans as Seneca, Cicero, and Macrobius. About the same time Hugh of St. Cher composed extensive scripture commentaries, long popular, and a *Mirror of the Church* (c. 1240); and the English Provincial, Simon of Hinton, a *Summary for Young Students* (c. 1250), Aag of Denmark, *A Handbook* (*Rotulus Pugillaris*, 1254-1284) and, at the end of the century, John of Freiburg whose *Summary for Confessors* (1298) was the most popular of all. Such works provided solid, integral instruction in Christian living based on patristic texts.

Other Dominicans besides Peyraut took interest in Christian

education. Thus the encyclopedist, Vincent of Beauvais, while tutor to St. Louis IX, wrote *On the Education of Noble Sons* (1261) and *Principles of Moral Instruction* (1263), only the first part completed; William of Tournai, *On the Instruction of Boys* (1264); and James of Cessole of Genoa in 1290, a frequently translated text book comparing Christian life to a game of chess. The vernacular guide of Laurence of Orleans, *La Somme de Roi* for Philip III (before 1285) on the ethics of government, for a medieval took an unusually positive view of the laity's married life.

The first seven friars Dominic sent to Paris were not well received by the secular faculty, but a letter from Honorius III got for them from the Regent Master, John of St. Albans, his house and chapel of St. Jacques from which they were nick-named "Jacobins." John also supervised their studies, thus incorporating them in the university, the first religious college so received. Jordan of Saxony, then John of St. Giles, occupied a chair in theology, and Roland of Cremona, a Master from Bologna, a Dominican since 1219, seized the opportunity of a strike by the secular faculty over a fracas between students and police, to take office as a Regent Master in 1229 giving the Order a second chair in theology. He wrote a still unpublished *Summa Theologica* and a *Commentary on Job* in which he already made extensive use of Aristotle and exhibited wide knowledge of medicine, the natural sciences and witchcraft.

Roland was succeeded in his "French Chair" by Hugh of St. Cher and then by several less notable Masters, while the "Extern Chair" was occupied by Guerric of St. Quentin who got entangled in the first important doctrinal controversy of the Order. The Bishop and the Masters of Paris in 1241 (1244) condemned ten propositions relating to the beatific vision influenced by the Greek Fathers' view that the blessed see not God's essence but only his "energies." The Dominican Chapters of 1243 and 1244 warned against these theories and the controversy served permanently to fix Catholic doctrine on the face-to-face vision of God.

The next occupant of the Extern Chair was the most remarkable German, St. Albert, known soon as "the Great," and then (after one Elias Brunet) Albert's still greater pupil, Thomas Aquinas. St. Albert, born in Lauingen on the Danube in Swabia about 1200, eldest son of a rich noble, studied at Padua, a university always noted for study of the natural sciences, some day to produce Galileo and William Harvey. In 1223 he was drawn to the Order by Jordan of Saxony and was sent for further study in Bologna and then became a lector of theology in Germany in several houses and finally at Cologne. About 1240 he taught at Paris for four years and, skipping the degree in Liberal Arts, became a Regent Master of Theology.

At this very time the Arts Faculty was fascinated with the many new works of Aristotle not known before in the West which were becoming available in translations through Arabic or directly from Greek, along with commentaries by Islamic scholars, chiefly Averroes (Ibn Rushd, d. 1198). Such studies were already begun at Oxford by Grosseteste and were being continued by the Dominican Robert Kilwardby and the Franciscan Roger Bacon. Although in 1210, 1213, and 1231 church officials had discouraged this enthusiasm as a pagan influence on theological students (and with some reason). Albert seized upon these works and in spite of the many administrative and pastoral duties which were laid on him as he founded a Dominican studium in Cologne, became German provincial, and finally Bishop of Ratisbon in 1260, produced a series of commentaries covering a great part of the Aristotelian corpus along with some works intended to fill out gaps in the Greek's scheme of sciences. After his retirement as bishop Albert hoped to write a great *Summa Theologiae* but was unable to complete it.

Albert's systematic doctrine has still not been satisfactorily studied but he held the traditional view that theology is a *scientia ad pietatem*, i.e., primarily a practical doctrine directed to the sanctification of the student, consisting primarily in growth in charity.

> Since the human being is open to God through intellect and affection, no one can be perfect unless he grasps God as He is Wisdom through intellect and as He is Virtue through love (*Commentary on Matthew* 11:28).

All are called to this perfection by keeping the commandments; religious also by the vows; and pastors in the Church by the duties of their office. The contemplative life is the goal and reward of the active life but is impossible without the active exercise of the virtues, yet action should be informed by contemplation and contemplation should overflow in action (*Commentary on Luke*, 9:37). "In contemplation truth is drawn out [from the well] which then is poured out in preaching" (*Ibid.*, 4:14). Contemplation reaches its height in the "rapture" of the negative mysticism of the Eastern Fathers, but except in special cases like St. Paul's, this remains faith and not vision in this life. The Holy Spirit's gifts of understanding and wisdom give a certain "vision" and "taste" of God.

Although the numerous works on Mariology attributed to Albert are spurious, throughout his works he manifests a great devotion to the Blessed Virgin and the Eucharist. Above all, Albert inculcates a spirit of dedication to the Truth as the Word of God, which he says alone can give us true freedom.

From Albert two extremely important lines of influence descend. One resulted from his commentaries on the works of the Pseudo-Dionysius and reached to Meister Eckhart in the next century. The Middle Ages believed these pseudonymous writings by some Syrian mystic of the fifth century were by that Athenian Dionysius whom St. Paul converted by his sermon in the Areopagus on the unknown God (Acts 17:34). They transmitted to the Latin West the Neoplatonic theological tradition of Origen and the Cappadocians in a more radical form than St. Augustine's. Bishop Bartholomew of Breganza (Vicenza, d. 1271), a novice of St. Dominic and founder of the Militia of Jesus Christ (a society of aristocratic laity to work for peace), wrote spiritual treatises dependent on this Pseudo-Dionysius: a *Treatise on the Deification of the Soul* and *The Search for Divine Love* as introductions to his *Commentary on the Song of Songs* dedicated to St. Louis IX.

The Aristotelian side of Albert's thought was chosen by his greatest pupil Thomas Aquinas, who used Dionysian works copiously but did not accept their Platonic metaphysics. Thomas was born in 1224/5 in Roccasecca Castle near the great Benedictine monastery of Monte Cassino between Rome and Naples, son of a knight of Norman ancestry, whose first marriage produced three sons, and his second, five daughters and three sons of which Thomas was youngest. Two of his brothers fought in Emperor Frederick II's army, and the family considered Rinaldo (a troubadour whose songs Dante admired) a martyr because Frederick killed him for siding with the Pope against the Emperor.

As a boy, Thomas was placed with the monks of Monte Cassino as an "oblate." From 1239-1244, however, he studied liberal arts at the University of Naples where he was counseled by a Dominican John of San Giuliano, and in 1244 entered the Order. He then traveled to Bologna with the Master of the Order, John of Wildeshausen, who had been visiting Naples and was going to the General Chapter. On the way Thomas was kidnapped by Rinaldo and another brother. Landulf had recently died and the family took it hard that a son of such promise should join a begging Order rather than enhance the family fortunes as an abbot. Thomas was confined by the family for a year at home and his brothers vainly attempted to have him seduced by a prostitute to change his mind. Thomas, encouraged by his old counselor, John of San Giuliano, refused to remove his habit and spent his time in study. At the end of the year the family gave up and let him go his own way.

From 1245-1248 he made his novitiate in Paris and began study of theology under Albert, with whom he was taken to Cologne when Albert was sent by the Chapter to start a studium there for the German Province; and there in 1250 Thomas was ordained priest. In 1252-1256 he was back in Paris as a Bachelor teaching the *Sentences* of Peter Lombard and was made a Regent Master from 1256-1259. In 1259 he began his *Summa Contra Gentiles* to aid preaching to Muslims and Jews. The same year when the friars were attacked by the secular William of St. Amour, Thomas was asked to teach at Naples in his own Roman Province where he continued work on this *Summa*. From 1261 to 1265 he was lector at Orvieto, then Urban IV's residence, where Thomas composed the Corpus Christi liturgy in 1264 and completed the *Contra Gentiles*. Urban died that year and Thomas went to Rome as sole professor of a new studium for his province and began the *Summa Theologiae*. In 1267 he was in Viterbo where Pope Clement IV was resident, but next year was back in Paris for a second regency, 1269-1272, to meet a university crisis.

The Arts Faculty was teaching an Averroist Aristotle, including the eternity of the world and the mortality of the individual soul. This provoked a condemnation by Archbishop Tempier in 1270. Furthermore, the attacks on the friars by William of St. Amour had been revived even more violently by another secular, Master Gerard of Abbeville. Aquinas actively joined the fray but by 1272 returned to Naples to teach and continue the *Summa Theologiae*. Here on December 6, 1273, his health broke but he attained new spiritual insights. When his faithful companion Reginald of Piperno asked him why he could no longer write, Thomas replied, "After what I have seen, what I have written seems as straw." In 1274 he set out for the Council of Lyons but injured his head in a fall from his horse and died March 7, 1274, in the Cistercian Abbey of Fossanova, southeast of Rome, leaving the *Summa* incomplete, but disciples finished it with a "Supplement."

Thomas, a quiet man, large in body and mind, was no recluse. Raised in a political family, he taught and preached at the great academic centers of the age, engaged in current controversy, and frequented the courts of kings and popes, who sought his counsel. He served his Order in many ways and was often asked by its superiors for theological and pastoral advice. His inner life was hidden, since in line with his methodology in philosophy and theology his writing is cooly objective. As for his preaching, only dry outlines survive. But his companions testified to his intense devotion to Christ and the Eucharist and his rich mystical experience. He lived the Dominican life fully, intensely centered in thought, dictating to two or three secretaries at the same time, burning himself out at 49.

His theological synthesis, permeated by his basic conviction that theology is a wisdom which guides human life to the contemplation of the mystery of the Triune God, is seen most fully in three works, the *Sentences* commentary, the *Summa Contra Gentiles*, and the *Summa Theologiae*. In the last he aimed to help theological students with a textbook more orderly, concise, clear, and complete than Peter Lombard's; but during the Middle Ages it never managed to replace the *Sentences*, and was only gradually recognized as of unique value. To these works should be added the incomplete *Compendium of Theology* (counterpart to St. Bonaventure's completed *Breviloqium*), written for the *fratres communi*.

Yet the *Summa Theologiae* only summarizes much preparatory work not only in the *Sentences* commentary and *Contra Gentiles*, but in many shorter works. Aquinas, like most medievals, considered theology to be reflection on the Bible. He wrote commentaries on *Job, Psalms 1-54, Isaiah, Jeremiah, Lamentations*, the Gospels of *Matthew* and *John*, and most of the *Epistles of St. Paul*, along with the *Golden Chain* of comments by the Greek and Latin Fathers on the Four Gospels, and two brilliant sermons on the value and scope of the Bible. These commentaries were written at various times and some are only student *reportationes*.

Many topics in the *Summa Theologiae* are treated more fully in Aquinas' academic disputations *On Truth, On the Power of God, On Evil*, etc., and the *Quodlibeta* (Miscellaneous questions). His commentaries on Boethius' *De Trinitate* and *De hebdomadibus* clarify the relation of the human sciences to theology. The commentary on the Pseudo-Dionysian *On the Divine Names* is important for spiritual theology and that on the Pseudo-Aristotelian *De Causis* for his criticism of Platonism. Other important treatises fill out this magnificent synthesis.

Aquinas was sensitive to pastoral concerns and wrote replies to many queries from correspondents, *Against the Errors of the Greeks* (1263) to assist Pope Urban IV prepare for ecumenical discussions at the Council of Lyons, and *On the Rule of Princes* (incomplete, 1267) at the King of Cyprus' request. Some of his works deal directly with the spiritual life: *Against Those Attacking the Worship of God and Religious Life* defends the friars against William of St. Amour (1256) and both *Against Teaching that Obstructs Vocations to Religious Life* (1271) and *On the Perfection of the Spiritual Life* (1270) against Gerard of Abbeville. Extant also are a brief letter (probably authentic) *On Study* for a Brother John, and a few sermons (many difficult to authenticate) of which those on the Creed, *Our Father, Hail Mary*, and *Ten Commandments* are certainly genuine. Finally, there are the *Office of Corpus Christi* and a few prayers and poems of uncertain authenticity.

The originality of Aquinas is seen if we compare his work to that of his great Franciscan contemporary St. Bonaventure, their works reflecting the different spirits of their Orders.

Bonaventure remained faithful to the philosophical position of Augustine but Aquinas (although like all medievals he was deeply indebted to Augustine) abandoned Platonism and remolded all of theology on Aristotelian lines. He saw, as no Christian theologian before him (and not too many afterwards) had done that Plato's dualistic conception of what it is to be human, is ultimately incompatible with the Christian doctrines of Incarnation and Resurrection.

For Platonists the human person is the soul, and its body only a burden to be laid down. Truth does not come to us through our senses but from an inner light. But for Aquinas the human person is not the soul, but soul and body, because the human soul attains truth by using its bodily senses to explore the material world of change. Only from knowing this world can it extend itself by analogy (not simply by symbol) to truth about the wider spiritual world: its own spirituality and that of God. Even the truths of faith given us by God's grace have to be expressed by analogy with things accessible to sense. "Grace perfects nature," building on it but transforming it. The full implications of this rejection of Platonic dualism for theology are not yet recognized, though Vatican II has pointed the way.

Teaching with Aquinas at Paris was Peter of Tarantaise who was to be the first Dominican Pope, Blessed Innocent V. He had entered the novitiate at sixteen at Lyons where Humbert of Romans had been prior and Guillaume Peyraut and Etienne de Bourbon had lived. He studied in Paris and after some years as a lector became a Regent Master in 1259. The same year he served with Aquinas on the commission which defeated anti-intellectual tendencies in the Order by insisting that theological studies must be grounded in a solid study of the liberal arts and philosophy. In 1264 he was elected Provincial of France but the Chapter sent him to teach in Paris again in 1267, after Aquinas had declared that a series of 108 questionable propositions taken from Peter's *Commentary on the Sentences I* could be understood reasonably. The chief issue was whether such attributes of God as his justice and mercy, are really distinct in our understanding (as Peter maintained) though identical in God.

Peter, elected Provincial again in 1272, was made Bishop of

Lyons in 1274 by Pope Gregory X to quiet that troubled city in preparation for an ecumenical council to reunite the Eastern and Western Churches, and then made him cardinal. When Gregory died Peter was elected his successor, taking the name Innocent V, but his pontificate lasted only five months. In this brief time he tried to carry out the Council's work for Church unity and defense against Islam, while working for peace between the King of Sicily, Charles of Anjou and Rudolf of Hapsburg and (more successfully) between Charles and the city of Genoa. But as a Frenchman he too much trusted Charles whose idea of Church reunion was to make himself Emperor over the Byzantines. Some say Charles poisoned the Pope who died suddenly.

Peter's works, still not all published, show that he was more conservatively Augustinian than Aquinas, yet basically Aristotelian in his epistemology and independent in his solution of many problems. His answers in the *Sentences* commentary, while hardly equal to those of Thomas in profoundity and originality, are remarkable for their clarity and succinctness of expression. For example, he asks whether the gifts of the Holy Spirit differ from the virtues, special gifts, beatitudes, and "fruits" mentioned by St. Paul, but his answer disagrees with that of Aquinas:

> The virtues are given to act well, gifts to act easily, beatitudes to act perfectly, fruits to act joyfully. Yet these are not given by God or used at the same time (III, d. 34, q. 1, a. 4).

Although Paris was the chief center of Dominican study, after the Chapter of 1221 Dominic had sent twelve friars from Bologna to found houses at Canterbury, London, and Oxford. The first Dominican theologian at Oxford, a friend of Grosseteste and St. Edmund Abingdon, was Robert Bacon (d. 1248), probably a student at Paris before joining the Order. Not much of his writings, except his biography of St. Edmund, are extant. Apparently he was a conservative Augustinian. His pupil Richard Fishacre (d. 1248) introduced more modern methods based on an increasing use of Aristotle and used Lombard's *Sentences* as the basic theology text. Next came Simon of Hinton (d. after 1261) whose *Summa for Young Students* was mentioned earlier.

The most important English Dominican of the century, however, was Robert Kilwardby (d. 1279) who became Archbishop of Canterbury and then cardinal. He had studied at Paris but became a Master at Oxford, and wrote a commentary on the *Sentences* showing a vast knowledge both of Augustine and Aristotle, as well as useful concordances of the Church Fathers. An able philosopher, he commented on works of Aristotle, Porphyry, Priscian, and Boethius and wrote a very important *On the Origin of the Sciences*. His letter to Dominican novices on poverty, answering Franciscan criticisms, gives us insight into his Dominican spirit. But today he is best known as a severe critic of Aquinas. His attacks along with the Franciscan William de la Mare's *Correctory of Friar Thomas* produced a number of replies by the Dominicans Thomas of Sutton (d. 1315), Richard Knapwell (d. 1288), and William of Hothum, Archbishop of Dublin (d. 1298). By defending Thomas they established a firm tradition which preserved his reputation after the condemnation of 1277. Thus this century ended with the Dominicans thoroughly at home in the greatest university centers of Europe: Paris, Oxford, Bologna, and Cologne; with a strong tradition of study, and the great model of Aquinas, soon to be canonized in 1323, freed of any suspicion of heterodoxy.

Prayer

Since in the Middle Ages liturgical rites varied considerably from town to town, itinerant preachers needed their own rite. The Franciscans chose the Roman rite and invented the portable breviary. The Preachers also adopted the Roman rite but with some variations in the offertory and communion prayers, a preparation of the gifts at the beginning of low Masses and by the seated celebrant at solemn Masses, many special sequences, and a simplified chant. After several tries, they composed their own liturgical books, published by Humbert of Romans in 1256 and papally approved by petition of John of Vercelli in 1267. This "Dominican rite" was in use until Vatican II.

In the 1200s the Order made three special devotional additions to Catholic piety: First, Hugh of St. Cher (inspired by St. Julienne of Liège—not a Dominican) promoted the Feast of Corpus Christi, officially approved in 1264; and St. Thomas Aquinas, at the request of the Pope, composed (or revised) its liturgical texts. Second, responding to the protests of the Council of Lyons in 1274 against widespread blasphemy, John of Vercelli preached reverence for the Holy Name of Jesus. Third, in the time of Jordan of Saxony, the *Salve Regina* procession after Night Prayer was instituted to deliver a poor Brother Bernard from the devil. The antiphon was not new, but the procession from the choir (in medieval churches screened from the people) to the Virgin's altar to kneel there at "Turn then, most gracious advocate, thy eyes of mercy toward us," as the leader sprinkled them with holy water. So popular was this custom, many other orders adopted it. The friars (who knew the Psalter by heart) on rising also recited the Little Office of the Virgin (the gradual psalms) in the dormitory, and weekly the Office of the Dead with a procession through the cloister dedicated to them.

Dominic had retained monastic practices which made of the whole life of a friars' convent (only the nuns had "monasteries") into a liturgy. The brethren always wore the habit (it was all they had) and slept in it. They kept silence everywhere but the parlor, especially after Night Prayer. Generally, all slept in a common dormitory which had study cells around the walls, each with a desk and a bench. At meals in the refectory all sat on one side of the tables around three walls to be served from the other, while hearing the Rule or the Church Fathers read. The Hours were always sung in plain chant, with many gestures of bowing, kneeling, prostrating, and processing, as St. Dominic loved to pray.

After the midnight Matins (today's Office of Readings"), the brethren remained in Church for some time in silent meditation, often before some altar dedicated to a favorite saint. Each morning at a brief community meeting ("Chapter") after Prime, the *Martyrology* was read and the prior made announcements, corrections, or assigned the day's jobs. At times at a Chapter each friar confessed his faults against the Rule and publicly confronted others with their faults. Humbert of Romans also tells of a *circator* who made periodic inspections of every room in the house and at Chapter reported if the rule was anywhere broken. Then the prior corrected, punished, and forgave, or required a friar to beg another's forgiveness.

This prayer was supported by a rigorous asceticism. Friars kept the Lenten fast from the Feast of the Cross, September 14, until Easter and, except when sick, were vegetarians. They retired soon after sundown, slept on straw mattresses and rose between midnight and three. Only one change of habit and only scratchy woolen underclothing were permitted, since linen and cotton were for the rich. Each day some had to beg on the streets for food for the community which went hungry if they were unsuccessful.

In his commentaries *On the Rule* (cc. 46-71), *On the Constitutions* (cc. 23-68) and his *Offices* (Novice Master, cc. 15-20), Humbert thoroughly discusses the friars' prayer and penance, for example:

> As to meditation the novices are to be instructed to use the opportunities for it when traveling, or in the cloister, or the garden, òr walking elsewhere at leisure, or when praying privately in their cells, or when resting in bed but still awake. These meditations should concern sometimes the general or particular gifts of God, or the thanks due Him and the ingratitude of men, or the works of creation and those of redemption such as Christ's Passion, or the rewards of the good and the punishments of the wicked, or about justice already done and mercies granted, or creatures, or the Scriptures, or one's own defects and one's progress, or the devils' deceits and the ministries of angels, or the saints' examples and the perverted's perversities, or one's inner life and external behavior, or about events to be remembered and things to be done, or the omnipotence of God, his wisdom, goodness, severity, mercy, justice and his judgments manifest or hidden. From reflections of this sort are to be drawn various affections: now hope, now fear, sorrow, tears over evils, aspirations to the good, wonder, exclamation, thanksgiving, supplication, shame, reverence, and so forth, all better learned by experience than taught.
>
> They are also to be instructed not to be eager to see visions or work miracles, since these avail little to salvation,

and sometimes we are fooled by them; but rather they should be eager to do good in which salvation consists. Also, they should be taught not to be sad if they do enjoy the divine consolations they hear others have; but they should know the loving Father for some reason sometimes withholds these. Again, they should learn that if they lack the grace of compunction or devotion they should not think they are not in the state of grace as long as they have good will which is all that God regards.

Humbert praises liturgical prayer, insists also on the need for private prayer, and warns that prayer does not justify shirking assigned work. In keeping with his warning about excessive interest in extraordinary experiences, the friars of this century wrote little about interior life. Three exceptions, however, need notice. The first is Bl. Bartholomew of Breganza (d.c. 1271) already mentioned for his Pseudo-Dionysian treatises and also as a preacher of the great "Alleluia" revival. A second is Peter of Dacia (Sweden, d. 1289) who as a student at Cologne was fascinated by the ecstatic Bl. Christine of Stommeln and wrote in her honor a mystical poem with a prose commentary. To that he added an account of his visits to her and 63 letters exchanged among their friends and them, with also a biography and a separate account of her childhood by her pastor. This material gives not only a vivid (and somewhat odd) picture of Bl. Christine, but also of her Dominican friends, e.g., the report of how a Cologne abbess invited four friars from different countries to meet Christine and to debate in scholastic manner the question, "Which gift of Christ was greater—his gift of the Church to Peter or of his Mother to John?"

A third, very different type of writer was Robert de Usèz (d. 1296), a French aristocrat who already had a reputation as a prophet when he was received into the Order by a provincial Chapter. He wrote two brief works, *The Book of Visions* and *The Book of the Lord's Words*, partly autobiographical but mainly in the prophetic, apocalyptic style. The first foretells the coming of the Antichrist, the Bark of Peter drifting rudderless, a great schism. The second, cloaked in allegory, sides with

Celestine V against Boniface VIII who urged that Pope to
resign and then jailed him.

To look deeper into the interior life of Dominicans in the
1200s we must turn from the public objectivity of the Preachers
to the women of the Order who lived the enclosed contemplative life. Besides what we know of St. Dominic's own
foundations of nuns recounted in Chapter 1, we also have the
primitive *Constitutions* of San Sisto Vecchio in Rome and the
recollections of Bl. Cecilia Caesarini, a founding member also
mentioned in that chapter. These *Constitutions*, extant in a
slight adaptation, were approved for the Penitents of St. Mary
Magdalene by Gregory IX in 1232. Essentially the same as the
friars', they provided for a stricter cloister, but with a small
adjoining community of friars, just as at Prouille in Dominic's
time. These friars were the nuns' chaplains and agents for their
economic and external business. The nuns, however, elected
their own prioress and other officials, yet to be exempt from
the bishop's control were visited by the friars' provincial who
could remove the prioress when necessary for peace or observance.

Also preserved are the important letters from Bl. Jordan of
Saxony to Bl. Diana d'Andalo, whose story was told in
Chapter 1. Jordan was much older than Diana and treats her
as his spiritual daughter, but he also puts great trust in her,
relying on her understanding and encouragement, especially in
his deep grief over the loss of his friend Henry. The tenderness
and humanity of these letters reveals that the austerity of
Dominican life and the urgency of its mission did not stifle
affective life, even if it tempered it.

Not all the brethren, however, shared Dominic's and
Jordan's respect for women or their understanding of women's
role in an Order of Preachers, although St. Peter of Verona
and St. Raymond of Pennafort each left a letter like Jordan's.
The Chapter of 1228 actually forbade the brethren to affiliate
any further convents of nuns to the Order for fear too many
friars might be tied down to chaplaincies and thus taken from
preaching. Acceptance of such affiliation also made the friars
responsible for the economic needs of the nuns. This ban was
tightened by the Chapters of 1234, 1238, and 1242. The nuns
succeeded in their appeal to Pope Innocent IV, but John of

Wildeshausen in 1252 was finally able to stop this affiliation. It was through the efforts of Cardinal Hugh of St. Cher and the acquiescence of Humbert of Romans that this was gradually reversed until Clement IV in 1267 finally provided a legal process for affiliation.

Humbert occasionally has some hard things to say about women but his model "Sermon to Women" in his *Treatise on Preaching* gives a number of reasons why women are *superior* to men: Adam was created outside Paradise; Eve in it. He was made out of mud; she out of his living body. Moreover, she was created not from his feet but from his very heart. Again, God could have taken flesh from a man, but in the Incarnation he took his flesh from a woman. Pilate's wife alone tried to prevent the crucifixion of Christ and in his resurrection Christ first appeared to Mary Magdalen.

By the end of the century there were 141 monasteries of nuns (74 in Germany) directly under the jurisdiction of the Order and many more under bishops but affiliated to the Order by habit, rule, and spiritual direction. This rapid proliferation of communities of women can be partially explained by the condition of medieval women. Because of many wars there was a marked surplus of women over men. Women were expected to marry very early, with little or no formal education, and to husbands chosen by their parents largely for economic and political reasons. The one way to escape from oppressive domestic situations or loneliness and perhaps to obtain a little education and freedom of spirit was through religious life.

Some of the convents were refuges for women of the aristocracy, others were more middle-class. It is not clear that women of the working and peasant classes were often received, since a dowry was necessary to assist in the support of the community. The nuns had to read Latin if they were to be choir-sisters and some nuns achieved learning, but not many. All had to learn crafts for the support of the community, such as weaving, sewing, manuscript copying and illumination.

Since the 1100s there had developed in the Church, especially in northern Europe, a type of consecrated life for women called *beguines* and for men called *beghards* (the names probably meant "beggars"). They sometimes lived with their families or as hermits or wanderers, or they formed communities called *beguinages*. Such communities, however, differed from convents or monasteries because they had no strict cloister and the members did not take vows enforced by church law.

The relation of these individuals and communities to the local bishop was canonically vague, and outside episcopal control they could become eccentric or scandalous in behavior and heretical in the notions they spread among the faithful impressed by their ascetic way of life. Hence the bishops and ultimately the Popes and councils repeatedly attempted to control and even suppress this form of life. From the time of Innocent III the problem was solved by encouraging or forcing these pious people to enter canonical religious orders or affiliate with them. Since the older orders often refused to accept them, they turned to the mendicants. Thus in addition to the nuns who constituted the "Second Order," the First Order of Preachers took under its wing a large number of beguines into its "Third Order," its own form of the much older Order of Penance, as did the Franciscans. These communities of women tended to develop a style much like that of the cloistered nuns but remained distinct either by the fact that they were not exempt from episcopal control or by a less rigorous and restricted style of life. Outstanding examples of these two types of Dominican life for women are the nuns St. Margaret of Hungary and a beguine related to the Order, Mechtilde of Magdeburg.

Margaret (1242-1271) was the daughter of the King of Hungary, Bela IV, dedicated by her parents from birth in petition for the freeing of the country from the Tartars. Her father built a royal monastery, St. Mary of the Isle, for her at Veszprem where she received the habit at the age of four and at 12 made profession to Humbert of Romans at a meeting of the General Chapter at Buda in 1254. Her sister Constance became Queen of Ruthenia and Cunegund, Queen of Poland, and her ambitious father sought to have Margaret dispensed from her vows when she was eighteen so she might marry the King of Bohemia, but Margaret refused three times to marry him or anyone else and obtained the solemn consecration for virgins which made dispensation impossible. She would not become prioress as Diana d'Andolo had done. A vivid picture of her character is furnished in her *Acts of Canonization* by the nuns who lived with her. She lived in total humility, engaging in the most menial tasks even in winter when her hands bled from the cold. She constantly fasted and refused nice clothes and royal comforts, remarking she preferred the odor of sanctity when dead to smelling sweet only when alive. She spent her days in prayer and caring for the poor war-stricken people, lavishing on them whatever gifts her royal family sent her.

Mechtilde of Magdeburg is still better known to us by her *The Flowing Light of the Godhead* in verse and prose. From it we learn she was born about 1209 in East Germany, probably of upper-class parents.

> I, an unworthy sinner, was greeted so powerfully by the Holy Spirit in my twelfth year, when I was alone, that I could no longer have given way to any serious daily sin. The loving greeting came every day and caused me both love and sorrow (IV, 1).

She educated her younger brother Baldwin and secured his entrance to the Dominican Order, where he became a sub-prior and manuscript copiest. Although her home life was happy, at about 23 she entered a beguinage at Magdeburg. When she was 43, she wrote her revelations at the request of her Dominican director, Heinrich of Halle, and when he expressed amazement a woman could write so deeply, she replied that if the Holy Spirit could speak through mere men such as the cowardly apostles, the indecisive Moses, or the boy Daniel, why not through a female sinner? When Heinrich published the work, many were shocked and urged her to burn it, but in prayer God reassured her: "The Truth may no man burn." Worn out by this opposition and perhaps after the death of Heinrich, her health and sight failing, in 1270 Mechtilde at the age of 63 found refuge with the Cistercian nuns at Helfta.

The Helfta community was a real haven since it included St. Mechtilde of Hakeborn (1241-1298) and St. Gertrude the Great (1256-1301) who were to become two of the major mystical writers of the Middle Ages. These learned women, who knew

Latin and had Dominican spiritual directors, make copious reference in their writings not only to the Bible but also to Augustine, Bernard, Albert the Great, and Aquinas. No doubt the aged Mechtilde of Magdeburg was an important influence on these younger nuns. During her last years she completed her own revelations which after her death the nuns collected. They were translated from her Low German to High German about 1345 by Henry of Nordlingen, a secular priest closely associated with Dominican mystics of the Rhineland, the only extant version of the whole, although the part written at Magdeburg survives in Latin translation by a Dominican. This incomplete Latin version of Mechtilde's writings was probably known to Dante, who in the *Divine Comedy* (Purgatorio XXVIII) beautifully pictures her (or a composite figure of both Mechtilde's) as that Matelda who guards the Earthly Paradise, gathering flowers on the river bank in the freshness of the morning light.

Although Mechtilde of Magdeburg remained a beguine, her spirituality is clearly Dominican. She herself exclaims, "Dominic, my dear Father! I have a small share in thee for which I have longed many a day," and she recounts how:

> On St. Dominic's day I prayed to our Lord for the Order of Preachers. Our Lord deigned to honour my request by coming Himself and bringing St. Dominic whom I love above all saints.... Our Lord said, "I will tell you two things more. When Dominic laughed he laughed with real sweetness of the Holy Spirit and when he wept he wept with such fidelity that he thought first of his brethren and set them before my eyes, this he did also for Holy Church.... Two things I cherish so dearly in the Order of Preachers that they always rejoice my heart. The first is the holiness of their lives; the second their great service to Holy Church. Added to that they greet my Holy Trinity with seven things, sighing, weeping, living desire, earnest self-conquest, sorrow of exile, true humility, joyful love. They also honour my Three Names with seven outward things: praiseful singing, true preaching, real absolution, compassionate comfort, friendly help, holy example, and are also a vigorous body of Christian believers." Our Lord said, moreover, "Their alms

which they give to the poor for love of me are so holy that the sins of the poor who receive them are thereby diminished and the devil can never stay where their alms are eaten. That comes from the holiness of their poverty."

Her mysticism is a form of the bridal mysticism (*Brautmystik*) scripturally based on *The Song of Songs*. Devotion to the Sacred Heart of Jesus as the symbol of His love for the Church and for sinners (based on *John* 13:25 and 19:31-37) was well known in Dominican circles, e.g., by the mystic Jutta de Sangerhausen (d. 1260) who also lived near Helfta and had a Dominican director, Bishop Heidenreich of Kulm. But Mechtilde is the *first* person in the history of Christian spirituality to mention actual visions of the Sacred Heart. For example:

> During a grave illness which troubled me, God revealed himself to my soul and showed me his wounded heart, saying, "See what they have done to me!" And my soul answered: "Alas, Lord why have you suffered such an injury? Your pure blood which you sweat so profusely when you prayed [in Gethsemane] would have sufficed to redeem the whole world!" "My Father," he replied, "was not satisfied with that alone. My poverty, labors, sufferings, and mockery were only a knock at the door of heaven until that hour when my Heart's Blood flowed over the earth. Only then were the gates of the Kingdom opened."

Like St. John the Evangelist, Mechtilde is convinced that Love is Light (that is, that God can be truly known only by those who love Him), but that Light is also Love (that is, that enlightened faith is necessary to love God truly) and that this Light and Love are made known to us in the humanity of Jesus Christ. It is this equation that connects her poetry with the Dominican spirituality of the Word.

Although Mechtilde is the only notable Dominican spiritual writer of this century it was a time rich in Dominican women known for their sanctity. Besides those already mentioned, one should note Margaret of Ypres (d. 1237) a penitent (not a nun) who died when only 21; Bl. Zedislava Berka (d. 1252), a

Slavic married woman, inspired by St. Hyacinth of Poland who during the Mongol invasions of Eastern Europe established a hostelry for refugees; Heneln of Hungary (d. 1270), novice mistress of St. Margaret and a stigmatic, Ingrid of Sweden (d. 1282) and her sister Christine, wealthy women and friends of Peter of Dacia, who founded a monastery of nuns in Skanningen after a pilgrimage to the Holy Land and several trips to Rome; Bl. Beneventura Bojani (d. 1292), a penitent, and many others.

Preaching the Word

By the end of the 1200s some 557 convents of the Order of Preachers housed some 15,000 members, but not all preached. Many simply lived a monastic life. Most of many extant sermons are in Latin for the clergy not the laity; few of them have been published, translated or analyzed. At first reading, those published seem dry, moralistic, heavy with far-fetched biblical allegories and tiresome catalogues of virtues and vices. But these "sermons" are usually mere *outlines* to aid the preacher's memory, skeletons lacking the flesh and blood of actual delivery. What held the laity were the *exempla* or stories which, like the illuminations of medieval manuscripts, vividly illustrated these sermons.

A fair sample of a Latin sermon is that for the feast of the martyred soldiers, St. Maurice and his Companions, to the Dominican students at St. Jacques in Paris on September 22, 1230, by John of St. Giles, with the Master of the Order, Bl. Jordan of Saxony present. John, an Englishman, had studied medicine at Oxford, Paris, and Montpellier, served as physician to King Philip Augustus, taught medicine at Montpellier, and then turned theologian at Paris.

Medieval preachers, unlike the Church Fathers, seldom commented on an entire biblical passage. To be more topical and directly relevant, a preacher usually began with a "text" or "theme," usually a single sentence from the day's liturgy. John announced his text: "Is there any numbering of His troops? Yet over which of them does not His light rise" (Jb 25:3). Then his "pro-theme," a second text to be related to the principal theme and used to catch the listeners' attention, on this occasion: "Keep these words in your heart" (Lk 9:44), therefore, "Keep the words of Scripture in your hearts, not just your notebooks." John warned them not to be like the proud mountains of Gelboa (II Sm 1:21) which shed the rain from their stony flanks but yielded no harvest. Rather pray for God's rain of grace to soften their hard hearts and inspire John to sow the seed of the Word.

Then John applied the first half of the text, "Is there any numbering of his troops," to St. Maurice and his fellow martyrs, subdividing it into four points, each illustrated by copious quotations taken widely from the Scriptures: (1) If kings have many soldiers and honor them, so must God. (2) None of Maurice's companions fled martyrdom, although they were not vowed religious. (3) They even competed to die first. (4) They threw down their arms and fought only with the weapons of faith. Then he applied the second half of his text, "Yet over which of them does his light not rise?" directly to the students, offering them as spiritual arms: (1) The light of grace. (2) The light of reason, not to be abused by reducing theology to philosophy or by deserting their vows for worldly riches. Was not the story of the widow of Naim in the day's Gospel (Lk 7:11-17) an allegory of the Church mourning over her sons, the clergy, dead from avarice? (3) The light of good intentions leading to conversion. (4) The light of faith, which enabled the martyrs to achieve their victory over the devil. John concluded, "While you have the light, believe in the light that you may be sons of light" (John 12:36).

But before he finished, John, struck by the application of the Word to himself, a courtly physician and ambitious academic, suddenly stopped, came down from the pulpit and begged from Master Jordan the habit of the Order, then returned to finish his sermon as a Dominican novice! As a Dominican he taught at Paris, Toulouse and Oxford, noted as a peacemaker, dying c. 1260.

To realize why the elaborate divisions and subdivisions of such sermons and their allegorical exegesis, tedious to us, appealed to the sensibility of that age, compare them with its poetry, architecture, and art. A Gothic cathedral charms not by simplicity or symmetry, but by its hierarchy of forms within forms and the variety and fantasy of its symbolism. It synthesizes the abstract with the concrete and picturesque. Similarly, this sermon style interested by the ingenuity of its symbolism, allegory, and curious stories of events both marvelous and earthy, yet fitted these firmly into rigorously logical outlines to fix doctrinal and moral principles in the hearers' minds, always emphasizing humility and our need for grace. Luther echoed such sermons.

We can appreciate the evangelical spirituality of this age best, not from these extant sermon outlines, but from the great flood of *preaching aids* these Dominicans produced in the 1200s and which preachers used for many years. At a time when the high cost of hand-copied books made such handy helps popular Dominicans worked in teams to produce them. Foremost were the Bible study aids. Dominican novices had to memorize the *Psalms*, the *Gospel According to St. Matthew*, and St. Paul's *Epistles*, but Dominican sermons all made a wide-ranging use of the whole Bible. Hugh of St. Cher (1200-1263), a student of the first Dominican theologian at Paris, Roland of Cremona, twice Provincial of France and Vicar General of the Order, was the leader in this field. Made Cardinal of Santa Sabina by Innocent IV in 1244, he attended the ecumenical Council of Lyons, reformed the Carmelite rule and liturgy, and was papal legate to Germany, where he first approved the feast of Corpus Christi. Under Alexander IV he sat on the commission that condemned William of St. Amour's attack on the mendicants. In the midst of this busy life, however, his great love was the Bible of which he wrote:

> St. Paul tells Timothy, "Until I arrive, devote yourself to reading Scripture, to preaching and teaching (1 Tm 4:13) . . . as if you could see in a mirror what you should be like and how to teach others. . . . This text applies alike to contemplatives who should listen to reading, to preachers who themselves should listen to preaching, and to teachers whose office is to teach but first must learn. Before you are judged, examine yourself, and before you speak, learn" (Si 18:19).

Therefore, besides many other works including a commentary on the Mass, Hugh prepared three fundamental Bible study aids: (1) Probably the first *Concordance* of the Latin Bible; (2) *Postillae* or exegetical notes on the entire Bible in its literal and spiritual senses; (3) *Correctorium* or textual correction of the Latin Bible, much needed because hand-copied Bibles often varied wildly. Although it led to some rivalry with Franciscan scholars, its ultimate fruit was the Gutenberg Bible which was based on the Bible of the University of Paris. The commentaries on much of the Bible by Nicholas of Gorran (1232-1295) of that university also were widely used.

Since the biblical Word of God must always be understood in the light of the living Tradition of the Christian community, the medieval preacher confirmed his reading of the Bible from the Church Fathers, as well as secular *auctoritates* on the sciences and arts. The most comprehensive attempt to supply preachers with such information was undertaken by Vincent of Beauvais (d. 1264), who anthologized excerpts from a wide variety of authorities on natural science (*Mirror of Nature*) and biblical and world history (*Mirror of History*). To these a later author (c. 1325) added the *Mirror of Morals*. This vast treasury of facts and quotes continued to be copied or printed into the seventeenth century. Thus our modern encyclopedias began as handy treasuries of illustrations for preachers.

Similar motives led the Dominicans of St. Jacques to collect *exempla* or stories for sermons which were partly published by Étienne de Bourbon (d. 1261) in a vast collection, entitled from its arrangement, *On the Seven Gifts of the Holy Spirit.* Étienne was an Inquisitor known for his efforts to eliminate superstitions such as the cult at the tomb of a saint who was really a dog! The same fund of *exempla* was used in the more famous *Bible of the Poor* published by Nicholas of Hanape (d. 1291), Patriarch of Jerusalem who died heroically in the Muslim siege of Acre. These collections of *exempla* delight historians by the vivid light they cast on medieval culture. To them should be added Nicholas of Biard's the *Poorman's Dictionary*, and the *Alphabet of Stories* attributed to Étienne de Besançon (1294).

Since sermons on saints' days had been made popular by the Pseudo-Gregorian *Dialogue on the Lives and Miracles of the Italian Fathers* (c. 700), all preachers needed a handy book of saints' lives. This was supplied by the *Golden (or Lombard) Legend* of the Archbishop of Genoa, Bl. James of Voragine (Varazze, d. 1298), one of the most popular books of the Middle Ages, later used by Ignatius of Loyola and Teresa of Avila, and the favorite handbook of artists. One of its many sources was the earlier chronicle of Jean de Mailly.

Today even when we have learned to stomach the hyperbolic, oral style of medieval hagiography in these *legenda*, we are still troubled by a faith so preoccupied with external, physical signs of sanctity, odd miracles and gruesome asceticism, and so little with the quality of that sanctity itself. These narratives, constructed of folk-tale motifs, little resemble our experiences of Christian life. Yet, in my opinion, the 1200s and 1900s differ only in that: (1) They exaggerated the number of miracles, but we minimize them. (2) We judge an event miraculous only if scientifically verified; they feared to doubt such reports lest they be thought impious. (3) We exaggerate the subjective element in our perception of the world because of our pluralistic culture, while they, because of their cultural uniformity, minimized it.

Thomas of Cantimpré (or of Brabant, i.e., Belgium; d. c. 1272) was interested in the saints of his own time. His curious work, *The Whole Good from Bees,* like the *Lives of the Brethren* of Gerard de Frachet (cf. Chapter 1), collects traditions about St. Dominic and other early Dominicans. He also wrote biographies of a number of holy women who were not Dominicans and an encyclopedia of natural science similar to Vincent of Beauvais' *Mirror of Nature,* entitled *On the Nature of Things,* to provide illustrations from which moral lessons might be drawn, since for medievals nature was no less wonderful than were miracles.

Still another kind of aid for preachers who had to dispute with Jews and Muslims was encouraged by Raymond of Pennafort (c. 1220-1284) who, after he retired as Master of the Order, urged Thomas Aquinas to write the *Summa Contra Gentiles* to meet unbelievers on their own grounds. Raymond and after him another Master of the Order, Humbert of Romans (1200-1277) founded schools with faculties of eight or nine for the study of Hebrew and Arabic and the theological literature written in them at Barcelona and Tunis. William of

Tripoli (d. after 1273) wrote a *Treatise on the Condition of the Saracens and on the Pseudoprophet Muhammad* based on Arabic sources. It is said he converted many Muslims in Palestine, acted as ambassador of St. Louis IX to the Mongol Kahn, and tried to join Marco Polo's expedition.

Thomas Agni (d. 1277), Latin Patriarch of Jerusalem, wrote another work on Islam, and Raymond Martin in 1277 published a great one, *The Dagger of the Faith,* used for centuries as a fund of information and apologetics. A Belgian, William of Moerbeke (d. 1286), participant in the Council of Lyons and in 1278 Archbishop of Corinth, worked for church reunion and translated many works of Aristotle and other Greek authors with remarkable accuracy, some at the request of St. Thomas Aquinas. While Master of the Order, Humbert of Romans, in his *On Preaching the Cross Against the Saracens* urged missionaries to read the Qur'an and in his important memoir on church reform at the Council of Lyons he treated relations with the Orthodox and Muslims. These works could not anticipate the ecumenical spirit of Vatican II, yet they sought to share the Gospel with all humanity. Humbert's great *Treatise on the Formation of Preachers* gives us the clearest view of the motivation of these Dominican preachers; they saw their preaching as a supreme work of love, yet a harder life than the asceticism of the Cistercians.

Humbert argues that preaching even excels celebrating Mass and the sacraments since without the faith that comes from hearing the sacraments cannot be effective. But how can we relate these lofty motives to the fact that the office of preacher was so often joined to that of *inquisitor* to which many Dominicans were called by the popes? One of these, Bl. William of Arnauld, was martyred in 1242 along with eleven companions including Franciscans and two other Dominicans; and then in 1252 St. Peter Martyr of Verona was was, after St. Dominic, the first of the Order to be canonized. But today we are more likely to sympathize with the heretics than those they martyred. Is it not a bitter, even demonic irony that an Order founded to preach the Gospel of peace should so quickly have become a persecutor!

Yet to view the Inquisition from the perspective of modern ideas of the rights of conscience is anachronistic. Medievals saw heresy as subversion of both church and state. The Inquisition was started to prevent by peaceful means (and by force only if the former failed) the spread of this subversion. Hence the inquisitors were first of all preachers, striving to free those innocently "brain-washed" by heretical tactics and to convert the leaders by theological debate. If they failed they released the "stubborn" heretics to the government for the harsh criminal justice of those times. The Inquisition's own methods of inquiry, which seem to us barbarous, were based on current secular legal procedures and were then thought to be moderate and just, carefully observing "due process" as then understood.

The popes entrusted the Inquisition to Dominicans precisely because they were theologically trained preachers. Theirs was a dangerous task requiring courage and prudence. St. Peter of Verona's life shows he was no fanatic but a man of peace. In 1233 when the Inquisition began, Bl. Guala of Bergamo and Bl. John of Vicenza were successfully preaching "the Great Alleluia," a peace movement to reconcile the Emperor and Pope and end feuding among the cities of Lombardy. Similarly, the zealous preacher of the Spanish Crusades, St. Peter Gonzalez (d. 1246, often confused with St. Elmo, as patron of sailors), urged easy terms for the Muslim enemy after the surrender of Cordoba in 1226. Ultimately, Inquisition and Crusades failed although led by brave, often saintly men driven by evil times to solve by force what can be solved only by prayer, preaching, and martyrdom.

Yet this first century of the Order of Preachers yielded a rich harvest of the sown Word.

3

Mystics (1300s)

Community

The fourteenth century, called by Barbara Tuchmann *A Distant Mirror* of our own, was a time of declining population, economic regression, and political and religious turmoil. The Great Famine of 1317 was followed by the Black Death of 1347 with outbreaks throughout the century. In 1337 began the Hundred Years War in which the French fought to expel the English, while in the East the Crusades no longer gave hope of stopping the advance of Islam.

The papacy fell under the control of the French Kings and moved to Avignon in the "Babylonian Captivity" from 1309-1376. In 1311 an ecumenical council was held at Vienne, which at Philip the Fair's behest suppressed the rich Order of Knights Templar. John XXII (1316-1334) carried on a bitter struggle against the claim of Louis of Bavaria to be emperor, and condemned the extreme views on poverty of the Spiritual Franciscans led by William of Ockham whose "modern way" of Nominalism in philosophy and theology came to dominate the universities. When Gregory XI (1370-1378) finally returned to Rome the election of his successor Urban VI (1378-1389) was repudiated by the French cardinals and a Great Western Schism splitting the Church into a Roman and Avignon obedience began. Meanwhile at Oxford John Wyclif (d. 1386) put forward a radical ecclesiology that anticipated the Protestant Reformation.

Yet this was also the time of Dante (d. 1321), Petrarch (d. 1374) and Boccaccio (d. 1375) in Italy and in England of William Langland (d. c. 1400) and Chaucer (d. 1400), of Perpendicular and Flamboyant Gothic in architecture and International Gothic in painting and sculpture, a brilliantly elegant style with a taste for such morbid themes as the *danse macabre*. Chivalry in warfare waned, but as a life style for the aristocracy flowered in courtly love, music, poetry, fantastic dress and armor.

In these complex times Dominican community life suffered one of its sharpest declines in the Order's whole history. Although by 1303 it had reached 20,000 friars, the Black Death carried away a third and perhaps half. Even earlier community life was falling apart, because of frequent dispensations to own income-producing properties and for individuals to keep gifts and stipends. This abandonment of strict mendicancy had led Boniface VIII in 1299 by the bull *Super Cathedram* to tax one fourth of their income in favor of the seculars. Benedict XI, a Dominican, suspended this decree but the Avignon popes reinstated it

A class system grew up because the Masters of Theology and Preachers General (distinctions eagerly competed for and abusively multiplied) could claim one of the better preaching territories ("terms") and keep its rich stipends to live a private life in their own apartments on an upper floor of the convent, with a lay brother servant to serve each his own meals, while the *fratres communi* lived the common life on the ground floor, often lacking even necessities. After the Plague instead of consolidating their diminished communities the survivors struggled to maintain half-empty buildings. Night office was often neglected and Masters and Preachers General were exempted from choir altogether. Friars competed for office, condemned authority, quarreled over elections, and stubbornly resisted correction. As the Church fell into three parts so did the Order.

For the first half of the century the General Chapters were hampered by the rapid turn-over of Masters. Albert Chiavari (1300) died after three months; Bernard de Jusix in two years;

Aylmer of Piacenza's (1304-11) longer term was frustrated by his resistance to the revival of the *Super Cathedram* tax and to Clement V's suppression of the Templars. Berengar of Landorra (1312-1317) attempted reform and imposed the following of Thomism. Hervé Nedellec (1318-23) confirmed this and obtained Thomas' canonization. Barnabas Cagnoli of Vercelli (1324-1332) continued these policies and saved the growing Third Order from papal suppression. Hugh of Vaucemain (1333-1341) resisted a project of the former Cistercian, Benedict XII, for general reform of religious orders because Hugh feared this would mean the end of the Mendicants. Gerard of Domaro de la Garde (1342) after four months in office was made cardinal. Pierre of Baume-les-Dames (Palma) (1342-1345), Garin de Gy l'Eveque (dead of plague in 1348), and Jean de Moulins (made cardinal in 1350) were ineffective leaders, although Jean, who had assisted the Pope's efforts to end the Hundred Years War, is also remembered for urging Humbert II, King of Dauphine, to resign his crown, become a Dominican, and will his kingdom to France.

Simon of Langres (1352-1366) had a long term, but was so harsh and so frequently absent on papal business that only the Pope's favor prevented his removal by the General Chapter. Elias Raymond (1367-1389), who recovered the body of St. Thomas for the Order and tried unsuccessfully to end the privileges of the Masters of Theology and Preachers General, remained Master in the Avignon obedience of the Great Schism after Bl. Raymond of Capua's (1388-1400) election for the Roman obedience.

Raymond, born in 1330 at Capua of the noble family Delle Vigne, studied law at Bologna under the famous canonist Giovanni d'Andrea and his daughter Novella (so beautiful she lectured behind a curtain!). He was called in prayer at the tomb of St. Dominic to enter the Order for the Province of Sicily about 1347. After his studies he taught and then became confessor to the nuns founded by St. Agnes of Montepulciano and wrote her life. Elected prior of the Minerva in Rome in 1367, and appointed in 1374 Regent and Lector in Sacred Scriptures at Siena, he became confessor to St. Catherine whose life he was also to write. During the Plague he risked his life caring for the poor. On Catherine's peace mission to

Florence he was present when she received the stigmata. Prior of the Minerva again in Rome in 1377 he witnessed the disputed election of Urban VI, whose legitimacy he always defended. In 1379 he was made Master of Theology and in 1380 elected Master of the Order.

Catherine died just before Raymond's election, but under her inspiration he began the reform of the Order in earnest. He relates in a letter how he arrived at a method of reform when requested by Conrad of Prussia to permit him and some companions to form a house of strict observance:

> . . . I did not want to refuse them without their having an opportunity to observe those things instituted by the Holy Fathers, and so I granted what they sought, with the intention of later, after they were confirmed in their regular observance, to disperse them through diverse convents, that they might be, as it were, a leaven for others, and thus that the whole Order might be strengthened and reformed, without any coercion at all, replacing the dispersed with others in the same convent who meanwhile had learned perfect observance, and after they taught, to disperse them also, like the ones before (Opus. et Lit. VIII, p. 57-70).

Raymond then answers objections. The observants, he claims, will not divide a province since the Order's unity comes from its Founder and *Constitutions*. Nor will a change in customs cause a schism since only volunteers will be asked to live in the houses of observance. No public scandal will arise because a reformed house will be the only one in a city. Moreover, the laxity of many houses is already notorious. Finally, Raymond apologizes for not giving an example of keeping the constitutional fasts himself. He has tried repeatedly but fainting spells and even fever have forced him to dispense himself.

The reform began in Germany under Conrad of Prussia, first at Colmar, then at Nuremberg and also at Utrecht in the Lowlands; some other attempts failed. Its second locus was in Italy led by Catherine's disciples: Bartholomew of Siena, Thomas Caffarini, and especially Bl. John Dominici into the next century. On the whole Raymond's method succeeded, but it was based on the assumption which today must be

St. Catherine
the Great

questioned that religious renewal can be a literal return to "primitive observance" in the face of historical changes. He failed to distinguish between those elements of Dominican life which define its permanent purpose and those which had become obsolete.

Hence Raymond's reform, though it saved the Order, also had some unhappy consequences. "Monastic observance" came to overshadow St. Dominic's single-minded goal of an Order of Preachers. Also the government of the Order became more centralized in order to empower the Master to defend the "observants" against the hostility of General Chapters elected by "conventual" majorities. Hence after 1370 Chapters met not annually but only every two or three years. Finally, the conventuals remained the majority in many provinces and their dislike of the observants made for constant faction and friction. Fortunately, unlike the Franciscans, Carmelites, and others, the Dominicans never split into separate orders.

While the First Order underwent this drastic decline and slow revival, the Second Order flourished especially in Germany, although the sad state of the friars led some of the nuns to disaffiliate, so that the Second Order only increased slowly in this century. For economic reasons the Master of the Order allowed no monastery to have more than 50 nuns. The Master or a local provincial appointed a friar as vicar for these convents and often several priest confessors and a lay brother or two to help with manual work resided at a convent. At that time the cloister was not as strict as later, but we read of frequent efforts to enforce it and to prevent the friars from exploiting the nuns' hospitality or interfering in their life. The vicar's supervision was to assist the nuns economically, provide them the sacraments, and protect them from the heretical movements of the time.

Especially significant in this century was the rise of the Third Order. We have seen that the bishops urged the beghards and beguines to affiliate to an order. Many had already lived according to an old *Rule of the Brethren of the Order of Penance,* of unknown origin. In 1221 the Franciscans made a revision of the Old Rule to give it a distinctively Franciscan character. Innocent IV in 1247 asked them to make a canonical visitation of the Italian members, but some did not affiliate to the Franciscans, or, especially in Germany, attach themselves to the Dominicans. For example, in Cologne there were 39 houses of beguines under guidance of the Dominican priory. Consequently, in 1285 Munio Zamora made a Dominican version of the Old Rule. The Franciscan rule received papal approval in 1289, but the Dominican, not until 1405 by Innocent VII through the efforts of Thomas Caffarini, a disciple of Catherine and Raymond. Caffarini mistakenly believed it had originated with the *Militia Jesus Christi*, a sort of military confraternity supporting the Albigensian crusade.

After Munio revised the rule, the Third Order spread widely in Italy, as at Siena, Florence, Lucca, etc. Members wore a white tunic, black mantle and belt; brothers, a black capuce and sisters, a white veil. In Lent and Advent and all Fridays they fasted, and ate no meat Mondays, Wednesdays, Fridays, and Saturdays. Their office was a certain number of Our Fathers recited at the canonical hours, and they kept vigils on great feasts.They were not to take part in public festivities, nor without the director's consent to leave the city. Each chapter elected its prior or prioress with the consent of the older members who could expel any who failed to live by the Rule. Some women's chapters lived in community, supporting themselves by manual work, caring for the poor, and praying in the local Dominican church, and some of these communities eventually affiliated to the Second Order as cloistered nuns.

Study

This century was not a great period of Dominican scholarship, but it saw some important developments in the intellectual life of the Order. The Paris condemnation of Averroistic tendencies in the Arts Faculty in 1277 had cast a shadow over the thought of St. Thomas Aquinas which many thought was tainted by the same tendencies. Thomism was strongly opposed at Oxford, as we have seen, by a prominent Dominican, the Archbishop of Canterbury, Robert Kilwardby. When Kilwardby was made a cardinal in 1272, his successor was a Franciscan John Peckham (d. 1292) who was even stronger in his opposition. I have already recounted in the last chapter how a group of Oxford Dominicans sprang to Aquinas' defense and then others at Paris.

There was, however, another current of thought in the Order which also stemmed from St. Albert the Great promoted by those who followed Albert's Neo-Platonic rather than his Aristotelian interests. It was this tradition which culminated in Meister Eckhart's mysticism. Hugh Ripelin of Strasbourg and Ulrich (Engelbrecht) of Strasbourg were both pupils of St. Albert. Hugh, prior of Zurich, 1232-42 and again in 1252-1259, and who lived to 1268, wrote a *Compendium of Theological Truth*, a simple textbook which followed the plan of St. Bonaventure's *Breviloquium*, but was closer to Aquinas. It was used by Henry of Suso and many later writers. Ulrich (d. 1277) was more original. He produced an Aristotelian and a *Sentences* commentary, but his chief work is *On the Supreme Good*, a kind of summary of all theology explaining the *Divine Names* of the Pseudo-Dionysius. Ulrich conceived God as the Absolute Truth or Pure Intellectual Light from which all reality flows out in lesser rays of truth.

This "light metaphysics" is also evident in Theodoric (Dietrich) of Fribourg (d. 1310) who was at the University of Paris by 1276, provincial of Germany in 1293, and probably Regent Master at Paris in 1297. He wrote on a wide range of philosophical and theological subjects and in his theology followed the Neo-Platonic tradition. His most remarkable work, however, was in the science of optics. Using a truly Aristotelian method he produced the first satisfactory mathematical theory of the rainbow in a work written at the request of the Master of the Order, Aylmer of Piacenza in 1304. In a major work *On the Intellect and the Intelligible* (which curiously contains one of the first references to the discovery of eyeglasses), he closely follows the Neo-Platonist Proclus in his theory of knowledge.

Nicholas of Strasbourg (f. 1323-1329) wrote a *Summa philosophica* synthesizing the work of Albert and Thomas. He was a lector at Cologne, a vicar of the Master of the Order in reforming the German Province, and a defender of Eckhart. As a result of this defense he was excommunicated by his bishop but rehabilitated by the Pope. Basing himself on writings of John Quidort (d. 1306), he produced a work, *On the Advent of Christ,* and left German sermons. His contemporaries were the brothers John and Gerard Korngin (of Sterngassen), natives of Cologne, who both knew Eckhart. John was a lector at Strasbourg and prior and probably Regent of Studies at Cologne in 1320. He left a *Sentences* commentary. Gerard wrote a *Meadow of Souls or Remedy of the Sick Soul* (*Pratum animarum aut Medela animae languentis*). Bertholdus of Moosburg, a lector at Ratisbon and Cologne and Vicar of Bavaria (d. after 1361), wrote a huge Neo-Platonic *Exposition on Proclus' Elements of Theology* which was to influence Cardinal Nicholas of Cusa in the next century.

A second non-Thomistic current within the Order favored the "Modern Way" of Nominalism, which under the leadership of the Franciscan William of Ockham (c. 1300-c. 1350) came to dominate the universities during this century. Nominalism was a style of thought which put great stress on logical technicalities and rigorous methodology with the result that it "deconstructed" (as philosophers today would say) the efforts at a grand synthesis of faith and reason in theology at which the "Old Way" of the great thirteenth-century scholastics had aimed. The Dominican James of Metz, teaching at Paris 1300-1303, departed from Aquinas by denying that our knowledge is wholly derived from our senses, that material things are individuated through their matter not their form, and that each angel is a distinct species. Such views are more like those of the Franciscan Duns Scotus (d. 1308) against whom Ockham reacted than those of Ockham himself.

More truly Nominalistic were the views of Durandus of St. Pourçain (d. c. 1334). In his *Sentences* commentary Durandus put forward many novel opinions: he denied the reality of universal concepts, of all relations except causality, and the passivity of the human intellect in relation to its object. The General Chapters of 1278, 1279, and 1309 had already demanded with increasing strictness respect for "Brother Thomas'"teachings. Now, as a result of these dissenting voices, the Chapter of Metz under Berengar of Landorra in 1313 delcared that:

> Since the teaching of our venerable doctor, Friar Thomas Aquinas, is regarded as sounder and more common and our Order is especially bound to follow it, we strictly command that no brother in lecturing, in solving questions, in answering objections, dare to assert anything contrary to what is commonly believed to be the opinion of the aforesaid doctor.

Thus in preaching, teaching, and writing, silence was imposed on anyone who could not plausibly argue that his views were consistent with those "commonly believed to be the opinion" of Aquinas. This phrase indicates there was already disagreement as to just what Aquinas' opinion was on a good many matters. Hervé Nedellec, head of the commission (which included Peter de la Palu, John of Naples and seven other luminaries) which in 1314 condemned Durandus, himself rejected the composition of essence and existence in creatures which later Thomists were to consider the touchstone of Thomistic authenticity! Hervé carried on his controversy with Durandus for twenty years, while Durandus first toned down his views, then reasserted them, escaping the control of the

Order by becoming a bishop. Besides the works of Hervé, a work *Evidences Against Durandus* (c. 1330) by an author known only as Durandellus seems to have ended Durandus' influence in the Order.

Hervé himself was not only Master of the Order, but also the outstanding Dominican theologian of this not so outstanding century. His own commentary on the *Sentences* dates from his teaching at Paris in 1302. He became a master around 1307 and was the first Dominican to write against Duns Scotus. He was an opponent of Jean de Pouilly who had revived the old secular campaign against the mendicants at Paris, but he also wrote a treatise *On the Poverty of Christ* against the "spirituals" not only among the Franciscans but within his own Order. He wrote some forty works, including ones on logic, commentaries on philosophical works, on the Scriptures, theological treatises, disputed questions, polemical works, etc.

Peter de la Palu who taught with Hervé was the second most distinguished theologian of the period. He was of noble family, served in the case of the Templars (to whom he was rather favorable) and was Regent Master at Paris in 1314-17, succeeding Durandus, whom he opposed. He, too, was a vigorous opponent of Jean de Pouilly. As an ambassador to Flanders for the King of France he was accused of treason but escaped conviction. He became very involved in the poverty question and favored the liceity of the conventual form of poverty which with a superior's permission allowed religious to keep gifts and stipends for personal use. In 1329 he was made Patriarch of Jerusalem and worked unsuccessfully for a crusade. After much service to the popes, however, Peter fell into disfavor with Pope Benedict XII, who undertook to reform the Order in a way to which Peter objected. He apparently was forced into retirement as bishop, dying in obscurity at Paris in 1342. He was a prolific writer, and besides his *Sentences* commentary, left many Scripture commentaries, a treatise on poverty, a concordance of St. Thomas' *Summa Theologiae*, two treatises on the power of the pope, polemical works against Jean de Pouilly, sermons, and saints' lives. His works show great knowledge as a canonist and a moralist, but he is by no means consistently Thomistic.

Besides the controversies already referred to concerning

poverty, the legitimacy of the mendicant orders, and the status of Thomism, others occupied a good deal of thought and writing during these times. First, we have seen the struggle of Boniface VII and King Philip the Fair of France who led Durandus, Hervé Nedellec, and Peter de la Palu to write on papal authority, its extent and limits. Later in the century many wrote in defense of the election of Urban VI or contrariwise for the Avignon popes. To these political controversies must be added the Dominican participation in the trial of the Templars where Peter de la Palu showed his fairness, and in the trial of St. Joan of Arc in which Dominicans were on both sides, but later worked successfully for her rehabilitation.

Second, was the fending off once more of renewed attack by the secular master of Paris Jean de Pouilly on the right of mendicants to hear confessions. Third, was the role they played in the almost comical controversy over Pope John XXII's opinion that the blessed do not enjoy the beatific vision until the Last Judgment. John XXII was always favorable to the Dominicans, but before his election had put forward his eccentric opinion and as Pope is said to have favored in his appointments theologians who supported this opinion. In 1233, however, the Faculty of Paris with Dominican support condemned his view as heretical, and in the next year the Pope was forced to declare that it was merely a private opinion and not his teaching *ex cathedra*. Nevertheless, this matter became a charge against him by Louis of Bavaria whose claim to be emperor the Pope had refused to recognize. Dominicans were at the Pope's death-bed to make sure he fully submitted his theological opinion to the future judgment of the Church.

The fourth and undoubtedly most notorious controversy of this time was over the doctrine of the Immaculate Conception of the Blessed Virgin Mary. On this question St. Thomas Aquinas, just as St. Bernard of Clairvaux, St. Bonaventure, and almost all the great scholastics except the Franciscan Duns Scotus, had taken a conservative, negative position. Aquinas taught that Mary, like every merely human person, had been cleansed of all sin only by the merits (in her case foreseen) of her Divine Son and that this cleansing took place before the angel's message came to ask her consent to the Incarnation;

but that for some time, however short, she must have been in the state of original sin.

Scotus, after Aquinas' death, was the first to point out that Mary's redemption could have been "preventative" so that she came into personal existence not in sin but in grace. This explanation cleared the way for the general acceptance of the doctrine in the Church after the establishment of the feast by Sixtus IV in 1476 and its solemn definition by Pius IX in 1854. Clearly if Mary had to be perfect in grace in order to be prepared in the name of the human race to speak her "*Fiat*" in perfect faith, it was necessary that she be free not only of personal sin, but also of original sin and all its effects by which her faith might have been weakened.

Thus Aquinas had already granted the essential premises of the doctrine without yet seeing how they concluded. His hesitation should be attributed to his theological honesty and sobriety, as Scotus' solution to *his* theological genius but even more to the inspiration of the Holy Spirit without which divine mysteries are impenetrable. Unfortunately, after the official approbation of Aquinas as the Doctor of the Order, most Dominicans felt bound to reject the doctrine and combat the Scotistic explanation.

The controversy broke out when John of Montesono (d. 1412) of Valentia on incepting as Master of Theology at Paris proceeded in lectures and sermons to attack the doctrine with the result that 14 articles taken from these were condemned by the Faculty of Paris in 1387. John appealed to Clement VI of the Avignon obedience only to be excommunicated in 1389; whereupon he transferred to the Roman obedience and wrote in his own defense and that of Urban VI. During the rest of the century a whole flood of literature from Dominicans and a counter flood from Franciscans poured out. The result was the exclusion of Dominicans from Paris degrees for some years and, paradoxically, an increase in devotion to Mary in the Order as a way of proving that the Thomistic position was not impious.

Prayer

The 1300s were a time of great mystics, especially in two

centers, first Germany, and then Italy. In Germany was the great Meister (i.e., Master of Theology) John Eckhart, at Hochheim near Erfurt where he entered the Order. He studied philosophy at Paris under the Averrorist Siger of Brabant about 1277, five years after Aquinas left there, and theology at Cologne where he probably met the aged St. Albert who died in 1280. In 1293-94 Eckhart returned to Paris to teach but was soon elected prior in Erfurt and Vicar Provincial of Thuringia. Again in Paris in 1302, he became a Regent Master and taught during 1303, only to be elected provincial of the new province of Saxony in 1304 and to hold that office until 1311, as well as that of Vicar General to reform the ailing Province of Bohemia. He then taught for two years in Paris, but returned to Stras-bourg 1314-1322 or 1324 as vicar of Masters Berengar of Landorra and Hervé of Nedellec for the nuns of Alsace and Switzerland, becoming famous as their preacher and spiritual director. Again in Cologne as Regent of Studies, he also had a great following as a preacher.

His preaching in German soon raised accusations to the Archbishop of Cologne of heresy both from Dominicans and Franciscans. Eckhart had already been cleared by Nicholas of Strasbourg, then papal visitator of the province, and when the archbishop's commission was about to condemn a long list of heretical statements taken from his sermons, he appealed to the Holy See. Accompanied by his Dominican superiors he traveled to Avignon to defend himself before Pope John XXII (himself accused of heresy by Dominicans for novel views), but soon died there in 1328. A year later the papal commission reported that Eckhart had faithfully accepted the decision of the Church in advance and therefore was not a formal heretic, but that some 17 propositions excerpted from his works were, as they stood, heretical and 11 theologically rash.

Eckhart's own *Defense* has facilitated a critical edition of his authentic Latin and German writings. He planned a vast *Work in Three Parts* to consist of a General Prologue (extant), a First Part of over 1,000 "propositions" (theses) each with its commentary (only its Prologue consisting in the first proposi-tion "Existence is God" survives), a Second Part to consist of a series of disputed questions following the order of Aquinas' *Summa Theologiae* (nothing extant except five questions against a Franciscan Gonsalvo of Spain) and a Third Part to consist of a series of commentaries on books of the Bible along with sermons, which were themselves commentaries on selected texts. Its Prologue and commentaries, *Genesis, Exodus, Wisdom, Sirach, Chapter 24, The Song of Songs* (fragments), the *Gospel of St. John*, and 56 Latin sermons, many little more than outlines, survive.

The Middle High German works include the 86 sermons established as authentic by the modern editor Joseph Quint, as well as several short treatises, *Counsels of Discernment* (probably his earliest work, written for young Dominicans), *The Book of Divine Consolation* (written for Queen Agnes of Hungary on the assassination of her father, to which was added a sermon *On the Noble Man*), and *On Detachment*. The Latin works make clear Eckhart's essential orthodoxy by their exact scholastic terminology and the fact they were edited by him and not merely reported as were the sermons, but it is the German sermons which have been most influential by their sometimes shockingly paradoxical and thought-provoking style.

Eckhart, though well versed in the works of Aquinas and respectful of them, was no Thomist but followed the other Neo-Platonic, Pseudo-Dionysian aspect of the teachings of St. Albert the Great. In German Sermon 53 he sums up his favorite themes:

> When I preach, I am accustomed to speak about detachment, and that a man should be freed of himself and of all things; second, a man should be formed again into that simple good which is God; third, he should reflect on the great nobility with which God has endowed his soul, so in this way he may come to wonder at God and, fourth, at the purity of the divine nature, for the brightness of the divine nature is beyond words. God is a word, a word unspoken.

Eckhart's theology is radically *negative* (*apophatic*) since ultimately it names God only as The One; while Aquinas, though he admits that "we rather know what God is not than what He is," yet seeks to name Him positively by analogies taken from creatures. Aquinas interprets God's answer to

Moses, "I am who am," to mean that God is Existence (Being); but for Eckhart this answer means "Do not ask my unknowable name," and says that if we are to give Him any other name than One it should not be "Being" but "Mind." Hence in the 1800s the German idealists called him their forerunner. He accepted Aquinas' central thesis that in God essence and existence are identical, but in creatures really distinct, but unlike Aquinas, understood this to mean that creatures have no existence of their own, but exist only by God's existence within them. Thus he can say that "the creature as such is simply nothing." He even speaks of the need to transcend the Trinitarian nature of God to enter into the formless "wilderness" or "desert" of the Unity of the Three Persons. Yet he still affirms the Trinity as a procession or "bubbling up" (*bullitio*) within the One, just as creation is a "boiling over" (*exbullitio*) outside the One. Unlike the Neo-Platonists, however, he holds that creation is not a necessary but a free act of God.

It follows from this conception of God that union with God is not primarily through love but through "letting go" (*Gellasenheit*, detachment). Love is great because it compels us to undergo all suffering for God, but detachment "compels God to love," since God cannot refuse the soul that is empty of self and open to Him alone. Then the Word is born in the soul and the soul is "formed again into that simple good which is God." This union takes place in the very *ground* of the soul where intelligence and will are one, its "inner castle" or very "isness." Yet since we have no existence of our own but exist only by the presence of God within us, this divine spark (*vünkelîn* or *scintilla animae*) is not something of the soul itself, but is simply God present to the soul, and hence Eckhart (to the alarm of the inquisitors, and no wonder!) could say that the ground of the soul is "neither created nor creatable." This separation from creatures as they are separated from God by creation and entrance into God's own eternal unity is called by Eckhart a *durchbruch*, "breakthrough" or, better, "penetration," or total return from the state of "unlikeness" (St. Augustine), plurality, or alienation from God which creation or the going out from God entailed.

Although Eckhart's writings were suspect, his influence was great. One who fell under his spell was a younger man of great

literary gifts, Henry Suso. Suso was the friend and director of
a Dominican nun of the monastery of Töss, Elsbeth Stagel,
who composed from the notes she had taken of his confidences
to her a *Life of the Servant of Divine Wisdom* which is the
first spiritual autobiography in German and which, although
chronologically vague and very incomplete, provides a vivid
account of his spiritual development considered by specialists
authentic, though somewhat dramatized. He was born on the
shores of Lake Constance in Switzerland about 1295 of a
knightly family. His mother was spiritual but his father, a
coarse man, seeing his frail and sensitive son was not fit for
anything else let him[6]enter the Dominican novitiate at
Constance at only thirteen (an abuse of the time). He says his
first years in religious life were spiritually shallow, but at
eighteen he began to seek God in earnest. Under the influence
of courtly literature, his life was at first very dreamy and
romantic because, as he says, "he had a heart made for love."
     Henry delighted in gathering flowers for the Virgin's altar
and heard angels singing with him in choir. The Eternal
Wisdom was his lady love to whom he composed songs as
would a courtly knight. Yet this Wisdom was also his friend
Jesus to whom he swore fidelity and whose Holy Name he
actually carved in his flesh over his heart. During this time his
life was full of ups and downs of poetic ecstasy and deep
depressions over troubles of conscience, including fear his vows
were invalid because his parents had paid to get him admitted
to the novitiate. Yet, though he dreaded pain he began to
realize he needed a life of penance if he was to master his
temperament and become conformed to the Crucified. With
characteristic impetuosity he began a life of extreme rigor,
relentless fasting, bloody flagellations, vigils, cold, thirst, silence
in imitation of the Desert Fathers, but it was hardly impetu-
ousity that enabled him to maintain this for twenty long years
of agony!
     Henry was a gifted student and in 1324 he was sent to
Cologne for higher studies. Here, Meister Eckhart relieved his
scruples about his vows and taught him the spirituality he
followed the rest of his life, but the other theologians at
Cologne seemed to him to be playing intellectual games and
he had no desire to share in their competition for academic

advancement. Eckhart himself at this time was being investi-
gated for heresy and Suso probably suffered with him and at
his death in 1327.

At about this time Suso returned to Constance as Lector
where he was to continue his life of rigorous penance in the
convent located on an island in the lake, spending as much
time in solitude as his duties permitted. At this time, it seems,
he finished his first work, *The Little Book of Truth*, a very
expert explanation in an orthodox sense of the points of
Eckhart's doctrine which had been found suspect. This work
makes clear that while Suso had thoroughly grasped and
accepted the Meister's principal ideas, he also recognized their
dangers and had been able to understand them in a manner
completely free of pantheism or Pelagianism.

Somewhat later about 1328 he wrote a much more personal
work *The Little Book of Eternal Wisdom* in which in vivid,
poetic language he developed his chief theme of a spiritual
marriage to the Crucified as the Eternal Wisdom through total
emptying of self and a sharing in His Passion. After Henry's
twenty years of penitential life and commitment to solitude,
the Eternal Wisdom said to him:

> You have spent enough time in the elementary school and
> are ready to take up higher studies. Follow me: I will con-
> duct you to the spiritual graduate school where you will be
> instructed how to bend your stiff neck to the divine yoke.
> This will establish your soul in holy peace and bring your
> devout beginning to a blessed end.

This meant he must put aside his external penances and give
himself to the work of preaching and the guidance of souls. A
voice told him to look out the window, where he saw a dog
playing with an old rag, and the voice warned him that now he
would be like "the dog's plaything, tossed about and tattered
by the tongues of men." The *Life* gives a whole series of
adventures by which this prophecy was fulfilled, a colorful
picture of the trials of an itinerant preacher in those days.
Among these incidents was the story of how he converted an
ex-nun, his own sister. During these years Suso preached
widely in Alsace, Swabia, and down the Rhine to Holland,

especially ministering to the nuns of that area. Unfortunately, we have only two authentic sermons, but a considerable number of letters of spiritual direction. These, along with the *Life, The Book of Truth,* and *The Book of Eternal Wisdom,* were put together with a spurious *The Soul's Love-Book* to form his works in German under the title of *The Exemplar.*

Suso was also elected prior of the Constance convent. His concern for reform appears especially in his later work in Latin, *The Clock of Wisdom,* so titled because it is divided into 24 meditations for the hours of the day. Written a little after 1331 it uses materials from *The Little Book of Eternal Wisdom* but is an independent work sent to the then-Master of the Order, Hugh de Vaucemain. During this time, according to the *Life,* Suso was accused by a prostitute to whom he had given alms of fathering her child and the story was widely believed. Suso was almost driven to despair but was finally vindicated. In 1339 because of the troubles between the Pope and Louis of Bavaria, the Dominicans of Constance, most of whom took the Pope's side, had to flee to Deissenhofen until 1343, where Suso seems to have been re-elected prior, but when they returned to Constance, Suso was assigned to Ulm where he remained until his death in 1366, continuing to preach and counsel.

The other great disciple of Eckhart was John Tauler, who did not leave us a spiritual autobiography (the *Life of the Master* is fictional). He was born in Strasbourg about 1300-04 and was probably with Suso a student of Eckhart during the time of the Meister's troubles with the Inquisition. He never became a Master of Theology but devoted himself to preaching, with Strasbourg as his residence. He favored the Pope in his struggle with Louis of Bavaria and as a result had to move to Basel before 1339 and was still there in 1346, as we know from Henry of Nordlingen's letters. Sometimes he visited Cologne to preach there, but died at Strasbourg in 1361 in the garden of the convent of St. Nicholas where his sister was a nun.

These bare facts do not tell us much, but from Henry's letters we see that Tauler was the leading figure of the Rhineland "Friends of God" of whom we will hear more later. His *Sermons* (or *Spiritual Conferences*) is the first important collection of sermons in the German language and became enormously influential not just among Catholics but later among Protestants. They are not his own writings but *reportationes*. Older editions contained sermons by Eckhart and the great Dutch mystic (not a Dominican) Jan Ruysbroeck, but criticism has established about 80 as authentic. These are not parochial homilies but conferences to nuns and other "Friends of God." While Eckhart shocked his audience by paradoxes, Tauler is determinedly pastoral. He presents Eckhart's essential themes, yet is careful not to mislead his hearers in their lives and prayer. Thus he insists that "detachment" requires the practice of the virtues:

> Our preparation requires four things: detachment, self-giving, interiority, and unification. The outer man should be at peace and practiced in the natural virtues, and the lower faculties rightly governed by the moral virtues, then the Holy Spirit will clothe the higher faculties with the theological virtues. All must be guided and ordered by the virtue of discretion, so we may discover if all our actions and our life are lived ... for God. But if we find anything in our life which is not for God alone, we must so correct it (Sermon for Sunday after Ascension).

Tauler, although respectful of Aquinas, explicitly prefers Eckhart's views on spirituality as "incomparably more sublime" (XXIX, Second Sermon for Feast of Trinity), but like Suso insists the only way to God is through identification with the Crucified.

The development of Eckhartian mysticism grew out of and in turn stimulated the phenomenal growth of the Second Order in Germany not through aristocratic foundations as in most of Europe, but largely from the middle-classes. The wars and other troubles of the century had led, it would seem, to a great excess of single women over men and thus to social pressures favorable to entrance into religion. In 1303 out of 141 convents of nuns in the Order, 74 were in the German and Saxon Provinces, but some communities actually dropped their affiliation with the Order during this century. Today, of the 74 houses of 1303 only Linz, Regensburg (Ratisbon, from which many American houses have descended), Schwyz, and Spire still survive.

The biographies of certain outstanding nuns have been preserved in the chronicles of the cloisters of Adelhausen, Diessenhofen, Engeltal, Kirchberg, Oetenbach, Töss, and Unterlinden in the Rhineland. The earliest of these, the *Chronicle of Unterlinden* (the only one in Latin) written during the years 1330-40 by Sister Catherine von Gebweiler, sketches the lives and virtues of some 43 aristocratic and middle-class women, and some working-class lay sisters. Catherine wrote to Venturino of Bergamo about these nuns' distress that the interdict launched by the Pope in the conflict with Louis of Bavaria sometimes deprived them of the Eucharist. His letters assured them they still had access to the graces of the Eucharist through prayer. He recommended they meditate on the Five Wounds of Christ while flagellating themselves and cultivate mutual charity within the convent.

Adelhausen at Freiburg im Bresgau had a chronicle composed by Anna von Munzingen during her term as prioress beginning in 1327. This cloister had been visited by Hugh of St. Cher and St. Peter Martyr in 1244, who had preached to them in Latin which many of them understood. This Chronicle is replete with visions and prophecies. More convincing is that of Töss in Switzerland written by Henry Suso's friend, Elsbeth Stagel (c. 1300-60) which relates the lives of some 37 nuns from its founding in 1233 until 1340. Besides editing Suso's life and letters, she also wrote a life of Elizabeth, grand-niece of St. Elizabeth of Hungary which shows Stagel knew Latin, had a good theological education, and a sense of literary style. The anonymous chronicle of Oetenbach stresses the inner purgative trials of contemplatives. Thus Ida von Hohenfels suffered for five years from temptations against faith and another five as if she was already forever in hell, until she cried out, "Even if I shall never see God, I will serve him faithfully," and Ida von Hutwell underwent six years of the "dark night" but then experienced a vision of the Sacred Heart from which the light of love and mercy streamed over land and sea. The chronicle of Kirchberg near Wurtemburg was written by a Sister Elizabeth, perhaps of Jewish ancestry. In this convent many Sisters received what they called "the grace of rejoicing," often at communion, which they sometimes experienced for many days or even years. Thus one Sister Eite von Holzhausen says when she was granted this grace she felt "like a bread crumb dipped in a honey jar" so permeated was her whole being with the joy of heaven.

Engelthal, near Nuremburg, had a chronicle titled *The Little Book of Grace* written by Christine Ebner (1277-1356). This chronicle is marked by its emphasis on the ethical aspects of the spiritual life, as well as extraordinary phenomena, and one sister is especially praised who admitted she had no such experiences. The cloister of St. Mary Magdalen at Medingen near Dillingen did not preserve a chronicle of this sort, but it was the residence of Margaret Ebner (only a remote relative of Christine's) (1291-1351). Born at Donauwörth, Swabia, she entered the Medingen convent at 15. At 21 she became chronically ill and often bedridden for the rest of her life, but she did penance as she could and devoted herself especially to meditation on Christ's Passion, with a special devotion to the Lord's Infancy. In 1325 the war forced her to leave the cloister with a lay sister to stay briefly at home. After she had returned she met the secular priest Henry of Nordlingen, first known to us at Avignon in 1335 as a strong supporter of the pope against the Fraticelli and Louis of Bavaria. Returning to Germany, Henry became an itinerant preacher, often in danger from Louis' party.

About 1332 Henry began to write letters to Christine Ebner at Engelthal and Margaret Ebner at Medingen, among the first of this literary form in German. The warmth of these letters is sometimes a bit embarrassing as when Henry (who had a taste for relics) requests one of Margaret's nightgowns that he may wear it to protect his chastity! Yet generally, they exhibit his great prudence and skill as a spiritual guide. Free of Eckhartian language, they are very Scriptural and Thomistic. Henry insists on strict orthodoxy for the nuns and moderates their more extreme penitential practices. It was he who translated into High German Mechtilde of Magdeburg's work. In 1339-49 he settled at Basel, where he became one of Tauler's "Friends of God," which included the mystic, Margaret of the Golden Ring (c. 1320-c. 1404), a lay woman and her Dominican brother John, and there were other "Friends" at Strasbourg.

If today this style of spirituality seems to us somewhat too fanciful, too colored by unresolved neuroses, and lacking proper physical and mental hygiene, we cannot deny that a good percentage of the members of these cloisters seems to have attained a high level of contemplation, selfless love of Christ, and dedication to intercessory prayer, the very purposes for which Dominic founded his Second Order. In northern lands outside Germany there was also a vigorous cloistered life but we are not very well informed about it. Italy provides us with a level of prayer life quite equal, but very different, from that in Germany. We have already seen that Venturino of Bergamo is a link between them through his letters to German nuns.

After Venturino the most important Italian spiritual writer of this period was Dominic Cavalca. He was born about 1270 at Vico Pisano perhaps of the Gaetano family, important in the Pisan government. After the novitiate at St. Catherine's in Pisa he was educated in the Roman provincial studium, which had an excellent library. Yet he never became a lector but passed his life in Pisa preaching and caring for the poor, sick, and prisoners, and monasteries of nuns, especially the Dominican monastery of St. Martha for converted prostitutes, which he founded. He died in 1342.

His writing seems a product of his preaching and he is more a popularizer than an original thinker, yet his works have considerable literary quality. He translated from the Latin the *Dialogue* attributed to St. Gregory the Great, the letter of Jerome to Eustochium, the *Lives of the Desert Fathers*, and finally the *Acts of the Apostles*. His own compositions include a pair of treatises based on *James* 3:1-12, one devoted to the sins of speech, *The Wounding Tongue* and the other to its good uses, *Fruits of the Tongue*, namely, praise of God, preaching, and confession of sins. He also wrote a guide for confession, *The Mirror of Sins; On Patience or the Medicine of the Heart; Thirty Follies* on the obstacles to true conversion and victory over temptations; *Discipline for the Devout* on the chief faults of those striving for perfection (vanity, presumption, rash judgment, contempt for manual labor); and an *Exposition of the Apostles' Creed* which was not completed. In these he drew a great deal from Guillaume Peyraut's *Summa of Vices and Virtues*.

Cavalca's masterpiece, which seems to have influenced St. Catherine of Siena, was his *The Mirror of the Cross* which he introduces by saying that since each of us will be judged by the talents God gave us, he has decided to write a book for the simple in which Christ himself, seated on the chair of the Cross, will teach us all we need to know for salvation. He shows that from the Cross flow the Seven Last Words, the Seven Gifts of the Holy Spirit, the Seven Corporal Works of Mercy, the Seven Spiritual Works of Mercy, and the Eight Beatitudes. He thus provides a complete catechesis of the Christian life. Because these works were so popular many spurious works are attributed to Cavalca.

As Eckhart was central to the development of Dominican spirituality in the first half of the 1300s in the North, St. Catherine of Siena was to the second in the South. She is known to us through the biography written by her confessor, Bl. Raymond of Capua, its supplement by another confessor, Thomas Caffarini, and other contemporary reports. Raymond's work, full of marvels, has undergone severe critical scrutiny by R. Fawtier, A. Grion and others, but has proved one of the most authentic of medieval saints' lives. The critics admit the authenticity of the over 300 letters written through much of her active life to a wide variety of persons which confirm the essential facts of her life and give a clear notion of her principal spiritual ideas.

Catherine was born in Siena March 29, 1347 (the year of the Great Plague), the twenty-fourth of twenty-five children born by her mother, Mona Lappa. Her father, Giacomo di Benincasa, was a well-to-do wool dyer. She grew up in the parish of San Domenico under the preaching and pastoral care of Dominican priests and at the age of six had her first vision of Christ, dressed as the Pope and seated on his throne over the entrance of the parish church. At seven she vowed her virginity to Christ and later steadfastly refused the exasperated efforts of her mother to have her married like the rest of her daughters. She began to practice severe penances and to receive spiritual guidance from Tommaso della Fonte, a brother of her brother-in-law, who had lived with the family after his parents' death from the plague in 1349 until he became a Dominican priest.

From seventeen to twenty-one Catherine lived as a contemplative in her own room which in that crowded household her father had reluctantly assigned her, and at twenty-one experienced a mystical espousal to Christ and an exchange of hearts with Him. He then commanded her to take up active social work in the care of the poor, sick, and imprisoned. She wore the habit of the Third Order, which she managed to join in spite of the reluctance of the elderly women who chiefly constituted the parish Chapter. Her charities brought her into contact with many different sorts of people who were so attracted to her (though she was no beauty) that they formed a *bella brigatta* or "fair company" who called her "Mama" and hung on her every word. She was in effect their spiritual director, but she herself from 1368 was under the direction of a Dominican, Bartolomeo d'Dominici. In 1370 she underwent a "mystical death" for four hours. She had visions of St. Dominic, the Virgin, the Trinity, purgatory and hell. In 1372 she received permission (then rare) for daily Communion and found herself no longer able to eat or sleep.

About 1373 or 74 she visited Florence for the first time and met with her future biographer Raymond of Capua who then became her confessor and one day as she confessed to him saw her transformed into the image of Christ. She worked miracles of multiplying bread and of healing and converted many. She also began to write letters to political figures calling for social reform and to the pope Gregory XI calling for a crusade, which he actually undertook in 1373 ordering Raymond to preach it in Italy. To win support for this crusade in 1375 Catherine journeyed to Pisa and Lucca. At Pisa she received the stigmata of Christ but prayed that she might suffer the constant pain without the wounds being visible until after her death. She there also converted a young murderer Niccolo di Tuldo and accompanied him to the scaffold.

In June of 1376 with several companions she journeyed to Avignon to plead the cause of the city of Florence and to personally urge Gregory XI to end the Babylonian Captivity of the Church as he had vowed to do at his election and as he had been urged to do also by another mystic, St. Bridget, Queen of Sweden. This Gregory actually did in September. Returning to Siena by way of Genoa and Pisa she found that

Raymond had been made prior of the Minerva in Rome. In 1377 she founded a monastery for nuns at Belcaro just outside Siena and then stayed for a time at Rocca d'Orcia, some twenty miles from Siena, working for the reconcilation of feuding factions. It was here she had the vision which became the basis of her great work, the *Dialogue*. She also visited Sant' Antimo and Montepulciano where Raymond had been chaplain and where she venerated the incorrupt body of St. Agnes.

Again at Gregory XI's request she returned to Florence in 1378 to make peace and insure the continuance of the crusade, only narrowly to escape assassination. In March of 1378 Urban VI succeeded Gregory in a stormy election. When its validity was challenged by the French cardinals, the Great Western Schism began. Back in Siena Catherine wrote to many important people to support Urban as the true successor of St. Peter. Urban called her to Rome to assist him, and with a group of followers she went to Rome in 1378, but not before dictating her *Dialogue*. In Rome she was reunited with Raymond whom, however, the Pope soon sent on a mission to the king of France. He never got to Paris because of his fears of assassination, much to Catherine's sorrow, as she wrote to him. She was never to see him again.

From the beginning of 1380 Catherine suffered greatly, beginning with a vision she experienced in St. Peter's of the Bark of St. Peter (in Giotto's fresco over the entrance of the old St. Peter's, still retained as a mosaic in the present edifice) descending on her shoulders as she prayed for the end of the Schism and the reform of the Church. Each day she dragged herself the mile to St. Peter's for morning Mass and prayer until vespers. After a three day's illness in bed she died at the age of 33, April 29, 1380. She was canonized by Pius II in 1461.

Critics have minimized the actual influence of Catherine on Gregory IX's return, pointing out her lack of political realism in not foreseeing the conflicts between the Romans and the French cardinals which precipitated the disastrous Schism. Her efforts to promote peace in Europe, to further the Crusade, and to reunite, free, and reform the Church were all failures; yet because her efforts and those of other saints were not supported by the powers of the day, ecclesiastical and civil, the still greater schism of the Reformation some hundred years later became inevitable. Hers was the greater realism of vision and she gave her all to bring about the true reform which eventually took place. In reading about the many miracles recounted by her contemporaries we must also take into account the medieval perception of reality which I have already discussed. Perhaps most troubling are the suspicions that she suffered from *anorexia nervosa*. Yet as recent studies have pointed out, such a phenomenon can be the effect of very diverse causes, and Catherine's inability to eat reflected her intense love for God and suffering humanity and deep concern for reform of society and the Church.

What Catherine's life was really about can best be seen in the *Dialogue* written near her early death and summing up all that she hoped and worked for. It was dictated in ecstacy in a very short time, but probably by combining several shorter pieces written previously. Did her Dominican censors distort her thought in editing it? Probably not, since: (1) the ideas are also found in her letters as the critical edition by Cavalini has demonstrated; (2) the priestly editors, if they had dared, would have corrected certain passages in which Catherine makes some minor theological gaffes. The *Dialogue* contains themes that seem traceable to Augustine, Cassian, Gregory the Great, Bernard of Clairvaux, John Colombini, and the Dominicans Aquinas, James of Voragine, Passavanti, and in particular Dominic Cavalca, and even to Franciscans such as Ubertino di Casale. But Catherine who was almost illiterate could easily have known these authors from conversation and sermons. While her thought is in harmony with the Thomism of her Dominican guides, it was open to other influences as well.

The *Dialogue* is based on a letter she wrote in October 1377 to Raymond of Capua from Rocca d'Orcia (Letter 272) relating how one morning at Mass she made four petitions to God and received His answers. In the *Dialogue* written a year later Catherine somewhat modified these petitions but its structure is essentially the same. In a Prologue (c. 1-2) she relates the vision and the petitions. Then (3-12) God the Father answers her petition for her own sanctification by an instruction on discretion in penance and the love of God and neighbor. Next

(13-25) he replies briefly to her other three requests, but she asks for fuller answers, so in reply to her petition for the salvation of the world, God explains his plan of salvation by the metaphor of Christ the Bridge over which all must pass to heaven (26-87), and appends two special instructions, the first on the role of "tears" (affectivity) in the spiritual life (88-97) and another on how she is to give "light" (spiritual direction) to those who ask her counsel (98-109). Next, God replies to her petition for the reform of the Church by teaching her about the Mystical Body and the dignity of the Eucharist and the priesthood (110-134); and then to her petition for a special person (Raymond of Capua) by instructing her on His Providence and the cooperation of religious with it by their vow of obedience, since disobedience has been the cause of the decline of their orders (135-153). To each of the Father's replies, Catherine returns thanks, and the whole dialogue is completed by a summary and a magnificent, eucharistic prayer of thanksgiving to the Trinity (166-167).

What is most striking about Catherine's spirituality, as contrasted to that of Eckhart, is it objectivity and universality compared with his subjectivity and individuality. Her prayer moves from herself to the salvation of the world and the reform of the Church and the Order while his looks intensely toward the interior life of the individual soul. The Father instructs Catherine to seek him through service of the neighbor, and in spite of her intense contemplative life and intimate espousal to Christ, her love, like Dominic's, is expansively apostolic. Her spirituality is also much more ecclesial and sacramental than Eckhart's. For her, Christ in the Eucharist is the center of the Church and of the Christian life and in the Eucharist she sees Christ mercifully forgiving the world through his blood dispensed by the power of the keys given to Peter. She also sees Christ in the successor of St. Peter in whom the Church is united and who is the symbol on earth of Christ's mercy and forgiveness. Her love for the Dominican Order is equally intense, because she is profoundly convinced that without the light of faith, the *preached* Truth of the Word of God, the world remains blind and helpless. She longs to preach this truth and to give her life's blood in its witness.

It is significant that this most perfect disciple of Dominic, the inspiration for the reform of the Order, was a woman and a member of the Third Order or Dominican Laity. Her influence on the Order's subsequent history, as we shall see, has been profound. Because of her great loyalty to the Holy See she was declared (along with St. Francis of Assisi) a chief Patron of Italy by Pius XII in 1939. She and Teresa of Avila were declared Doctors of the Church by Paul VI in 1970, the first women so to be honored.

Preaching

In the 1300s Dominicans continued producing preaching aids. The *ars praedicandi* of Thomas Walleys (d. 1349) is called *How to Compose Sermons*. He was an Oxford professor famous for his attack on Pope John XXII's theories about the beatific vision, who got delated for his own theories on the subject. His preaching manual treats very technically in nine chapters all aspects of a sermon. Directed to more popular preaching is the large *Summa of Preaching* of another Englishman, John Bromyard (d. 1352), rich in *exempla* and painting a vivid picture of the practical difficulties a preacher faces. Jean Gobi the Younger (fl. 1323), lector at St. Maximin in France, in his *Ladder of Heaven* listed *exempla* alphabetically. Bartolomeo da San Concordio (d. 1347) of Pisa (author also of a popular *Summa of Cases of Conscience*) collected the sayings of many authorities on prose composition in his *Teaching of the Ancients* in Italian. Giacomo of Fusignano (d. 1333), Provincial of the Roman Province, then a bishop, counselor, and friend of Charles II of Naples, also wrote an *Art of Preaching*. Jacopo Passavanti (d. 1357) of Florence is notable for the eloquence of his Italian *The Mirror of True Penitence* filled with *exempla* skillfully narrated. Finally, Arnaldo de Podio, a Catalan (fl. c. 1379-97), wrote an important, still unedited *Art of Preaching*.

Another author of a *Book of Exempla and Similitudes* was Giovanni di San Gimignano (d. 1337), who also left some 480 sermons in Latin (but many delivered in Italian) for Sundays, Advent, Lent, and for funerals. He was a lector in many houses of his province and prior in Siena, and his sermons reflect the thought of Aquinas, under some of whose pupils he had studied. A fine example of his preaching is a sermon for the feast of St. Dominic in which he interprets the seven stars of *Revelations* as the seven great lights of the Order: Dominic, Raymond of Pennafort, Hugh of St. Cher, Albert, Thomas, Robert Kilwardby, and Peter of Tarentaise.

Giordano da Pisa (d. 1311) left a collection of vernacular sermons of which more from this century than from the thirteenth survive. During the Lent of 1305 Giordano preached at Santa Maria Novella in Florence twice every day and three times on Sunday, sometimes in church, sometimes in the plaza before it. The rest of the year he preached at least six times a week, sometimes to the clergy in Latin. In a sermon of March 26, 1304, on the Creed, he began by urging his hearers to believe not only about God, nor even merely believe God, but to believe *in* God. He first praised faith as the foundation of the whole Christian life; second, he showed that believers ought also to love; third, that lovers ought to serve God by doing good; and fourth, they must love faithfully unto death. He concluded with Jesus' word to the Samaritan woman "to worship in spirit and in truth" (Jn 4:24). On April 11, 1305, preaching on the text "Christ was made obedient for us unto death" (Phil 2:8), he referred to the brazen serpent Moses raised in the desert and then showed this serpent to be Christ crucified as a sinner, but a serpent that did not poison but healed. Therefore, look to Christ crucified, because only in the Sinless can spiritual health be found.

The most popular preacher of the times, however, was undoubtedly the sensational Blessed Venturino of Bergamo (1304-44) who had wanted to go to the eastern missions but was assigned instead to preach in northern Italy where he soon became famous. Of middle height, black hair, eyebrows, and beard, a brown complexion, with an oval, emaciated but striking face, beautiful hands and a habit of walking with bent head, sparing in words and fond of silent meditation, yet kindly and pleasant in expression and conversation, he profoundly impressed his audiences. He lived very simply, "hated money like poison," and became known for his cheerfulness and compassion and his visits to the sick, the poor, and the imprisoned. He was in frequent correspondence with the

Rhineland mystics and wrote a work on asceticism, *On the Spiritual Journey*, a very severe, penitential conception of Dominican living.

Venturino, to dramatize his preaching, organized converted penitents in bands of twelve, wearing white tunics and long blue cloaks with a red and white cross on the right shoulder and a dove with an olive branch on the left, girded with cords with seven knots to flagellate themselves while reciting Our Fathers and Hail Marys. They trudged the roads carrying pilgrim staffs after a leader carrying a banner of the Madonna and St. Martha. As they marched they proclaimed, "Mercy! Peace! Justice!" These penitents were often men who had once been mortal enemies in the many feuds of those days, especially between the Guelfs (the Pope's party) and Ghibellines (the Emperor's party). Now as brothers they traveled through the villages to pray for peace for Italy at the tomb of St. Peter in Rome. No doubt Venturino got the idea from the "Alleluia" preaching of the friars in the previous century.

The peace pilgrimage grew much larger than Venturino had anticipated and war-torn Rome, at that time deserted by the Avignon popes and hardly more than a village, was overrun by huge crowds. When the news reached Benedict XII at Avignon, he suspected that Venturino was seeking to be pope and denounced him as a "hypocrite." But Venturino, innocent of any such ambition, leaving the pilgrims to fare for themselves, hastened to Avignon to defend himself. The naive answers he gave to the papal inquiry have been preserved. The Pope accepted his good intentions but banished him to France, where he became spiritual advisor to Humbert II of Dauphine, whom he urged to join the Crusade which Benedict's successor, Clement VI, commissioned Venturino to preach, as he did with immense success. Humbert proved a poor leader and Venturino died in Syria while Humbert resigned his crown, willed Dauphine to the king of France, became a Dominican, and eventually a bishop. After Venturino's fiasco, it is hardly surprising the Master of the Order denounced the flagellant movements and at the time of the Black Death strongly opposed them in Germany where they became especially bizarre. Yet, St. Vincent Ferrer (d. 1419) adopted similar methods in his enormously successful preaching.

Outside Italy there were many other famous preachers, some of whose sermons have been preserved but remain as yet unpublished and unstudied. Jacques de Lausanne (d. 1322), professor at Paris and French Provincial, who besides a *Sentences* commentary, left *Moralities* (spiritual reflections on the Bible) and many Latin sermons enlivened with French proverbs, examples from the natural sciences, and satires on the clergy, merchants, and government officials. Though a Dominican, he preached the Immaculate Conception. Henry van den Castre (d. 1303) of Louvain left many vernacular sermons and a *Letter on Six Things Which Make One Live in Constant Union with God.* Henry of Cologne (Henry of Cervo?) also left many German sermons. Thus this troubled century added much to the Dominican heritage, especially a deeper interiority.

4

Humanists (1400s)

Community

The Renaissance of the 1400s was a time of expanding commerce and brilliant artistic expression, yet not a time of peace. St. Joan of Arc was burnt in 1431, but the Hundred Years War lasted until 1453. Italy was torn by feuds and Bohemia by the Hussite wars and schism. The ancient Byzantine Empire finally fell to the Muslim Turks and its scholars fled to Russia which thus became the Third Rome, or to Italy and the First Rome. The twelfth and thirteenth century rebirths of ancient learning were based only on translations of the Greek classics of logic, science, and philosophy. In this Renaissance, interest shifted to classical literature. Unlike the scholastics, the humanists cultivated rhetoric and poetry, and found their livelihood no longer in the universities but at court or by the patronage of the new capitalists, first in Italy, then Germany, France, and England.

This new culture had its economic basis in the growth of capitalistic commerce and of an educated laity which had breached the former monopoly in learning of the clergy. The control of the Empire declined and split into many independent states, as did Italy; while France, England, Portugal, Spain,

Poland and Bohemia became clearly defined kingdoms. Spain achieved its unity under Ferdinand and Isabella and with her rival Portugal opened the searoads to new worlds.

The Church *seemed* to flourish, although the Council of Pisa called in 1409 to heal the Western Schism only managed to elect still a third Pope. Yet the Council of Constance (1414-1418) finally forced two of the Popes to resign, excommunicated the third, and elected Martin V whom all accepted. Then, after the Council of Basel (1431-1437) became schismatic, the Council of Ferrara-Florence-Rome (1438-1445) consolidated the Western Church and reunited (temporarily) the Eastern Church to itself, but not soon enough to forestall the fall of Byzantium. The second half of the century became the great age of the Popes as patrons of the arts, worldly rather than spiritual sovereigns.

Danger signs appeared. A Czech priest, John Huss (d. 1415), influenced by the radical ecclesiology of the Oxford theologian Wyclif (d. 1384) bolstered Bohemia's rising national opposition to German oppression with a national church, with the result that he was condemned to the stake at the Council of Constance. The Council itself, however, favored the view proposed by John Gerson and Marsilius of Padua, and even by some Dominicans, that Councils, even apart from the Pope, had supreme power in the Church. Everywhere the reform of abuses that the Schism had so clearly exposed was demanded, yet the bishops, so deeply enmeshed in secular politics and often invested with several dioceses, resisted fundamental reforms and the Popes, similarly involved, gave no good example.

Abortive efforts at crusades, increased reliance on the Inquisition, misguided efforts to suppress superstition by witch burning, the repression of the Waldenses, Fraticelli, and Hussites, could not substitute for thorough reform. The century came to a scandalous end in the reign of the Spanish Pope Alexander VI who, although a capable administrator and favorable to the reform of religious orders, lived a dissolute life in the sacred office he had cynically purchased.

Nevertheless, the Renaissance was *not* a mere reversion to paganism. Although the popes tolerated lay humanists in the curia, some who lived as pagans and a few who even abandoned the Christian faith, many humanists remained sincerely Christian such as the Italians Marsilio Ficino or Pico della Mirandola, the Germans Jakob Wimpfelling and John Reuchlin, the French John Gerson and Jacques Lefèvre, and the English St. Thomas More and John Colet. What was really happening was a paradigm shift from the other-worldly clerical culture to a search for a Christian spirituality that could meet the necessarily this-worldly concerns of an educated laity. Vatican II still faced this problem.

The Order of Preachers, especially in Italy, was deeply affected by this shift. The Popes, worldly as they were, and the civil rulers both sought at this time to reform the religious orders, all of which had survived decline in the previous century. The Franciscans were divided into conventuals and observants by the reforming efforts of St. Bernardine of Siena and St. John of Capistrano, while the reform begun by Bl. Raymond of Capua spread among the Dominicans.

While the Order of Preachers never suffered such a formal division, throughout this century the successful progress of reform led to constant internal struggles between the Observant minority and the Conventual majority, chiefly over the practice of the vow of poverty. All agreed that the vow of poverty required all Dominicans to renounce all personal ownership of material goods. Yet even many Observant convents were forced to seek dispensations to acquire income-producing property. Finally in 1475 this trend was formalized by papal authorization for the whole Order to abandon mendicancy, although some Observant communities were able to continue its practice.

Furthermore, the Conventuals also permitted the friars, with permission of their superiors, to retain for personal use some of the stipends and gifts they received. They were even permitted to give or will these possessions, including their own apartments and preaching territories ("terms") to other members of the community. Some even were given ecclesiastical benefices with their annual rents. These dispensations combined with the special privileges of those who were Preachers General or Masters of Theology (for which offices there was great competition and absurd proliferation) to produce a system in which some friars lived a very comfortable private life while others lacked even necessities. This Conventual system often favored a general relaxation of traditional discipline. Many friars were dispensed from choir; fasting was mitigated; the habit, though always worn was fashionable in materials and cut; the cloister was ignored. The nuns followed suit and their monasteries sometimes became more centers of social life than of prayer.

The Observants on the other hand wanted to return to what they believed to be the Order's original lifestyle, to an exact observance of the Constitutions, and sometimes even added new customs and devotions to enhance this austerity. Though often cautioned by the Masters of the Order not to become self-righteous, the Observants sometimes expressed contempt for the Conventuals as "not real Dominicans." Since at first Observants had to struggle hard to survive the Conventuals' hostility, they increasingly sought to become as independent as possible of any control by the Conventual majority, who accused them of neglecting study and preaching. Yet by the end of this century the Observants seemed the most vital and productive part of the Order.

The reform initiated by Bl. Raymond had its first great promotor in Bl. John Dominici, born c. 1356 in Florence. He entered the Order at seventeen in spite of a stutter which in one of his letters (n. 550) he claims was cured by prayers to St. Catherine of Siena whom he had met as a student in Pisa and Florence when he was about twenty. He also studied in Paris, was prior in Florence, and lector in Venice. Urged by Raymond he established houses of observance in Venice (1388), Chioggia, Citta di Castello, Cortona, Lucca, and Fabriano and was made vicar of the reformed houses until 1400. Inspired by one of St. Catherine's companions, Bl. Clara Gambacorta (d. 1419), he also worked for the reform of the nuns and left over 80 letters of spiritual guidance to them.

When Raymond died in 1399 Pope Boniface IX put John in charge of continuing the reform, but as a result of controversy over his leading processions of "White Penitents" in Venice he was banished and lost papal support, yet was later allowed to continue the reform. In 1406 he founded the reformed convent of St. Dominic in Fiesole on the hills overlooking Florence. After numerous diplomatic missions, he was made Archbishop of Ragusa and then cardinal by the Roman Pope Gregory XII

St. Antoninus,

The Bishop

whom he supported but urged to call the Council of Constance and at the Council persuaded him to resign in favor of Martin V, ending the Great Schism. Martin sent him to Poland and Hungary in a hopeless attempt also to end the Hussite schism. He died in Budapest in 1419 and was beatified in 1832. Undoubtedly Raymond's reform would have faltered if it had not been for Dominic's tireless work.

Thomas Paccaroni (of Fermo; 1401-1414) was Master of the Order for the Roman obedience until it was divided by the Pisan Schism (which he accepted, leaving the Romans to be governed by a Vicar) and Jean Puinvoix (1399-1414) of the Avignon obedience, until the Council of Constance ended the Great Schism and the Order also was reunited under one Master, Leonard Dati (1414-1425). Paccaroni had favored Raymond's plan of reform but could do little during the Schism to implement it. Dati was a humanist, fond of Renaissance pomp, who took a notable part as defender of papal primacy at the Council, but he not only established vicars for the Observants as Raymond had wished, but even attempted, although with little success, to put through a plan for the Order's total reform. For the rest of the century the elections and tasks of the successive Masters centered on the Observant vs. Conventual struggle.

Bartholomew Texier was elected only after the refusal of Thomas de Regno, who did not want to occasion a rebellion of the Conventuals, since they knew he had been elected only by the votes of Observants who had been appointed as substitute delegates by himself as Vicar of the Order. Under Texier's long Mastership (1426-1449) the Order regained its vigor, taking a major part in the Councils of Basel and Florence and giving the Church over 100 bishops. Texier, although a Conventual himself, effectively supported reform. The Masterships of Peter Rochin (1450) and Guy Flamochetti (1451) were cut short by death. Martial Auribelli (1453-1462) was removed by Pius II in 1462 because, though generally favorable to reform, he strongly resisted the attempt of the Reformed Congregation of Lombardy (the first to be papally approved) to gain semi-independence from his authority. After a short interim under Conrad of Asti, Auribelli was returned to office (1465-1473) but was constantly under siege by Observants seeking to get him removed again.

Leonard de Mansuetis (1474-1480), a learned humanist, fond of pomp and ceremony, was the Master who finally in 1475 asked Sixtus IV to abolish the Order's strict mendicancy, when the Chapters hesitated to incur the (legendary) curse of St. Dominic on all who might change his Order's poverty. The popes and cardinal protectors imposed Salvo Cassetta (1481-1483), Bartholmeo Comazio (1484-1485) (who died ministering to the plague-stricken) and the aged Barnabas Sansoni (1486). Joachim Torriani (1487-1500), also aged, was an ascetic, learned, but weak Master who vacillated about reform and at 81 yielded to the plots against Savonarola and signed his condemnation.

Thus the centralization of government in the interest of reform begun by Bl. Raymond was now further aggravated by the constant interference of the Popes and cardinal protectors (Cardinal Oliver Carafa controlled the Order from 1478-1511) often by appointing substitute electors for those unable to attend a Chapter. These nullifications of the Order's *Consti-*

tutions were encouraged by Observants struggling to remain free of control by the Conventual majority. The Provincial Chapters began to meet bi-annually instead of annually, and the Masters of Theology in 1407 were made Chapter members for life, thus giving them great power over the elections and protecting their other privileges as an aristocracy within the Order.

During this period the Provinces of Portugal and Scotland were added to make twenty-two, and Ireland attempted to separate from the English province but failed. The monasteries of nuns grew beyond the 157 recorded in 1358, but we can only guess their number. The growth of the Third Order was greatly stimulated by the papal confirmation of its rule in 1405 and by the fame of St. Catherine, but by 1498 the General Chapter began advising women's Third Order communities, previously highly varied in lifestyle, to conform to that of the Second Order, except the strict cloister.

Raymond had wanted a house of observance in each province to renew the province itself and as the reform spread the Observant houses grouped together within a Province first under a Vicar appointed by the Provincial, then directly under the Master of the Order, thus weakening the provincial's control. Soon, some of these sought to become extra-territorial congregations including houses in several provinces under a Vicar appointed directly by the Master of the Order or even confirmed by the Pope. In time some came to elect their own Vicars and hold their own chapters. Yet they also had representation in provincial and general chapters and were still taxed by their provinces, although often they resisted or even refused to pay.

The first of these was the Reformed Congregation of Lombardy which against Auribelli's opposition gained legal status in 1459 and had houses throughout Italy and Sicily. Savonarola founded the Congregation of St. Mark, but to eradicate his influence it was fused with other houses in a Tuscan Congregation. In the north was formed the Congregation of Holland (1462) which came to embrace houses in France, Germany, and as far as Scandinavia. Congregations were also formed in Spain, Aragon, and Portugal, and observant Vicariates in Germany, Naples, Sicily, Hungary, Austria, and France, and dispersed reformed convents in England, Ireland, Poland, and Scandinavia.

Thus by 1500, although the Order remained united under the General Chapter and Master of the Order, it was like two Orders, with two life styles and largely independent governments. Most communities were conventual with much private life, a privileged class of Masters of Theology, and relaxed ascetic and liturgical discipline, while observant houses were growing in number, grouping in Congregations or Vicariates which enforced the minutiae of monastic life. Yet, as we shall see, even observant convents such as San Marco in Florence, had to accommodate to the Renaissance.

Study

As we have seen, Dominican theologians played a major role at the Councils of Constance and of Basel-Ferrara-Florence in ending the Great Western Schism, in opposing the views of Wyclif and Hus, and in working for the reunion of the Eastern Church. Thus Thomas of Claxton was a member of the committee that in 1411 condemned Wyclif's errors and was a theologian at Constance, while John Nider (d. 1438), a disciple of Conrad of Prussia the leader of Dominican reform in Germany, and dean of theology faculty at the University of Vienna, was prominent at Basel, Ferrara, and Florence. He was also author of numerous Thomistic works, including the encyclopedic *Ant-Heap* and spiritual works such as *On How to Live Well* (often attributed to St. Bernard), *On the Reform of Religious*, and the oddly titled *Twenty-Four Golden Harps Showing the Nearest Way to Heaven*.

Guided by Aquinas' high view of papal primacy, most of these theologians vigorously opposed conciliarism, although the brilliant John Stokjkovic of Ragusa (d. 1442), after acting as a legate of the Council of Basel to end the Hussite Schism and persuade the Byzantine Emperor and the Patriarch of Constantinople to come to negotiate for reunion, himself went into schism with the Council when it elected the anti-pope Felix V, who made him a cardinal. The greatest of these defenders of papal primacy was Juan de Torquemada

(Turrecremata, 1388-1468, not the Spanish Grand Inquisitor!).
After studies at Paris and teaching in Spain he became prior at
Valladolid and Toledo, and then was Eugene IV's theologian
at Basel. He wrote on the Eucharist against the Hussites, on
the papal primacy, and against the Immaculate Conception,
but approved the revelations of St. Bridget. In 1434 he became
Master of the Sacred Palace. When the Council moved to
Ferrara he debated with the Greeks on purgatory, and at
Florence helped draw up the Decree of Union with the Greeks.
For his great oration against concilarism he was entitled
"Defender of the Faith" and made cardinal. As cardinal he
undertook a mission for peace between France and England
and crowned his labors by writing a history and defense of the
Decree of Union and his *Summary on the Church*, the first
systematic exposition of the Pope's universal jurisdiction.

Besides these applications of Thomism to the great issues
with which these Councils were dealing, the Preachers, after
being readmitted in 1403 to the University of Paris (from
which because of their opposition to the Immaculate Conception they had been excluded since 1387) at their Chapter of
1405 renewed the Order's commitment to Thomism. Aquinas
was now no longer called just the "Common Doctor" but also
the "Angelic" and even the "Divine" Thomas. This new enthusiasm became fully effective in the work of John Capreolus, (c.
1380-1440), called the "Prince of Thomists." He was born in
Rodez and died there after teaching only briefly at Paris for
many years in his own province at Toulouse. His life's work is
the great *Defense of the Theology of the Divine Thomas*, the
spirit of which is expressed in a brief aside at its beginning:

> Before I set out any theses, I preface one of my own: I want
> the reader to assume throughout that I intend to add
> nothing of my own but only to state the views which seem
> to me to have been those of St. Thomas; nor, except rarely,
> to propose any arguments for these theses except Thomas'
> own. But I propose to state in their places the objections of
> [Peter] Aureoli [O.F.M.], a conceptualist, [Duns] Scotus
> [O.F.M.], Durandus [of St. Pourcain, O.P., a nominalist],
> John of Ripa [O.F.M., Scotist], Henry of Ghent [a secular
> Master adopted by the Servites and anti-Thomistic], Guy

[Terrana] the Carmelite [nominalist], Warro [of England, O.F.M., Scotist], Adam [Wodham, O.F.M., Ockhamist] and others [chiefly Gregory of Rimini, O.S.A., nominalist] against St. Thomas, and answer them in his own words.

Capreolus achieved his aim with such a comprehensive, accurate and penetrating knowledge of Aquinas' thought, including a recognition of his development from the *Sentences* commentary to the *Summa Theologiae*, that this work became the basis of all later Thomism. Another major contribution was made by Peter Niger (Schwartz) of Bohemia (1434-1483), rector of the University of Budapest in his *Shield of Thomists*, also directed against Nominalism. Peter was also one of the first Christians to publish a Hebrew grammar. In 1474 he debated with Jewish scholars for seven days and published in Hebrew characters a treatise for their conversion, the German edition of which was called *The Star of the Messiah*. Such works mark the decline of the Nominalist domination of the universities and the revival of Thomism and Scotism that began in this century, along with a renewal of a radical Averroistic Aristotelianism at Padua and other schools.

The work of Capreolus and Schwartz led in the last half of the century to a shift from the use of Aquinas' *Sentences* commentary as the basis of theological instruction to the *Summa Theologiae*, first in Germany by such Thomists as Gerhard of Elten (fl. 1475-84) at Cologne and then in Italy, and soon by numerous non-Dominicans. At Padua in direct competition with Scotism Thomistic metaphysics and theology began to be taught about 1442 and 1490 respectively. Internationally there were many lesser commentators of the *Sentences* and the *Summa*.

Dominicans were involved in two special controversies. First, in spite of the influence of Juan de Torquemada, the Council of Basel forbade preaching against the Immaculate Conception, but (since Basel became schismatic) St. Antoninus of Florence, George Orter of Frickenhausen (d. 1497) in a controversy at Leipzig, and a Master of the Order, Vincenzo Bandelli, continued the traditional Thomistic opposition, although in 1476 Sixtus IV (a Franciscan) extended the feast to the universal Church, a clear sign that the Thomistic position was lost. Second, the controversy on the Precious Blood debated in the previous century was revived by a sermon given by a great Franciscan preacher, St. James of the Marches (with St. John of Capistrano and St. Bernadine of Siena, the great leaders of the Franciscan Observants). Following a metaphysics of the plurality of forms which had been involved in the "condemnation" of St. Thomas' Aristotelianism, St. James maintained that the shed blood of Christ was no longer united to his divinity. Relying on St. Thomas' contrary teaching, a Dominican, James of Brescia, attacked this sermon, and the matter was finally appealed to Pius II before whom it was solemnly debated by James and two companions against three Franciscan theologians (one was the future Sixtus IV). Pius II (who did not want to offend the Franciscans on whose support for a crusade he counted) imposed silence, but among modern theologians the Dominican position on this question has prevailed.

Other Dominicans dealt with special theological problems and with editing. Thus Cardinal Juan de Torquemada was one of the first patrons of Gutenburg's invention of printing and saw to it that works of Aquinas were among the first to be so published. Also Paul Soncinas (d. 1494) in Venice edited his works and a compendium of Capreolus, while Peter of Bergamo, regent at Bologna, produced a *Golden Table* or Thomistic index and his disciple Dominic of Flanders (d. 1422) a useful *Summary of Divine Philosophy.*

As the crisis of Byzantium and the efforts to reunite the Eastern Church progressed, certain Greek scholars became interested in Thomism and translated and used works of Aquinas. Thus Manuel Calecas of Constantinople (d. 1410) used the Thomistic teaching on the simplicity of God to which he had been introduced by a Dominican Maximus Chrysoberges and another Greek Thomist Demetrius Cydones to refute the hesychastic theology of Gregory Palamas. He eventually became a Catholic and, after a time in exile at Milan, he returned to Constantinople and then lived in Lesbos where in 1404 he became a Dominican. Though never a priest he served as rector of the Chapel of St. John at Myteline and died there in 1410, leaving many writings directed to the issues between Catholics and Orthodox, some of which were used at the

Council of Florence. Other Dominicans, such as Boncursius, Phillip of Pera, John of Montenigro (d. 1444) and Andrew of Rhodes, also wrote on these topics.

Thomism, rooted in the universities, was now faced with Humanism centered in the princely courts. The Humanists cultivated not the logical, technical language of university scholasticism, but rhetorical, literary, Ciceronian Latin or classical Greek. They for the most part rejected Aristotelianism for Platonism, and preferred dialogue, diatribe, or polemic to the cool scholastic *disputatio*. Dominicans did not find this new style very congenial, but some of them experimented with it in an effort to gain an audience. Bl. John Dominici, who had already expressed his own educational program in a *Treatise on Family Care*, wrote against the Humanist Collucio Salutati's *The Glow Worm* (1405), replete with classical allusions, arguing that Christian education should not be based on pagan classics but on the Bible and the Fathers.

A more positive attitude became wonderfully exemplified when, as a result of John Dominici's preaching of reform, St. Antoninus, the greatest Dominican theologian of this time, with the patronage of Cosimo de Medici, founded San Marco in Florence. This Church and convent, with its great library and its works of art was a harmonious synthesis of the best in Christian Humanism. Antoninus Pierozzi (1379-1459) entered the Order at 15, inspired by Dominici's preaching. After his novitiate at Cortona he became a founding member of the reformed convent of St. Dominic established by Dominici at Fiesole. The schism produced by the Council of Pisa forced the friars to flee to Foligno, and Antoninus had only a course in logic, for the rest educating himself in philosophy and theology. He was prior in Cortona, Fiesole, Naples, and the Minerva in Rome, where under Eugene IV he was also a judge of the Rota and Vicar General for the reform in all Italy. On returning to Florence in 1436 he founded San Marco and was jointly prior of Fiesole. During the Council of Florence San Marco was host to the Dominicans and Eugene IV and all his cardinals graced its dedication in 1443. The Pope approved Antoninus' initiation of societies for the education of poor children, and the still existent Society of the Good Men of St. Martin to care for the poor.

As Archbishop of Florence from 1446 his ministry was marked by his personal simplicity of life, his care for the poor, his visitation of all the parishes, and his efforts to reform the religious. While in Rome to assist at a meeting for peace, he was at the deathbed of Eugene, and was almost elected pope, and then evaded an invitation by the new pope Nicholas V to be Cardinal. In his final years he served his city in many ways and was appointed by Pius II to a commission to reform the Roman Curia. On his frequent visitations and traveling he suffered much from a hernia. Both his asceticism and his sweetness of temper are reflected in his death mask which has been preserved and in the many portraits by Renaissance artists.

Antoninus' great work is a *Summary of Moral Theology* in four huge folio volumes, the first treatise of this type. While much of volume I on human nature and moral law, volume II on the classification of sins, and volume IV on the virtues and gifts of the Holy Spirit is compiled from Aquinas, canonists and other standard authors, volume III treats in a much more original and pastoral way the moral responsibilities of people in different states of life and occupations, including the first medical ethics, and a great deal on economic justice, based on his intimate acquaintance with Florentine business. Modern capitalism is said to have originated in the wool trade of Florence and its great financial families such as the Medici. Antoninus was an inveterate foe of usury, but he is also credited with beginning the adjustment of traditional Church teaching on business ethics required by the change from the medieval to the modern economic system. He made the results of this large work accessible in a *Confessional Summary* which for many years was one of the manuals most commonly used by priests. A more positive view of Christian life is found in his *How to Live Well* for the women of the Medici family and his many sermons. Finally he labored for 19 years over his remarkable *World History*, which he intended as a historical confirmation of what he had written in his *Summary of Moral Theology*. Although only the part on the Florence of his own day is original, it shows the humanistic desire to bring theological abstractions down to the concrete.

That other Dominicans were engaged in humanistic studies

is indicated by the fact that in a list of some 132 humanists and scholars in religious orders between 1400 and 1530 by Oscar Paul Kristeller, almost one-fifth are Dominicans, engaged in works of translation (including the Bible), poetry, eloquence, philosophy, and history (e.g., Peter of Prussia, fl. 1480, wrote 8 volumes of annals), and many were on close terms with noted humanists such as Salutati, Marsilio Ficino, and Pico della Mirandola. One of the most remarkable Renaissance works is *The Dream of Poliphilio*, a mysterious dream-vision which describes the spiritual journey under the symbolism of a romantic search amidst exotic architecture. An acrostic identifies the author as Francisco de Colonna, probably (but it is disputed) a Venetian Dominican. It has also been recently discovered that in some of the Dominican monasteries of Italy the nuns composed and performed "convent dramas" on religious themes. (The work of Dominicans in the plastic arts will be described later.)

Prayer

The liturgical life of the Order was enriched during this time by more solemn celebration of Corpus Christi, the Feast of the Sanctification of the Blessed Virgin (instead of the Immaculate Conception), the feasts of Dominican saints and of the patron saints of cities where Chapters were held, and the adoption by the German provinces of feasts honoring the mysteries of the Passion and the Blessed Virgin's sorrows, but otherwise was little changed except for corrections in the liturgical books made in 1405 and 1431 by John Nider and Guido Flamochetti. From 1474 breviaries were no longer copied but printed.

The progress of the reform movement gave rise to a good deal of spiritual writing, some of which has been mentioned, and other examples are the *Treatise on the Reform of Religious* by the Flemish John van Uyt den Hove (Excuria, d. 1489) of Ghent and the *Lament of Religion* of John de Bomal of Louvain, d. 1478. But the best indication of the intense interior life of the Order in this century is the great number of Blesseds which this movement fostered, some already mentioned, others who were great preachers to be mentioned later. They range from Bl. John Liccio, a miracle worker, fond of gardening, who is said to have lived 96 years in the Order (!) to the martyr Bl. Anthony Neyrot, who when taken prisoner by the Turks in Tunis, apostasized, but on hearing of the death of St. Antoninus who had been his novice master, repented and publicly confessed the faith on Holy Thursday 1469.

No less remarkable were the Dominican women of the reform, inspired especially by the example of St. Catherine of Siena. Bl. Clara Gambacorta (d. 1419) had been married at 12 and widowed at 15 when she met Catherine, and became a friend of Marie Mancini (d. 1431) who at 25 was also a widow who had lost her children. After Catherine's death Clara first tried to enter the Poor Clares but was removed by her family. Then Clara and Marie became Dominican Tertiaries and founded the monastery of St. Dominic in Pisa, Marie succeeding as Prioress at Clara's death. A princess, Bl. Margaret of Savoy (d. 1464) lived happily in marriage with the Marquis of Monferrato, working together in the service of the poor and sick for 15 years. When he died she was guided by St. Vincent Ferrer to join the Third Order and founded the monastery of St. Mary Magdalene at Alba which became the Second Order, where she lived a life of contemplation and great mystical suffering.

What characterizes the women of this period, however, is that like St. Catherine (or in the previous century St. Joan of Arc, whose rehabilitation in this century was largely the work of Jean Brehal, O.P. (d. after 1478), many were gifted as prophets to whom their cities looked for guidance and intercession against disaster, for example, Columba of Rieti (d. 1501) and Bl. Magdalen Pannatieri (d. 1503). An especially interesting example is Bl. Osanna Andreasi of Mantua (1449-1505), concerning whom we are well informed because in the very year of her death Francesco Silvestri of Ferrara, a noted theologian and future Master of the Order, published her biography. Also two years later Jerome of Mantua, an Olivetan (reformed) Benedictine, her spiritual son, published his conversations with her along with 43 of her letters to him. They give a more direct view of her spirituality than the many miracles recounted by Silvestri. She came from an upper-class family and wanted to become a nun at fourteen but received a special revelation that she was to remain with her family as a Dominican Tertiary, and did not take formal vows until she was 50. Her reputation as a holy woman grew and many came to her for counsel, notably the famous Duchess of Mantua, Isabella whose sister Beatrice d'Este of Ferrara presided over one of the great Renaissance courts and was patron of some of the greatest artists of the time. Isabella was the actual ruler of the Duchy, since her husband was disgraced and imprisoned, and she had many burdens. She came regularly to consult Osanna, and Jerome witnessed some of her visits.

Jerome had seen her repeatedly in Church in ecstasy and finally asked to talk with her. Although he was a traveling preacher he then visited her each time he came to Mantua and carefully recorded their conversations. She was then 56 and greatly appreciated the opportunity to open her heart to him. She told him that her visions had begun when she was five, that she had received the spiritual espousals to Christ at 18, and the stigmata over a period of years beginning at 28. She had a director, Dominic de Crema, O.P., whose notes concerning her, however, are lost. Living at home, and traveling out of the city only a few times, she occupied herself with household affairs and the care of the poor, while engaged in a life of continual contemplation that included both imaginary visions of Jesus and the saints, and of purgatory and hell, as well as prophecies, and "abstract" intellectual illuminations of God the Father in the Divine Word. She experienced a four-fold division of her heart by love, and the union with God in love through suffering is the central theme of her letters. She confessed to Jerome that humanly speaking she had suffered all her life from a lack of sympathetic understanding until she had been able to express herself to him. She communicated in visions with Columba of Rieti, but St. Catherine was her ideal. Remarkably in 1502 she predicted that God was soon to punish the Church for the corruption of its clergy.

As this intense, prophetic life was carried on by certain men and women in the Order, it was also concerned to share the contemplative life with the laity. This century was particularly marked by emphasis on new types of popular "devotions," such as devotion to the *Holy Name* initiated in the thirteenth century by John of Vercelli, but now revived by the Franciscan reformer, St. Bernadine of Siena, and theologically studied by Raphael de Pronasio, O.P. (d. 1465), the *Stations of the Cross* begun by Bl. Alvarez of Cordova, O.P. (d. 1430), confessor to the Queen of Castile, influential in ending the Western Schism, but then taken up by the Franciscans as custodians of the Holy Land, and the rosary which has remained associated with the Preachers.

Much research has been expended on the history of this last devotion. Although Jesus warned against quantitative rather than qualitative prayer, he also urged us to prayer always, which entails the repetition of basic themes which in the agony in the garden he himself used and the pondering of these in one's heart in meditation as Mary did. The use of piles of pebbles, cords with knots, or strings of beads to count prayers is an ancient practice common to meditative religions such as Buddhism and Islam as well as Christian monasticism. St. Dominic used genuflections to mark his own prayers but there is complete silence in the early Dominican records about the rosary of 150 Aves with meditations on the joyful, sorrowful, and glorious mysteries as we now know it, until Bl. Alan de Rupe (la Roche, van der Clip, 1428-1475) began to preach this devotion. He claimed he had received a revelation about 1463 that the rosary had been first revealed by the Blessed Virgin herself to St. Dominic, a legend which even today is fixed in the popular mind by its many depictions in art. At that time the Hail Mary consisted only of the first, biblical half, and Alan proposed a number of different ways in which the saying of the 150 Hail Marys (to correspond to the 150 Psalms) might be meditated. Only gradually was the present form universally adopted. No doubt Alan sincerely believed in his own vision, but history's silence shows it should not be taken literally.

Alan was a Breton, a member of the reformed Congregation of Holland, and the Preachers of this Congregation quickly adopted the rosary as a powerful instrument of their own reforming work. He founded the first Confraternity of the rosary while lector at Douay, c. 1464-1468 or 1470, and all its members were admitted to the merits of the Order. In 1475, Jacob Springer instituted it in Cologne, and Sixtus IV granted it indulgences in 1478, and in 1479 approved these for the whole church through which it began immediately to spread. Another member of the Congregation, Michel Francois, a Master of Theology of Cologne, Doctor, Prior, Inquisitor, and finally Bishop at the court of Bourgogne in 1479 published a theological *quodlibet* defending this devotion (he was also an author of a treatise *On the Time of Antichrist*, another *quodlibet* on the Seven Sorrows of the Virgin and *Art of Dying*). The special Dominican character of this devotion is seen in that it is a way that even illiterate people can share in the liturgy of the hours of the Church in which the psalms are recited by joining with the Blessed Virgin in her meditations on the saving events of Christ's life.

Preaching

It may seem inconsistent with this Renaissance task of harmonizing nature and grace that the two most famous Dominican preachers of this time were St. Vincent Ferrer (d. 1419) at the beginning of the century and Girolamo Savonarola (d. 1498) at its end, both of whom constantly preached the threat of the judgment of God on sinful humanity. The reform of the Church and of civil society was, however, an essential element of Renaissance spirituality which looked always to the realization of the ideal of the Creator in making the world and humankind.

Vincent Ferrer is a transition figure between the disasters of the fourteenth century and the more optomistic Renaissance. Born at Valencia in 1350, against parental wishes he entered the Preachers at fifteen. He studied at Tarragona for two years and then taught logic at Lérida, writing two treatises that reflect the highly technical logical problems which were the concern of the Nominalists: *On Dialectical Suppositions* and *On the Nature of the Universal*. He did his theological studies in Barcelona where he also taught the natural sciences and completed them at Toulouse. He described his life in those days as "study followed prayer, and prayer study." In 1379 he was ordained and soon after elected prior in Valencia and even then gained a reputation as a miracle-worker.

Vincent's treatise *On the Spiritual Life*, based on a work of

Venturino da Bergamo, probably dates from this time. It is very concise and Vincent deliberately omits the parade of scriptural and traditional "authorities" common in scholastic treatises. In the section on *poverty* he insists that this means seeking nothing but necessities in food and clothing and excludes the collecting of books, since the common library of a convent should suffice. Next he insists on the practice of *silence* except when the good of the neighbor requires speech but that speech should have been premeditated in silence if it is to do much good. Next, he speaks of *purity of heart*, which is not merely putting aside sexual thoughts, but is the desire "to think of nothing except of God or for God."

This search for purity of heart requires self-denial (Matt 16:24) both in temporal and spiritual goods through humility and companionship with those who give good example and not with those who complain and judge others. Even when one is criticized or frustrated in attempts to do good, it is necessary to mortify one's self-love by avoiding all flattery or making excuses and coming to know one's own faults and one's total dependence on grace.

At the same time Vincent warns against any tendency to scrupulosity or discouragement. He then assures the reader that if this way of humility is taken whole-heartedly love of God and neighbor will "begin to burn in the mind and like a fire consume all the rest of the inner man, so the whole soul will be so filled with love that nothing vain can enter it." Then one "can safely preach to others without risk, without the danger of vainglory." The knowledge that we can do nothing of ourselves and must depend wholly on God is our best protection. Thus three things: poverty, silence, and humble self-knowledge are the foundation of all truly good works. He then insists that the shortest and surest way to all this is by religious obedience, which, alas, he sees very much lacking in his own day.

In particular Vincent admonishes beginners that one of the best forms of discipline is the correct and attentive performance of the liturgy. He then gives this advice on preaching:

> In preaching and exhortation use simple words and familiar stories to make clear concrete behavior; and if insofar as

you can make your point with examples so that any sinner who is guilty of that sin will see it applies to him just as if you preached to him alone. But do this in such a way that all will see that your words do not proceed from pride or anger, but rather from a loving heart and a fatherly concern. . . . Such a method is usually helpful to hearers, for to talk about virtues and vices in the abstract does little to move your hearers.

When the schism began Vincent was convinced that the Avignon Clement VII was the true Pope and supported his claims. When Clement was succeeded by his good friend, a noted canonist, Cardinal Pedro de Luna (Benedict XIII) who had ordained him, Vincent was called to Avignon as Master of the Sacred Palace and Apostolic Penitentiary and, although declining the cardinalate, worked hard in behalf of Benedict but in favor of ending the schism. More and more discouraged, however, when Benedict procrastinated in keeping his oath to resign along with the Roman Pope, in 1399 Vincent obtained permission to undertake a preaching campaign which he continued for twenty years moving back and forth through Spain, southern France (in Dominic's footsteps), northern Italy, Switzerland, northern France, and the Low Countries, usually remaining in one place to preach only for one day and then going on. Often he traveled on a donkey, preceded by bands of men and women flagellants, and working constant miracles, including raising the dead.

A remarkable feature of Vincent's preaching was the large number of Jews he converted, a fact which gave still further credence to his proclamation of the imminence of the Last Judgment. When the Pope queried him on these prophecies, Vincent replied that he was doing no more than preaching what Scriptures had to say about "the signs of the times" and pointing out how the events of the days seemed to correspond to these. Later theologians have generally explained his apocalyptic prophecies as *conditional*, i.e., he was warning that unless the people repented, God's judgment would fall upon them.

As the Councils of Pisa and of Constance strove to settle the schism, Vincent twice, in 1408 and 1415, tried to persuade

Benedict XIII to resign. Finally seeing he was obdurate, for the good of the Church, Vincent repudiated his allegiance to Benedict. So great was Vincent's reputation that although he did not accept the invitation of the Council itself to attend, his example moved the King of Aragon, Benedict's last royal supporter, also to abandon him. The Council then proceeded to depose him and elect Martin V who was quickly accepted by all the countries of Europe. Benedict XIII, conscious of his expertise as a canonist and convinced of his legitimacy because he was the last survivor of the cardinals at the time of schism, never gave in, but retired to an island fortress to die. Vincent continued his preaching until his own death in Vannes, Brittany in 1455.

Many of Vincent's sermons have been preserved and they show that he followed his own advice quoted above. These sermons are simple, vivid, and concrete, As a preacher his appearance, emaciated, with glowing eyes, powerful gestures, and a great voice by which he made himself heard in the open air to vast crowds, many of whom did not understand his language yet caught his message, made him one of the two most popular preachers of the century. His only rival was the Franciscan St. Bernardine of Siena (d. 1444), whose preaching was confined to Italy and was devoted primarily to promoting devotion to the Holy Name of Jesus. A number of Dominicans, possibly because this devotion originally had been entrusted in the thirteenth century by a Pope to the Master of the Order of Preachers, Bl. John of Vercelli, opposed Bernardine's preaching, claiming it led to a kind of idolatry of the monogram of Jesus, but the Franciscan successfully defend himself against this accusation. His sermons themselves well exemplify the same principles of popular preaching that Vincent had taught and followed.

The following brief passage from a sermon for the Third Sunday of Advent illustrates the directness and simplicity of Vincent's style:

> "What will it profit, my brothers, if one should say he has faith and is without works? Can faith without works save him?" Further on St. James gives the answer (2:14): "So faith also, if it has not works in itself is dead." Therefore, it

is necessary to continue in doing good; that is, what we believe interiorly we must exhibit exteriorly. For example: Do you believe Christ came down from heaven, and humbling himself, entered the Virgin's womb? To express this belief in works you must humble your pride and vanity. Do you believe that Christ was poor in the world: that he willed to possess nothing? Show this belief in your works by avoiding usury, avarice, and theft.... Do you believe that Christ was most diligent? Then be not slothful in spiritual works. This is faith in action.

An apocalyptic and charismatic tendency was to be found in much of the preaching of this century, but there were also emphases on the reform of the religious orders and the intensification of popular devotion. In Germany and the Low countries John Nider effectively preached reform of the friars and nuns and Johannes Mulberg (d. 1414) the reform of the beguines. John Herolt (d. 1468) lector, prior, and chaplain to the nuns at Nuremberg, left a very popular collection of sermons called *The Disciple* (with supplements) and a *Book of Instruction for Christians* which went through 11 editions by 1521, based on Aquinas but using many other authors. Servatius Franckel also wrote doctrinal sermons based on the *Summa Theologiae*. In Cracow, Poland, Nicholas of Brest was a famous preacher. In France Antonine Defour (d. 1459) was both a renowned preacher and inquisitor, confessor to Louis XII, and Bishop of Marseille.

In Italy there were a host of noted preachers led off by Bl. John Dominici, followed by Manfred of Vercelli (d. after 1431), who was an apocalyptic preacher against the Fraticelli and against St. Bernardine's preaching of the Holy Name. Many others not only preached but gave such good example that many are beatified such as Bl. Stephen Bandelli (d. 1450), who had been a Master of Canon Law at the University of Pavia but became a "second St. Paul" in fiery eloquence, and Bl. Peter Geremia (d. 1452), a civil lawyer at Bologna, a rigorous ascetic whose preaching was admired by St. Vincent Ferrer.

Some of these preachers were also Inquisitors because of the close relation of the two offices. Bl. Bartholomew de Cerverii was martyred at this task in 1466 and Bl. Aimon

Taparelli professor at the University of Turin and confessor to the Duke of Savoy took this dangerous post but lived to be 100. Sixtus IV in 1474 renewed the Inquisition in Latin countries and the Master of the Order, Leonard de Mansuetis, appointed a number of friars to these posts. Two Spanish Dominican inquisitors were denounced to Rome as over severe, yet the King persuaded the Pope to appoint Tomas de Torquemada (d. 1483) who became notorious for his long term of implacable severity for which the Spanish Inquisition has remained infamous as more political than religious.

The Inquisition was always concerned with the suppression of superstition, including the practice of witchcraft which theologians argued could be effective only by a compact with the devil. Until the last quarter of this century trials for witchcraft were relatively rare but for reasons about which historians are still not in agreement they became much more common, climaxing in the next century. Unfortunately the theological arguments and inquisitorial procedures for such trials received their most persuasive formulation in a famous handbook *The Hammer of Witches* by two Dominicans Heinrich Institoris and Jacob Springer (Cologne, 1486)—the same Springer we have seen as one of the great popularizers of the rosary! Yet this book went out of print before the craze reached major proportions and was revived in the next century only by those already involved. I will only note here that the error was not so much the theory of the reality of commerce with demons, as the juridical processes by which guilt was determined, resting on testimony obtained by torture. Such procedures, however, were not invented by the Church, but accepted by it from Roman law and the procedures of secular courts in this period. Indeed most of the trials were secular not ecclesiastic.

Dominican preachers were also active in the missions. In Spain and France Vincent Ferrer is reputed to have converted thousands of Muslims and Jews—the exact facts are hard to verify—but he saw this as a sign of the End Time. Dominicans followed King Henry of Portugal's (d. 1463) explorations in Ceuta and the Madeira Islands, then in Benin and the Congo in 1486, and Guiana after 1491. Diego de Deza, the Dominican Bishop of Palencia, was an important advocate of Christopher Columbus' great enterprise of 1492, although the Franciscans were ultimately more directly involved with it, and, as we shall see, were soon ready to open up missions in the New World.

Another form of preaching which Dominicans have used throughout their history, the glorification of God through the fine arts, was especially active in this century, and three of its artists have been beatified by the Church. Bl. Andrew of Abellon (1375-1450) was an important figure in the spread of Bl. Raymond's reform of the Order in France, as prior of the great shrine of St. Mary Magdalen at St. Maximin in southern France. He was also a skilled illuminator of manuscripts and he encouraged and taught this art both to his friars and to Dominican nuns as a means of support, compatible with the reformed ideals of poverty. In Florence, the great center of Renaissance art, St. Antoninus at San Marco, encouraged the development of these arts for the same economic reasons, but also to a view to using them to lead to religious contemplation. In his convent he found several talented artists who were illuminators, such as Fra Benedetto, but most especially Benedetto's brother Giovanni del Mugello of Fiesole (c. 1387-1455) commonly known as "Fra Angelico" and recently beatified by Pope John Paul II, recognized as one of the greatest artists of the Early Renaissance.

Angelico, with Antoninus, had been a member of Dominici's reformed convent at Fiesole, but became prior of San Marco and with the aid of assistants filled the convent with remarkable murals, including crucifixes in each cell, and painted numerous panel pictures. He was later called to Rome to paint the small chapel of Pope Nicholas V which in a modest way bears comparison with Michelangelo's Sistine Chapel. It has been observed that Angelico had two styles: the panel pictures that were for the public are brilliant in color and narrative in contents; those in the interior of the convent are quiet and symbolic in tone, intended to awaken contemplation. Those in the Vatican chapel, which depict the charity of the deacons Stephen and Lawrence, are a whole theology of the diaconate and are in Angelico's most advanced style, especially in their realistic yet tender depiction of the poor. Critics see in Angelico in many respects not just a medievalist but an innovative painter, conscious of the advances in perspective, anatomy, lighting, and the use of classic models, but what is evident to all is the luminous spirituality of his work which comes perhaps closest of all Renaissance paintings to a true Christian Humanism.

In Bologna Bl. James of Ulm (Jacob Griesinger, d. 1491) was a lay brother who became famous both for his sanctity and his art of making stained glass. It may be that some of his work is still extant but it has not been certainly identified. He is credited with a number of important technical inventions in the art and had a number of successful pupils including Fra Ambrosio of Como and Fra Ambrogino of Soncino who was praised by the noted Renaissance critic Leander Alberti as an "unequalled master." Soon after his death James was regarded as the patron saint of artists in glass.

Girolamo Savonarola, the great preacher of the age, is often remembered because of his "bonfire of the vanities" including obscene art, but he continued this tradition. He lived with Bl. James in Bologna and later became prior of San Marco and proved himself a close friend of many of the Renaissance artists, and it has been shown that his sermons influenced their art. The descriptions of the spirituality which he inculcated in his novices, which included dancing, singing, and pageantry, show that stern ascetic that he was, he shared in the Renaissance spirit. He was born at Ferrara in 1452 and was encouraged to serious study of the classics, Plato, Aristotle, and Aquinas by his devout but severe grandfather, a Michael Savonarola, and became a medical student. Disappointed in love, he wrote poetry on the corruption of society and the Church.

At age 22 while on a trip to Faenza he was moved to repentance by an Augustinian preacher and, without parental permission entered the Dominicans at Bologna. When he was first assigned to San Marco in Florence, the weakness of his voice, his un-Florentine accent and rough gestures caused his preaching during this period to be so poorly received that he almost gave it up. When working on a sermon in the churchyard of the monastery of San Giorgio he experienced his "first" (as he called it in his confession) prophetic illumination with an insight into the seven reasons why the Church must be punished and reformed.

He then began to preach in a new way. After teaching in

Bologna and laboring as an itinerant preacher in many towns, he finally returned to San Marco in 1490 as a lector, and first attracted large audiences not by his homilies but by evening "lectures" in the rose garden at San Marco in a direct, non-rhetorical style on the *Apocalypse*, stressing three points: the renewal of the Church, the troubles Italy would have to suffer before this would come about, and that these events were imminent. He says that he based these themes not on the prophetic insights which he had even then received but simply on scriptural arguments. Since even this raised considerable objections, he repeatedly decided to give up preaching this message but found he could not without boring his hearers and himself! Finally in 1491 while preparing a sermon for the Second Sunday of Lent he struggled all day Saturday and throughout a night of thunder and lightning which struck the cathedral to make up his mind to say no more about these matters, until, exhausted, he heard a voice saying, "Fool, don't you see God wills you should proclaim these matters in this way?" He arose to give, he says, a "terrifying" sermon. Lorenzo the Magnificent lay seriously ill and took the storm as a sign of his death which occurred three days later, but only after Savonarola, who before had always refused to meet him, had come and blessed him.

Soon elected prior of San Marco he reformed it according to his own ideas of strict poverty, intending at first to move it out of the wicked city, but then with the recently elected Alexander VI's permission he joined it with Fiesole and Pisa as a reformed congregation independent of the Lombardy Province. In Advent 1491 he began a series of sermons on *Genesis* which continued until 1494 (except for a Lent preached in Bologna in 1493). His hearers remarked that these sermons paralleled the sequence of events occurring at that time in Florence and that it was taking him a very long time to get to the story of the Flood. In 1492, probably especially troubled by his knowledge that Alexander VI's election had been simoniacal, during the night before his last Advent sermon he saw in a vision a hand with a sword on which was inscribed, "The sword of the Lord swiftly and speedily over the earth" and above it the words, "True and just are the Lord's judgments." He then saw that the arm belonged to One with three faces shining in one light, each of which in turn spoke of judgment and mercy. Then he saw the whole globe to which countless angels in white, carrying red crosses descended, as the hand turned the sword toward earth amidst thunder and lightning. The angels then walked among the peoples of the earth offering them chalices of pure wine which some eagerly drank, others refused, and others hesitated to drink.

After this Savonarola began to predict the coming of a second Cyrus, namely, Charles VIII of France, to punish Italy but that Charles would spare Florence if it did penance. It seems he had also predicted the death of Innocent VIII and Lorenzo de Medici, and the revolution and reform of the Florentine state. But in September when, as he had been predicting for a long time, Charles VIII of France finally invaded Italy, conquering every city that resisted him and marching toward Florence, the preacher arrived at the text, "Behold I will bring the waters of the Flood over the whole earth" and his hearers realized where all these sermons had been leading. The great humanist, Pico della Mirandola, was present at this sermon and says that it made his hair stand on end.

In these sermons Savonarola often repeated sayings he had received in visions:

> Rejoice and exult, you just, but prepare your souls for trials by reading, meditation, and prayer, and you will be freed from the second death. But you, worthless servants who live in filth, wallow in it still! Fill your bellies with wine, ungird your loins for lust, pollute your hands with the blood of the poor; for this is your portion and destiny! But know that you are body and soul in my hand and soon your bodies will be torn by scourges and your souls cast into everlasting fire!

On the approach of Charles he again saw the threatening sword and began fasting on bread and water until he was so weak he could hardly preach. On All Saints and for the next two days he called the people to penance, before he accompanied an embassy to make peace with Charles. Charles bypassed Florence but otherwise failed to heed Savonarola's admonitions and eventually was forced to withdraw from Italy.

Savonarola then carried through his great reform of Florence as a Republic after the model of Venice.

But his enemies, which included the friends of the expelled Medici and the libertines of the city, in particular the active homosexuals, were urging Alexander VI to silence him, which happened in July of 1495. He excused himself from going to Rome to answer because of his poor health but he retired to Fiesole and wrote a *Compendium* to explain what he was preaching, namely, under certain conditions the approaching punishment and reform of the Church, the conversion of the Turks and Moors in the life time of his hearers, and unconditionally the glory of Florence. The first seems to have been fulfilled in the Reformation, the second can be interpreted as the great extension of the Church's missions fulfilled not in Islam but in the New World discovered in 1492. The third was certainly not literally fulfilled, but perhaps can be taken as we do the prophecies of Jerusalem's glory in a spiritual sense as applying only to the remnant who repented.

While Savonarola was preparing this answer, Alexander sent a letter accusing him of heresy and announcing he must be examined by a theological commission of his Order. He promised to obey and did so when he received a repetition of the order to cease preaching, but in 1496 the commission cleared him and the Signoria of Florence obtained verbal permission from Alexander for him to resume preaching. Alexander then revoked his permission for the Congregation, thus putting Savonarola under the Vicar of Lombardy who did not favor him, but the friars of San Marco objected and Savonarola awaited the answer to their appeal.

In 1497 the Arriabati ("the Enraged") renewed their plots and tried to assassinate him. In May the Pope in a highly non-canonical way excommunicated him as a heretic and for resisting the abolition of his Congregation and forbade attendance at his sermons. Savonarola observed this excommunication out of respect for papal authority, although he believed it unjust and canonically invalid, and wrote his great apologetic work *The Triumph of the Cross* which is entirely orthodox and recognizes papal authority. But the situation of the reform of Florence rapidly deteriorated and Savonarola finally felt justified in returning to the pulpit to prevent the Republic's collapse.

The Franciscans, however, dared one of his disciples to prove the Prophet's authenticity and sanctity by an ordeal by fire, and reluctantly Savonarola accepted the challenge. On the day of the ordeal the Franciscan challenger temporized and a rainstorm extinguished the fire. The infuriated mob that night stormed San Marco and dragged the Prophet and his companions to prison, where he was in the power of his enemies who tortured him ruthlessly. Savonarola confessed under torture, but withdrew his confessions each time the torture ceased. Finally his examiners produced a confession (probably forged) and he was condemned to death. To the Order's shame the aged Master of the Order, Torriani, signed the condemnation. The Prophet and his companions were hanged and the bodies burned May 23, 1498, in the public square, but only after receiving the sacraments and a plenary indulgence from Alexander VI! Thus with prophecies of the coming punishment and reform of the Church the century ended.

5

Reformers (1500s)

Community

In the 1500s the prophecies of Savonarola and many others of divine punishment on the Church were fulfilled: the Church (and the Order of Preachers) lost one-third of Europe, England, Scandinavia, and came close to losing France and Poland, and Bohemia as well. At the same time the prophecies of renewal were also fulfilled by the Catholic Reformation of the Council of Trent (1545-1563) and the missions of the Church were extended to the vast New World.

In Germany Martin Luther, an Augustinian friar and doctor of theology, in 1517 brought to a head both the long festering resentment of the Germans against the political and worldly Renaissance Popes and the yearnings of German mysticism for an experiential, personal interpretation of the Gospel. Huldryck Zwingli in Switzerland and John Calvin in France formulated a more rationalistic and radical Reformed Church. Both Lutherans and Calvinists were influenced by the Humanism of the times to rest their interpretations of the Gospel on the biblical text independent of the living tradition of the Catholic Church which they regarded as hopelessly corrupt, while they also shared some of the apocalyptic anxieties we have seen in the previous century. Moreover, they pressed the emphasis on the preached Word, rather than on the sacraments, which we have seen was characteristic, in a more moderate form, of the mendicant friars. Thus, in some respects Protestantism took up certain themes dear to Dominicans but in a one-sided way. Was this one-sidedness in part the result of the fact that the Nominalism in which Luther was raised cut him off from the balanced views of Thomism, with whom it seems he had only a remote acquaintance?

On the other hand this tragic schism within the Christian fold at last forced the Catholic Church to complete its own reform which had begun much earlier with the inspiration of prophets like St. Catherine of Siena and Savonarola, and this reform gave it the energy to take one of its greatest expansions, the missions to the Americas and beyond.

The Catholic reform of the Church had become a concern of the papacy even before the Lutheran crisis. Leo X, who provoked this crisis by using indulgences as a means to building a new St. Peter's in Rome, had convened the reforming Council of the Lateran V in 1512 but failed to implement its decrees effectively. Throughout this century the Popes in their reforming efforts tended more and more to centralize church government in their own hands, including control over the religious orders. To promote reform or political interests the Popes and Cardinal Protectors regularly overrode the Dominican *Constitutions* and transferred elective Chapters to Rome under Vicars who were their candidates for Master of the Order. Vincent Bandelli, 1501, an observant of Lombardy was a brilliant and amiable Master, yet was rumored to be the model for Judas in the great *Last Supper* painted by Da Vinci in the convent where he was prior. Bandelli founded the observant Congregations of Ragusa in 1501 and of Ireland in 1505, but his general policy was to try to reform whole Provinces into which he incorporated the reluctant Observants, as when in 1505 the Province of Spain accepted reform he suppressed its Congregation. He did not suppress the Congregation of San Marco founded by Savonarola, but he discouraged the Prophet's cult and special customs. Yet he was blocked from reforming the royal convent of St. Maximin by its prior, Pierre Bonnetti, who had amassed the revenues of the offices of provincial, royal counselor, and superior of two

Benedictine priories! Thus when in 1505 the Master reported on his visitations he had to lament, "On my way I found some consolations, but the reasons for sorrow and shame were greater." In 1506 he issued a new edition of the *Constitutions* and foiled Julius II's and Cardinal Protector Caraffa's efforts to set definite limits to the terms of superiors.

After Bandelli's death in Sicily in 1507, John Clerée, of the Congregation of Holland, a noted preacher, confessor to Louis XII, and reformer of the nuns and of St. Jacques in Paris, was elected by the King's favor (to Julius II's displeasure), but promptly died, some say by poison. Because the forced conversion of Jews in Spain had made their orthodoxy suspect, Clerée was the first Master to forbid their reception into the Order. His successor was the greatest Master of the century, Thomas de Vio, called "Cajetan the Brief" both in height and speech. His nose was large and aquiline, eyes squinting, intelligence incisive, will and temper powerful. A certain Duke on meeting him whispered to another Dominican, "Do you receive abortions into your Order!" At 26 the youngest Dominican, except Aquinas, to receive the doctorate, he taught at Padua and Pavia, and then became by Cardinal Caraffa's favor Procurator General and finally in 1508, against much opposition, Master of the Order. His first encyclical, only nine lines long, simply urged poverty and study.

Cajetan created the Province of Betica and divided the Congregation of Holland into the Gallican Congregation and the Province of Lower Germany. Unlike Bandelli, he did not insist on more rules, but on their prudent observance and he forbade for ten years, talk of visions and revelations by the San Marco Savonarolians. He opposed the schismatic Council of Pisa, called by the Emperor and King of France against Julius II, while urging Julius to summon the reforming Lateran Council V in 1512, at which Cajetan stoutly defended papal authority against the concilarists and the mendicants against the bishops. He also revised the *Constitutions* and the liturgy, before being made cardinal in 1517. His major role in the Reformation crisis caused him to be ridden backward on an ass by a Lutheran mob through the streets of Rome in the siege of 1527. To his death in 1534 he continued to write innovative works.

Cajetan's Vicar, Garcias de Loaysa, a Spanish observant, frail in health, smooth of manner, was only forty when elected. His first encyclical enforced common life, forbade friars to keep money longer than 24 hours, and ordered priors to see all their friars ate as well as themselves. The elective Chapter approved the reform of the Scotch Province and an observant Congregation for Ireland. Loaysa visitated Naples, Sicily, and Spain where he became Charles V's confessor, angering those Dominicans who opposed Charles' succession and thought Loaysa a "climber" when in 1524 he resigned to become bishop, cardinal, and Grand Inquisitor, and a bitter opponent of Bartolomé de Las Casas in the Indies.

The famous theologian, Francisco Silvestri of Ferrara, an observant, was elected Master in 1525. He had been the director and biographer of Bl. Osanna D'Andreasi, and had written to defend the phenomena of stigmatization among Dominican mystics. The elective Chapter promoted studies and forbade exclaustrated friars (evidently then numerous) to wear the habit. In 1528 Silvester visitated North Italy and South France where he reformed the nuns, but on his way to Spain by boat, this over-weight theologian fell overboard, took cold, and died. The contemporary historian Sebastian Olmeda says that Paul Butigella promoted his own election to Master in 1530, although sick of the gout which a year later killed him. During his term in 1530 the Congregations of St. Mark and Tuscany were converted into the reformed Roman Province (most of the conventuals then became exclaustrated or secularized), the noted Congregation of Lombardy into the Province of the Two Lombardies' and those of Calabria and of Aragon into reformed provinces. Thus the only observant congregations left were the Gallican congregation and those of Naples, France, Ireland, and Poland. A single province, Holy Cross, centered in Santo Domingo, was created in the New World.

Jean du Feynier was elected in 1532 after the Cardinal Protector had so often changed the Chapter's location that the delegates wandered all over Europe before their arduous journeys again ended in Rome. Feynier was an amiable French conventual from Berne, reputed to grant dispensations too gratefully for gifts. Yet, after he visitated Spain and Portugal,

Bartolomé de las Casas

in France he was jailed not only as a friend of Emperor Charles V, but also for refusing to permit Francis I to impose the noble Jeanne D'Amboise on the unwilling nuns of Prouille as prioress. Feynier died shortly after his release in 1538. The Chapter of Lyons in 1536, if not stopped by the Pope, would have changed the constitutional alternation of chapters of provincials and elected delegates.

Although Feynier accomplished little as Master, this period saw great events. From Luther's protest in 1517 to 1538 the Preachers had led the opposition, but in 1538 the Society of Jesus was officially approved with no little help from the Dominican theologians consulted by the Pope as to the orthodoxy of this radically new form of religious life. Meanwhile, the second American province, St. James of Mexico was founded in 1532, then St. John the Baptist of Peru in 1539.

Augustinus Recuperati, elected in 1539, died the next year (St. Catherine de Ricci is said to have seen him in a vision in hell!). His attempt to reform the Province of Portugal by sending in Spanish observants was resisted, and his methods in reforming the convent of Genoa were rebuked by the Pope. He witnessed the ruin of the English Province, isolated by the tyranny of Henry VIII since 1523, when the King made John Hilsey and Richard Ingworth successively provincial and then bishops. Six out of 53 convents apostatized but most Dominican friars and nuns fled to their families or the continent and the Order ceased to exist in England.

Albert de Casaus of the Province of Betica, the Emperor's candidate, was elected in 1542 but soon wished to resign, and in 1544 died suddenly at Valladolid, again with rumors of poisoning. A student of Garcia Loyasa and the historian Sebastian Olmedo, Albert had a speech impediment and was an authoritarian but able administrator who wished to set a term for the Mastership and to alternate an Italian and a non-Italian in the office. In 1542 at the urging of the Dominican Cardinal of Toledo, Juan Alvarez, Paul III instituted the Congregation of the Holy Office, although the Spanish Inquisition remained under royal control.

Francis Romeo de Castiglione loved solitude, but was taken by Feynier as a companion on visitations. On one such visit he became a friend of St. Catherine de Ricci. Elected in 1546 he visitated France (against royal resistance) and Spain where he rebuked the observants for their excessive concern with externals rather than interior spirituality. The Chapter of 1551 in Salamanca restricted the Master of Theology degree to veteran teachers in one of the Order's 27 Old and New World universities. Romeo attended the end of the first period (1545-47) of the Council of Trent and much of the second (1551-52), which many Dominicans attended. By this time the order had lost to the Reformation the five provinces of Scandinavia, England, Ireland, Scotland and Germany, but gained five new ones in the Americas when it divided the Province of Peru to form that of the Indies (St.Vincent) and of New Grenada (St. Antoninus). After Trent ended, Romeo died in Rome of a stroke.

Between the second and third period of Trent, Stephen Usodimare was Master (1553-57). A Genoese of a Spanish family, an observant, he was the Pope's candidate. His health made visitations impossible, so he occupied himself with writing a work to protect the privileges of the Order from Trent's restrictions on exemption. He also founded a hospice for the many brethren who came to Rome. Made Cardinal in 1557, he died the same year.

Next came another Genoese, Vincent Giustiniani, of a noble, wealthy family which gave many notable members to the Order. A student and Vicar of Usodimare, without papal pressure he was elected in 1558. His first letter lamented the ruin of the Saxon, Hungarian, and Bohemian Provinces. Soon the three French provinces were added to the list. The elective Chapter ordered each province to have only one novitiate and its many strictures on private life show conventualism was not yet dead. The Chapters also fought Protestant trends within the Order. Giustiniani's attempt at direct control of St. Jacques to maintain reform was prevented by the King, but he managed to visitate Spain, Aragon, Portugal, and even Southern France torn by religious war.

A Dominican, St. Pius V, was elected pope in 1566 and was present at the 1569 Chapter. He was born of a poor family. As a Dominican he had held the offices of novice master, prior of several communities, and inquisitor, known for his personal efforts to save the accused, and as bishop and cardinal for his concern for the poor. As Pope he continued this care, enforced the decrees of Trent on bishops, assisted the Oratorians and the Jesuits, sought to rescue Mary Queen of Scots, by prayer gained the rescue of Christendom for the Turks at Lepanto in 1571, but took the fatal decision to excommunicate Elizabeth of England. For the Dominicans he forbade apartments in convents, gave precedence to the Preachers among the mendicants, and interpreted the exemption decrees of Trent to permit Dominicans to preach in their own churches without episcopal license. He also sponsored new editions of the *Constitutions* in 1566 and of the works of St. Thomas in 1570. In the same year, Pius after sending Giustiani as a diplomat to Spain, made him cardinal. His nephew Cardinal Michel Bonelli was so long a Protector of the Order that his "protection" finally became near control.

St. Pius V also presided at the election of Seraphin Cavalli in 1571. Born at Brescia, tall, very thin, ascetic, but gracious in manner, Cavalli was nicknamed "The Pious." In 1559 as a

Commissar of the Holy Office he had almost been killed by a mob storming the Vatican on the death of Paul IV. He had accompanied Giustiniani in Spain and at Trent. He visitated Tuscany and Lombardy with its 69 convents and 17 smaller houses and 34 monasteries of nuns. At Pisa he was said to have miraculously cured Sister Malaspina who had been paralyzed for five years. He visitated France then enjoying a short peace from religious wars, and punished his Vicar for appealing to the King to retain his office. Cavalli also dared Calvinist persecution to visit the Low Countries. On the way to Spain, near Lyons, he escaped pursuing Huguenots by prayers that brought an unexpected ferry boat. In 1577 he dealt with the case of a convent in Spain which had become a refuge of criminals, visitated Sicily, and converted the Congregation of Abruzzi to the reformed Province of St. Catherine. After visiting the Province of Betica, he died at Seville in 1578. Crowds fought for his relics as those of a saint.

In 1580 Cardinal Bonelli pressured the electors to pass over Sixtus Fabri and take Paul Constabile from Ferrara, who because of dubious company as a young professor had been delated to the Inquisition, but who had himself become a zealous inquistor and finally Master of the Sacred Palace. He was an ascetic especially careful of chastity, who served the poor, longed for martyrdom, and proved a severe but just superior. He visited Naples and Sicily and praised the Spanish and Portuguese friars for their missionary zeal but rebuked the French for its lack. At this time the Philippine Congregation was being formed. Constabile died in Bologna in 1582 with a reputation of sanctity.

The delegates of the next Chapter in 1583 were at last free to elect Sixtus Fabri, who as an assistant to Cavalli had visited many provinces, but was then Master of the Sacred Palace. Much concerned for studies, he issued a new *Ratio Studiorum* and ordered negligent teachers and students to be jailed. He also enforced Trent's decrees for cloistered nuns. The Uniate Friars of Armenia (founded in 1344) were at last made a Province and allowed to wear the Order's white scapular with their own violet habit and striped turban. To face the Order's greatly changed situation in the Church, Fabri called a most general Chapter in 1588, but it never met. St. Catherine de

Ricci, whose stigmata he tested, prophetically warned him not to become involved in the case of another reputed Dominican stigmatic of Lisbon, Maria of the Visitation, but he did not heed. When Maria confessed she had faked her miracles to promote the liberation of Portugal from Spain, Sixtus V (at Bonelli's urging) deposed Fabri, who refused to resign. Exiled to Florence while the Pope lived, Fabri returned to Rome to die at Santa Sabina in 1594. Fabri's term, Mortier says, which saw the rise of the new Jesuit model of religious life, marks the end of the Mendicant Age in the Church.

Hippolytus M. Beccaria although frail in health proved a most energetic Master. Born at Mondovi in North Italy he taught philosophy at Bologna, then held a series of important offices before election in 1589 as Master at only 39. Yet to avoid the control of Cardinal Bonelli, he had to stay away from Rome until Bonelli's death in 1598. Tirelessly he visited Germany, Austria, Spain, Portugal, Bohemia, Hungary, Poland, traveling painfully by carriage, often amidst religious wars. The Polish friars treated him so badly he absented himself from St. Hyacinth's canonization in 1594.

Beccaria celebrated four Chapters which with papal support strove to resist adaptation of Dominican observance to fit the Jesuit model. Clement VIII also forbade the friars to bankrupt themselves by gifts to protectors and other dignitaries to obtain favors. Yet Chapters began to call the Master "Most Reverend" and Beccaria himself proposed to imitate the Jesuits by replacing the election of superiors with appointment. Fortunately, Cardinal Protector Bernieri, himself a Dominican, vetoed this radical change in the Order's government. The Chapters divided the Mexican Province of St. Hippolytus de Guaxaca from that of St. James. At the siege of Paris by the Huguenot Henri III, the friars of St. Jacques took up arms to defend their city. The fanatic young Dominican Jacques Clement, fired by the preaching of Prior Bourgoing, assassinated Henri. In France the Order narrowly escaped suppression, yet the Chapter of 1592 called these patriots (but not Clement) "martyrs."

Significant for the future was the reform of the Midi. Giustiniani in 1569 had converted the Congregation of France into the Province of Occitania as an enclave within the Provinces of Toulouse and Provence, but it languished until Sebastian Michaelis became its second provincial in 1588. He first reformed Clermont-Herault, a great convent ruined like most of the province by the Huguenots, but failed with the royal convents of St. Maximin and St. Baume. In 1599, however, Michaelis, no longer Provincial, became Prior of Toulouse and there the reform took firm root.

Under Beccaria, in 1599 the great controversy on grace (*de auxiliis*) began with the Jesuits. Beccaria maintained that truth and not rivalry with the Society was the only issue. He died the next year at the Chapter of Naples.

Study

The great theological battle of the century was over Luther's attempt to reform the Church by the principle of *sola fides, sola gratia, sola Scriptura*, or justification by faith based on the Bible only. Since Luther's first attack was provoked by the crass preaching of indulgences by a Dominican, John Tetzel (d. 1519), to raise money to build the new St. Peter's in Rome, it was fitting Dominicans should engage in the counterattack. Not only was Cajetan the pope's legate in dealing with Luther, but the first to censor his works was Leo X's theologian Sylvester Mazolinus de Prierio (Prierius, d. 1523), author of a much used confessor's manual, the "Silvestrina" (not to mention an inquisitor's manual on witchcraft) and a spiritual anthology, *The Golden Rose*. Naturally, this struggle was carried on mainly by German Dominicans, but others also vigorously participated.

Debate with the Protestants stimulated biblical study. While the French Dominican Spiritus Roterus (1564) opposed vernacular versions of the Bible, others such as Joannes Dietenberg (d. 1537) undertook translations into German (1524). The two outstanding Dominican biblical scholars were Santes Pagnino (d. 1541), a disciple of Savonarola, who produced a new translation of the whole Bible very faithful to the Hebrew (hence criticized by some as "too rabbinic" (Lyons, 1528)), a Hebrew dictionary and other Bible aids; and Sixtus of Siena (d. 1569), a baptized Jew who became a Franciscan.

Convicted of heresy he was saved by a Dominican inquisitor, the future St. Pius V, and wrote the first great introduction to the Bible, his two-volume *Bibliotheca sancta.*

The Council of Trent insisted against Luther on Tradition as well as Scripture as source of the Word of God, and a Dominican scholar, Giacomo Nacchiante (Naclantus, d. 1569), a fellow student with Pius V, was censored for his speech at Trent exalting the Bible over Tradition. The balance was struck by a Spaniard, Melchior Cano (d. 1560) in his treatise, *Theological Resources* (*De Locis Theologicis*, Salamanca 1563), which initiated a new branch of theology—positive theology or the study of sources. But at first, his confreres, still attached to the ahistorical approach of scholasticism, little appreciated its significance. While there was some attention to church history and patrology, most of the effort was devoted to the history of the Order.

The debate over Luther's central doctrine of justification came to a climax at the Council of Trent in which many Dominicans were participants—in all 18 bishops and 27 theologians. Important figures at the first session were the Master of the Order, Francisco Romeo, Bishop Ambrosius Catharinus (d. 1553, an independent-minded Dominican, defender of the Immaculate Conception and other non-Thomistic positions), Bartolomé Spina (d. 1546, who considered Catherinus a heretic and fought Cajetan's views on immortality), and Domingo de Soto (d. 1560). Prominent at the second session were Bartolomé Carranza, Archbishop of Toledo (d. 1576, whose famous *Catechism* led him to be imprisoned for many years by the Inquisition) and the theologian Melchior Cano (one of Carranza's chief accusers) and foe of the Anabaptists Ambrose Storch (Pelargus, 1557). At the third session were Master Giustiniani with his socius, Cavalli, the reformer Bartholomew of the Martyrs, Bishop of Braga (1582), Antonio Havet, Bishop of Namur, the inquisitor Camillo Campeggi, the Salamanca professor Joannes Gall, and others. At the completion of the Council the famous *Catechism of Trent* for preachers (1566) was chiefly the work of the Dominican bishops, Leonardo de Marino of Lanciano, Muzio Calini of Zara, Egidio Foscarini of Modena, and the Portuguese theologian Francisco Fureiro.

But Trent did not finish the debates over justification and

grace within the Catholic camp, especially over the interpretation of the views of St. Augustine which had so much influenced both Luther and Calvin. At the University of Louvain Michael Baius (d. 1589) proposed his own interpretation of Augustine on grace which resulted in a papal condemnation. In defense of this condemnation the rising Society of Jesus proposed new views, and a Spanish Jesuit, Prudencio de Montemayor, in 1581 provoked strong criticism from a student of Melchior Cano at Salamanca, Domingo Báñez (d. 1604). The *Harmony of Free Will, Grace, and Predestination* (*Concordia*) of another Jesuit, Luis de Molina (d. 1600) drew further attacks from Báñez in 1588. The debate then broke out at the University of Valladolid between Antonio de Padilla, S.J., and Diego Nuno, O.P., and was taken up at Salamanca, Saragossa, Cordova, etc. After Pope Clement VIII had queried the opinions of the universities he handed the matter to a commission of cardinals which after two examinations was unfavorable to Molina's work. In 1598 Clement asked the Dominican and Jesuit generals to attempt a reconciliation and then, this failing, entrusted it to a special Congregation which met for 68 sessions from 1602 to 1605, with Clement often present. After his death it continued under Leo XI, then Paul V, until Paul finally suspended it and ordered that neither party should call the other heretical. The chief Dominican presenters were Diego Alvarez (d. 1635) and Tomas de Lemos (d. 1629) and for the Jesuits, Gregory of Valencia and three others.

These controversies at least served to discredit the Nominalism which had long dominated the universities and which had in part given rise to the justification problem and stimulated what is called the "Second" or "Baroque Scholasticism" with a renewal of the high medieval systems of Augustinianism, Thomism, and Scotism in the universities, while Humanism reached it apogee in the rest of the culture. Among Dominicans the revival of Thomism begun by Capreolus in the previous period was taken up vigorously and with more originality by Cajetan, no longer so much in opposition to Nominalism as to Scotism. Cajetan's most famous works were his commentary on Aquinas' *Summa Theologiae* which the editors of the critical edition chose to include as the best of all such commentaries, concise, subtle, and witty, two special philosophical treatises, *On Being and Essence* and *On the Analogy of Names*, and the widely used *Summary for Confessors.* He wrote many short works on current topics, especially on papal authority, on usury and other moral questions, and extensive commentaries on the Bible, those on the New Testament from the Greek with considerable critical sense. Some experts detect certain influences in his works from the radical Averroists of his times against whom he fought, especially as regards his hesitations over Aquinas' proofs for the natural incorruptibility of the human soul, a point on which he was attacked especially by Bartolomé de Spina.

Cajetan when Master of the Order insisted on strict application to study and the Chapters from 1551 stressed that all teaching of philosophy and theology in Dominican schools must be strictly Thomistic. In 1567 Pius V declared Thomas a Doctor of the Church and insisted that Dominican professors teach philosophy several years before teaching theology. At this time Dominican students, after four years of humanities before or during the novitiate, then studied logic for two years, natural philosophy and metaphysics for three, and theology (with parallel courses in dogmatics and moral) for four. They first read the introduction to logic of Peter of Spain (Pope John XXI) and then the text of the major treatises of Aristotle with their commentaries by St. Thomas, and then the *Summa Theologiae*, article by article, according to the interpretation of Capreolus and Cajetan. This insured a strongly philosophical, Aristotelian understanding of Aquinas' theology often missing today. Teaching was by lecture with the student copying the lecture verbatim in his notebook on penalty of sitting on the floor of the lecture hall if he grew inattentive.

Paris was still by reputation the center of learning, but by the middle of the century the Spanish universities in this the Golden Age of the Spanish Empire were the real center. No Dominican could now be made a Master of Theology without having taught at least four years in one of the approved universities. Those of Spain were Salamanca, Valladolid, Segovia, Seville, Toledo, Alcalá (Complutum), and Valencia, but in its New World Empire were soon founded or partly staffed by Dominicans: Santo Domingo (1551), Lima (1551), Mexico

City (1553), Bogotá (1580), Guatemala (1589), Mexico (1589), Cuzco (1598).

The leader of this revival was Francisco de Vitoria (c. 1483-1546), whose parents were of the royal court of Castille. He studied in Burgos, entered the Order there when he was only 15, and was soon sent to Paris, which at that time was the center of a rich variety of intellectual trends, to study at St. Jacques under Jean de Feynier, later Master of the Order, and Peter Crockaert of Brussels (d. 1514, who had studied under the Scotch John Mayor d. 1550, nominalist and teacher of John Knox and himself an anti-papist), author of notable commentaries on the logic of Peter of Spain and Aristotle, on Aristotle's *Physics* and *De Anima* and on the *Summa Theologiae II-II.*Vitoria then taught philosophy and theology there from 1516 and edited the great moral work of St. Antoninus, the sermons of Pedro de Cordoba, and a dictionary of morals. He received his doctorate in 1522 and was sent to teach at the Collegio de San Gregorio in Valladolid and in 1526 to the "morning chair" at Salamanca. Salamanca was becoming the greatest university of Spain, but its students were turbulent, given to great banquets for graduation and demanding classes in the vernacular, and a professor had to earn his authority. Vitoria proved a great teacher, clear, incisive, and elegant in his mastery of classical Latin, praised by his university colleague, the great humanist Nicholas Clenardo. Evading academic regulations, he taught not from the *Sentences* but from the *Summa* in a style which did not belabor the obvious but took up the interesting and previously undiscussed points. For twenty years, except for some brief interruptions because of health, he was the leader and reformer of the university and made it the greatest one in Europe.

At Paris Vitoria had been sympathetic to the humanistic reform of the Church being proposed by Erasmus of Rotterdam, but now with his brother Pedro he joined (although with notable moderation and objectivity) in the efforts of the Inquisition to check its influence in Spain. He preferred the reforming ideas of Ignatius Loyola who (still under suspicion for his innovations) visited at Vitoria's residence, San Esteban, under the protection of its noted prior, Juan Hurtado de Mendoza. Vitoria composed a *Commentary on the Summa Theologiae*

II-II, q. 1-140 and numerous notes on his other lectures, notably on the sacraments are extant, but his greatest work is the series of *Relectiones* ("Repetitions" or summary of lectures which professors were required to prepare for the students on the completion of a course, and which amount to concise treatises on certain key topics).

Four of these treatises deal with the relations of church and state and of the pope and councils, in which Vitoria took the then radical view that the Pope's sovereignty over temporal rulers is only indirect, and that the Pope must, except for grave reasons follow conciliar decisions. Because of this Sixtus V almost placed them (and Bellarmine's works) on the Index. Two others concern the great question of just war and of the rights of the Native Americans, which made San Esteban a center for pro-Indian theologians and missionaries and gave Vitoria the title "Father of International Law." The others are chiefly on moral and sacramental questions, including notable treatments of the right ot life, marriage in reference to Henry VIII's divorce, and usury.

Vitoria and Domingo Soto had many brilliant students. Soto (d. 1560), who taught at Salamanca from 1532, effectively opposed Nominalism, which had been introduced there to compete with the university of Alcalá. In 1545 Charles V sent him as imperial theologian to the Council of Trent, for which he wrote the important *On nature and grace*, and in 1547 called him to Germany as his confessor. In 1550 he returned to Salamanca, was elected prior, and taught until 1556. He wrote numerous philosophical and theological works, of which his *On Right and Law* is especially notable. Among his Dominican students were Melchior Cano, already mentioned, whose work in positive theology was further pursued by Seraphinus Razzi (d. c. 1613) and Paul Grysaldus, (d. 1609); Martin Ledesma (d. 1594) who with Cano helped establish the important theological center of Coimbra in Portugal; Pedro de Soto (no relative of Domingo) who under Mary Tudor taught at Oxford; Bartolomé Carranza; Vincente Valverde, first Bishop of Cuzco, and Jerónimo Loaysa, first Archbishop of Lima, and less directly Bartolomé de las Casas. But his influence reached far beyond his Dominican brethren. Another influential Spaniard was Diego de Deza (d. 1523), inquisitor and Archbishop of Toledo who supported the cause of Columbus.

Outside Spain many other important Thomists taught in universities, such as Isidore de Isolano (d. 1522) who wrote on missiology, but innovatively on Josephology; Francesco Silvestri of Ferrara (d. 1525) who wrote the classical commentary on the *Summa Contra Gentiles*; and Chrysostom Javellus (d. 1538), author of an important manual on philosophy but a dissenter on the Thomistic theory of predestination. Dominicans (except Catherinus and some of the Spaniards) continued to argue against the doctrine of the Immaculate Conception, notably Cajetan and the German Wigandus Wirt (1519) who provoked a considerable controversy from which he was forced to retreat. Others such as Bartolomé Spina, Vincent Colzaldo (d. 1532), and Antonio Marrapha (d. 1550), wrote against Pomponazzi and Cajetan on the question of the immortality of the soul. Spina also opposed Cajetan's original views on original sin, baptism, necessity of confession, power of the Pope, marriage, etc.

The Protestant attack on the Sacrament of Penance and its renewal by the Council of Trent stimulated activity in moral theology. Along with more fundamental works like those of Vitoria, there was a flood of manuals and books of "cases of conscience" for confessors, such as those of Cajetan and Silvester Prierio already mentioned.

We should not forget two remarkable apostates from the Order. The first is Martin Bucer (Butzer, d. 1551) an Alsatian of a poor family who joined the Order to get an education, was influenced first by Erasmus then by Luther, left the Order in 1521 and married. He lived first at Strasbourg, then in England, where he considerably influenced the *Book of Common Prayer*. He is noted for his ecumenical efforts to reconcile the Lutheran and Reformed churches. The other apostate is Giordano Bruno (d. 1600), a Neapolitan, influenced by the notion of the "Ancient Theology" which many Renaissance Humanists believed underlay all religions and who developed a pantheistic philosophy. He wandered through all Europe seeking to make his living by teaching an "art of memory" which would communicate this philosophy. He was finally lured, by someone to whom he had tried to sell this art, back into Italy where he was denounced to the Inquisition.

When he would not consent to return to the Order, he was turned over to secular authorities who burned him at the stake as a stubborn heretic.

The fate of these two men makes clear that in this century underneath the prevailing Thomism there must also have been currents of other traditions of thought which have as yet been little researched by historians of the Order. Because of its great success in resolving many of the problems of the century in an orthodox manner at the Council of Trent, Thomism was now being adopted by other religious Orders, notably by some Augustinians and Carmelites and as the basis of education for the members of the new Society of Jesus.

Prayer

The forms of Dominican prayer did not change greatly in this century, since St. Pius V in 1570 required uniformity throughout the Roman Rite, according to the revision of the Council of Trent, in order to suppress changes made under Protestant influences, but explicitly excepted uses then more than 200 years old. While the Franciscans chose to accept the uniform Tridentine rite, the Dominicans with the Carthusians, Carmelites and others chose to retain their traditional usages. Yet in 1553 certain minor changes were introduced and Master Becaria's assistant Paul Castrucci edited the Missal in 1600 with new rubrics. Some of these changes influenced by the humanist style of Latin and baroque ceremony were unfortunate. The Chapters made several attempts to accommodate the new emphasis on formal meditation and finally in 1574 decreed that the friars should stay in choir in common prayer for a quarter of an hour after compline.

It was, however, a century marked both by many apostasies and by great holiness of many of the priests and cooperator brothers. Most remarkable were the women. Thus there were a number of women who followed the model of St. Catherine of Siena as Tertiaries, gifted as prophetesses, marked with the sacred stigmata and inspired by Savonarola's ideas of reform such as Bl. Stephana de Quinzanis (d. 1530); Bl. Lucia of Narni (d. 1544) who became the object of a struggle between the rival towns of Narni and Viterbo who wanted her to reside with each; Bl. Catherine of Racconigi (d. 1547) and Dominica of Paradiso (d. 1553).

The most notable of all was Catherine de Ricci, born in 1522 of an ancient noble family of Florence, and named Sandrina. Her mother died when she was four and she was raised by a stepmother and educated at the Benedictine monastery at Monticelli where two of her aunts were nuns. Still a child, she acquired a deep devotion to the crucifix, which set the pattern of her whole life. At nine she insisted on leaving the monastery because she was so shocked by a quarrel between the nuns over a pious book. In the summer of 1533 she met two Dominican nuns who were begging at her father's villa of San Vincenzo at Prato where her uncle Fra Timoteo, was confessor. At 13 against her father's wishes she joined their community of 130. As a novice she began to experience ecstasies as she kept vigil before the crucifix, especially on Thursdays and Fridays. She was professed in 1536, but the nuns agreed only because of Fra Timoteo and the Provincial who was a brother of Catherine's stepmother. Her health soon failed and she was subjected to gallstones, asthma, dropsy, and high fevers, and was bedridden for two years as incurable, until she was miraculously healed on the 22nd vigil of Savonarola's martyrdom in whose honor her father and the community had made vows. Timoteo was frightened by these events, and the provincial Francesco Romeo, the Master of the Order, Albert de Casaus and Cardinal Roberto Ducci on order of Paul III examined her and she was re-examined by every new prior at San Domenico every two years. She was still being accused to the Inquisition at her death.

In 1552, at thirty, she was elected prioress and had to deal with the many problems of the monastery, which was poverty-stricken and lacking a proper church. She held the office for seven terms interspersed by terms as sub-prioress. In her second term 1556-8 she began correspondence with the Grand Ducal family of Florence, the Della Rovere family of Urbino, St. Charles Borromeo, St. Mary Magdalen de Pazzi, St. Philip Neri, Alessandra Luzzago, and the reformed monasteries of San Giorgio and San Domenico in Lucca. In 1554 as a result of earnest prayer by herself and the community to be relieved of the pressures of constant visits by the public, her stigmata healed. She left over 1,000 letters in which her good sense and deep and balanced spirituality are clearly evident. In spite of the poverty of her convent she fed over 300 of the poor each day, sometimes miraculously multiplying bread, and was especially concerned to provide poor girls with dowries for marriage. At first she was guided in her visions chiefly by St. Thomas Aquinas. She died in 1590 and was canonized by Benedict XIV in 1746. Her letters give us a better idea of her spirituality than do the early biographies which over-emphasize the miraculous.

Two spiritual writers of this time are especially notable: Luis of Granada (d. 1588, certainly one of the chief of all Dominican authors on spirituality) and Bartholomew of the Martyrs (d. 1590). Born of a poor family, Luis entered the Order and with Melchior Cano and Bartolomé Carranza studied under Diego de Astudillo, a student of Vitoria. He intended to be a missionary but was sent to Cordova to reform a house which became under his direction a center of Dominican life. Here he met the famous Juan de Avila who had introduced the northern mystical tradition flowing from Eckhart into Spain. Luis was then prior at Badajoz and, at the invitation of the newly founded Jesuits, was called to Coimbra in Portugal where he was elected provincial and declined the archbishopric of Braga in favor of Bartholomew of the Martyrs. He attempted to save Carranza from the Inquisition but failed. After his provincialate he gave himself to writing and preaching and became famous as a spiritual director. His last years were saddened by the political troubles over Portugese independence of Spain and especially by the affair of Sister Maria of the Visitation, whom he had sponsored and who, as we have already seen, turned out to be a clever fraud.

Luis' spiritual works fill many volumes, but the most famous is the *Guide for Sinners*, a complete treatise on the Christian life for lay people. At this time there was in Spain a great controversy over mysticism. Melchior Cano, among others, feared this movement because it seemed to minimize the necessity of good works, the sacraments, and meditation in favor of inner "experience" and thus to be inclined toward Protestant individualism. Luis defended the higher forms of prayer as open even to the laity and sought to meet Cano's objections by a well-balanced view of Christian life. Cano himself wrote notable spiritual works expressing his own point of view.

Bartholomew of the Martyrs, a Portuguese and tutor to royalty, as Archbishop of Braga, played an important role at Trent and in his own church proved a model of a reforming bishop. His ideals and experience are embodied in his *Goal for Pastors* in which, using the writings of the Fathers of the Church, he lays out the role of bishops and pastors, and in his *Catechism* for the laity.

Preaching

The preaching style of this period continued and developed the florid oratorical manner which had been fostered in the previous century by Humanism. Simple instruction or tight theological argumentation were often replaced by a baroque theatricality and "amplification" of standard topics. Moreover, the religious divisions and theological controversies of the time were reflected in a highly polemical approach of exaggerated denunciation and even caricature of the opponent. Yet this also had the advantage of getting away from the excessive scholastic dryness, allegorization of Scripture, and lack of sensitivity to literary taste. The best preaching of the time is polished in language and addressed to the heart as well as the head. The concern of the Order for good preaching is reflected in the General Chapters which in 1518 required examinations for preachers, and from 1513 on, the Order began to accept the care of parishes in the Low countries and Saxony which meant a new field for regular preaching.

During this century preaching was especially aimed at three kinds of audiences: the instruction of the people in the fundamentals of Catholic faith and life as necessary to the Catholic Reformation and in opposition to Protestant deviations, the exhortation of the powerful in state and Church as to their obligations to the common good and the Faith, and the missionary evangelization of the New World. Every Province produced preachers who left behind collections of their sermons, a rich field for research.

One of the tasks of preachers in this time was to encourage the growth of lay confraternities centered on special devotions. For example, Diego de Vitoria did so for devotion to the Holy Name in Spain, and this spread to the missions in America and even to China. Thomas Stella in 1539 started a Confraternity of the Blessed Sacrament at the Minerva in Rome with solemn processions to take viaticum to the dying in order to offset the Protestant attacks on the Mass. The Rosary Confraternities remained very active and the second part of the Hail Mary (found as early as a manuscript of Savonarola and approved in the *Catechism of the Council of Trent*) was added officially in the Roman Breviary in 1568. Only about 1600 did the rosary take its exact present form of 15 mysteries, and its fame increased by the attribution of the victory of Lepanto in 1571 to its recitation. Attempts to ascribe its origin to the founders of the other Orders (Francis, Ignatius, etc.) and competing forms were suppressed by papal decrees and the exclusive control of the Rosary Confraternities was given to the Dominicans. The rosary became a frequent theme of Dominican preaching and some friars devoted themselves to it almost exclusively.

The Renaissance use of the fine arts as a form of preaching, which we have seen at San Marco, continued there and elsewhere. The most notable artist was the cooperator brother Fra Bartolomeo de la Porta (d. 1517) at San Marco. He was one of the originators of the High Renaissance style, as Fra Angelico had been of that of the Early Renaissance. Bartolomeo had been an artist before he entered the Order and a co-worker with Albertinelli. Raphael learned from him and he was an acquaintance of Michelangelo and many others of the great masters. His work is marked by Savonarolian influence and uses idealized, noble forms and warm, simple coloring. A companion at San Marco was the less gifted Fra Paulino whose work is similar but less powerful. Also in Florence was the Dominican nun Plautilla Nelli (d. 1587), recorded among the neglected number of excellent women painters.

Except for a few, not very notable poets, it is not easy to mention Dominican litterateurs, but one must remember Matteo Bandelli (d. 1555, brother of Vincent Bandelli, Master of the Order), Bishop of Agen in France, where he went to live to escape the troubles in Italy. He was acquainted with many of the literary people of his day and is known for his 214 short and not very edifying tales or *Novelle* which were translated into English and used by Elizabethan playwriters, including Shakespeare, as in *Romeo and Juliet.*

The greatest preacher of this time, Bartolomé de Las Casas (1474-1566), who was also the greatest of the Dominican missionaries to the New World, preached through written propaganda and gad-fly persusaion like the Hebrew prophets. His grandparents were all baptized Christians, but his paternal grandparents were of the Jewish *converso* Peñalosa family of Seville. Bartolomé studied at the cathedral school under the patronage of his uncle, Francisco de Peñalosa, a royal official, and then enlisted in 1497 in the militia to put down a Morisco rebellion in Grenada. When he returned to Seville, he studied Latin, probably in preparation for ordination to the priesthood.

At 19 Bartolomé saw Columbus return from his first voyage (for which Bartolomé's uncle, Pedro Peñalosa, had helped recruit) with seven Indians and samples of a strange new substance we call rubber. Bartolomé's father was a merchant whose poverty inclined him to take risks and with three of his brothers he decided to sail with Columbus on the second voyage. They returned with a little Indian boy whom Pedro gave to Bartolomé who made him his friend until Queen Isabella ordered the slaves returned to America. Pedro then took his son (who by this time was a cleric but not yet a priest) back with him to Hispanola (Haiti) in the expedition of the new governor of the island, Ovando (1499), to act as a catechist to the Indians from 1502-6. He witnessed the massacre of a tribe of Indians at Higuey when the gold mines were opened there. In 1507 Bartolomé went to Rome (where he was dismayed by the pre-Reformation situation), probably on business connected with the division of dioceses and was ordained there or a little later on his return to the island, where Diego, son of Columbus, was now governor. Diego gave the new priest an estate on the island, and Las Casas for a while as an *encomandero* with Indian slaves farmed and mined gold, while carrying on his catechetical ministry to the Indians. He now celebrated his solemn First Mass in La Vega, the first such event it seems in the New World. He also met Pedro de Córdoba, the saintly Dominican missionary. The first 15 Dominican missionaries to America had been sent by Cajetan in 1507, but only four arrived in 1509: Pedro de Córdoba (d. 1530), Antonio de Montesino (d. 1530), Bernardo de Santo Domingo and a cooperator brother. Montesino, profoundly shocked by the condition of the Indians whom he met, began in 1511 to preach publicly that the colonists who enslaved and mistreated them were in mortal sin and should be refused absolution and communion. In 1512 some 40 more friars arrived and Pedro de Córdoba founded a convent in Santo Domingo.

In 1513-14 Las Casas went to Cuba to act as a peacemaker with the Indians there, only to witness another massacre. Here he acquired some new properties on Arimao near Xagua and engaged in profitable farming and stock raising, but also helped rescue some shipwrecked Spaniards. Busy with these matters he seems to have done little teaching of the Indians. He had heard the reports of Montesino's famous sermons in Santo Domingo but was indignant when the next year a Dominican confessor refused him absolution as a slave-holder, and during the next three years stoutly resisted the arguments of other Dominicans. Only at Pentecost of 1514 was he moved to public conversion by reading in Sirach 34 that:

> Like the man who slays a son in his father's presence is he
> who offers sacrifice from the possessions of the poor.

After his conversion Las Casas went to Spain to plead for the Indians, studied law at Madrid and Valladolid, and finally got permission to return to America in 1517 with a plan of reform. This, however, was frustrated by the colonists. He quickly embarked again for Spain, narrowly escaping the orders to have him sent back in chains as Columbus had been. Las Casas took refuge with the Dominicans in Salamanca to continue his law studies, while awaiting the arrival of Charles V in 1518. Las Casas, this time with the support of Flemish Franciscans, persuaded Charles V, who was half Flemish, to approve a plan to experiment with peasant rather than soldier colonists. Las Casas made careful plans and obtained Dominican help in locating the colony in their missionary territory of Cumana, Venezuela (1520-21), but nobles and a treacherous aide made it hard for him to get recruits and these quickly took up the slave trade and provoked an Indian revolt in which a number of friars and officials were massacred.

Utterly crushed, Las Casas returned to Santo Domingo, convinced that his efforts had been vitiated by his compromises with the slavers and persuaded by Domingo de Betanzos, the Dominican superior, he abandoned all his wealth and entered the Order at Santo Domingo in 1522 to look to his own soul, and made his novitate and profession by 1524.

After almost twelve years quiet as novice, student, and prior of the isolated convent at Puerto de Plata, he was again stirred into protest when he saw Bahamian Indians dying on the beach. In response to his letters to Spain, a Reform Commission in 1530 obtained a law banning all Indian slavery. His sermons and confessional advice led his superiors to recall him to Santo Domingo and forbid him to preach for two years, while he collected material for his great *History of the Indies*. It was in this early period that Las Casas for a time argued for the importation of Black slaves from Africa in preference to enslaving the Indians, because he supposed they had been enslaved in a just war and were physically better able to survive in the mines. Later he came to greatly regret this mistake and to see that the oppression of the Indians and the Blacks was identical. Meanwhile in Spain some friar at court preached on the "sins of the Indians" and the friends of the *encomenderos* were able to get the anti-slavery repealed, against a campaign by both Franciscan and Dominican missionaries to retain it. Bartolomé then got permission to visit for a month the guerrilla camp of Chief Enriquillo (a Christian) who was gathering Indians and Blacks for a revolt. Las Casas succeeded in preventing this revolt, thus demonstrating that peaceful negotiation with the Indians was practical, and he wrote his first great treatise, *The Only Way to Bring All Peoples to the True Faith,* that is, not by force but by preaching and good example, and sent it to Court. This success induced his Dominican superiors at last to permit him to be a missionary on the mainland.

In 1534 as superior of a band of four Dominicans he left to accompany the new Dominican Bishop of Peru to his See.

Problems in the journey forced them to stop in Nicaragua; where they attempted to apply their peaceful missionary methods but were brutally expelled by the soldier colonists. Las Casas then went to Mexico City, and was appointed vicar for Guatemala by the provincial of the new Mexican province. In Mexico the first Viceroy was establishing better order, and the Ecclesiastical Conference of 1536 in Mexico City, after hearing Las Casas' eloquent pleas and with the support of the pro-Indian Bishop Zumarraga, adopted three resolutions: (1) No conquest or conversion by force; (2) Enslavers should be punished by the Church; (3) No adult baptisms without instruction. On this last point, the Franciscans, who had promoted mass baptisms, appealed to the Pope, and Bernadino Minaya, O.P., was sent with letters and treatises by Las Casas to Paul III, who then set up a commission headed by Cardinal Contarini, which in 1537 issued in Paul's name the encyclical *Sublimis Deus*, based on Las Casas' *Only Way*, decreeing automatic excommunication of enslavers, and providing rules for the administration of the sacraments and the celebration of feasts in the missions.

In Guatemala Las Casas had managed peacefully to penetrate the so-called "Land of War," had baptized a chief and was making progress, when he was again called to Mexico City for a provincial chapter, which sent him once more to Spain to recruit missionaries. At Oaxaca he wrote his *Abuses* and *Reforms*. His second great opportunity came when Charles V as Emperor again came to reorganize his Spanish kingdom, and in response to letters from Las Casas asked his superiors to retain him in Spain to be present at a Great Convocation for the Reform of the Indies at which Las Casas delivered his sensational *Account of the Holocaust of the Indies*, his *Sixteen Remedies for the Pestilences Destroying the Indies* and his *Twenty Denunciations of the Encomienda*, which charged many officials with corruption or intrigue. The Emperor was moved to enact "The New Laws of 1542" for gradual removal of the *encomendero* system. Las Casas' enemies therefore, to get him away from court, urged Charles to make him a bishop.

Thus in 1545 Las Casas came to Mexico for the third time as bishop of Chiapas, no longer restricted by religious obedience, but his poor diocese was almost ungovernable because of the intrigues of the colonists against him. Summoned to the Convocation of Bishops in Mexico City, he learned that the Emperor, who was in financial straits, had been bribed by the Peruvian colonists to revoke some of the laws protecting the Indians. But Las Casas did not hesitate to argue that the Viceroy and the Mexican High Court had incurred excommunication by cutting off the hand of an accused priest, and forced them to ask for forgiveness. He also forced the assembled bishops to agree with his stand on the Indians. He then left a Vicar General in Chiapas with secret rules for handling the absolution of violators of Indian rights, wrote *Ecclesiastical Exemption: A Warning*, threatening Prince Philip, then Regent for Spain, and left America for the last time. Back in Spain he refuted charges of treason and got the Revocation revoked and the Laws of the Indies strengthened, after successfully debating for five days the philosopher Sepulveda who had tried to prove that the Indians were naturally slaves. He then resigned his diocese, after emancipating all the slaves within its territory.

Las Casas was now the "General Representative of All the Indians" at the Spanish court. He resided at the Dominican college in Valladolid, where the court usually sat, and every day presented to it petitions and reports from the New World. When the Peruvian colonists sent eight million gold ducats for permission to buy their Indians in perpetuity, Las Casas wrote his Dominican brother Carranza to intervene with King Philip, then in England. He wrote *The Treasures of Peru* to show that Indians could buy their own freedom, but the last Inca died (perhaps murdered) before this solution could be put into effect. Las Casas himself died at 82 in 1566, while a friend was reading to him his last petition for a great convocation to free the Indies. This Junta Magna was held two years after his death with some effect. As priest, friar, bishop, retired writer, statesman at court under three popes and four kings, Las Casas had fought ceaselessly for fifty years for the human rights of the Indians and all human beings, and had crossed the Atlantic at least 10 times. The recognition of his prophetic sanctity by canonization has been held up by Spanish distrust of a man whose writings were misused by Protestants to discredit Spain by the "Black Legend." Only recently have they begun to see that he is one of the greatest glories of Spain and a tribute to the nobility of true Hispanidad, and the Master of the Order has begun the formal process which it is hoped will lead to his canonization. He is already recognized throughout the Third World as a patron saint of true liberation.

Las Casas' story is central to the history of the Dominican missions in the New World, but it is by no means the whole of it. There is no room here for an account of the missions throughout Latin America, in the Philippines, and in Japan, China and India. Nor should it be forgotten that the Dominicans continued their efforts to preach in the Balkans, Russia, and the Near East as far as Persia and to the Jews of Europe especially in Rome where Pius V founded a convent for Jewish Christian women. As we look back on these world-wide missionary efforts we are amazed by the immense sacrifices, frequently to lonely deaths, made by these men against much opposition by colonials and indifference and violence by natives. Sometimes these efforts were very imaginative and open to the good qualities of the pagans, but often limited by European prejudices which prevented the Spanish and Portuguese from accepting those of other races into the Order, a prejudice rooted in part in the history of Spain and its struggle to find national unity in the face of Moorish and Jewish minorities. Yet this missionary expansion of which Las Casas is only a shining example is the glory of this century.

6

Debaters (1600s)

Community

In the 1600s the division of Europe into Catholic and Protestant nations was consummated by the terrible Thirty-Year War (1618-48) and the struggles of the Puritans and Royalists in England. With the decline of the Spanish Empire French power and culture were at their height, while England, after its revolution of 1688, was rising. Most significant was the development of modern science with Galileo, Kepler, Harvey, and Boyle and of the "turn to the subject" in philosophy with René Descartes. Thus the Church was beginning to be faced by a new picture of the cosmos.

After struggles between Spain, Portugal and France and with the usual papal pressure for an observant, a noted preacher from Aragon, Jerome Xavierre, was elected Master of the Order in 1601. Xavierre supervised Dominican participation in the Congregatio de Auxiliis to its finish and began to restore San Sisto Vecchio in Rome, but otherwise achieved little. In France Sebastien Michaelis continued his efforts to reform the Province of Occitania against the resistance of its provincial, Joseph Bourgoing, who was supported by an aunt of Henry IV, Eleanor of Bourbon, Abbess of Fontrevault. She was formerly prioress of Prouille and had obtained the canonization of St. Agnes of Montepulciano. Michaelis, however, had on his side the King's Jesuit confessor, the famous Père Coton, and Henry, struck by Michaelis' custody of his eyes amid the splendor of the court, placed his reform under royal protection. Xavierre left Rome for Spain, where for two years he was Phillip II's confessor until made cardinal in 1607, only to die the next year.

To by-pass the constant rivalry between the French and Spanish kings an Italian, Augustino Galamini, Master of the Sacred Palace, was elected in 1608 rather than the noted scholar Nicholas Coffeteau, Henry IV's candidate. He proved a decisive, fearless Master, constantly traveling (while the Cardinal Protector ran the home office) and working effectively to promote reform and studies in face of the laxity and ignorance he found in Italian houses. He divided a Russian Congregation from the Province of Poland in 1608 and incorporated the ruined Saxon Province into that of Germany. The Chapter of 1611, held in Paris to placate the French crown, led to conflict with the University over Gallicanism and Conciliarism. Under royal pressure, it confirmed a reformed Congregation of Occitania, including St. Maximin, headed by Michaelis (but by an innovation directly under the Master). Galamini dramatically refused his blessing to St. Jacques which absolutely resisted his reform. His visitation of France and Spain was prevented by his elevation to cardinal in 1611, but he lived until 1639 as a zealous reforming bishop.

Galamini prepared the Chapter of 1612 by ending the abuse of swamping the chapters by the presence of crowds of non-delegates. In spite of pressure from the King of Spain, another Italian, Galamini's Procurator General, Seraphin Secchi de Pavia, was chosen. Called by the French "Le Sec" (The Dry One) for his concise speech and tenacious memory for names and details, he was also handsome, gracious, and a very just superior who never acted without taking counsel. Although Secchi was known greatly to admire the Jesuits, the elective Chapter excluded them and all non-Dominicans from preaching in Dominican churches. As usual it decried the proliferation of Masters of Theology and rebuked all recourse to the Holy See except through the Procurator General. For the first time in the history of the Order of Preachers, amazingly, it established special courses in preaching. A reaffirmation by Urban

VIII of mendicant exemption, which had been much restricted by the previous Pope, was obtained by the efforts of one Dominic de Molina.

Many friars, pleading expense, began to demand Chapters be held only every six years—a sign of the times. Secchi sent detailed questionnaires on observance to all provinces and then spent most of his term on visitation. In Spain he found Dominican life, especially studies, flourishing. Portugal was polarized by the issue of Spanish rule and in Italy he found many very small houses of very lax observance. To all the Provinces he could not himself visit he sent visitators: to Bohemia, Poland, and Russia, the New World, and the missions in Armenia, Persia, and India. He devoted much care to the Provinces of Toulouse, Provence, and France and the decadent Gallican Congregation, including St. Jacques. Against fierce opposition he solidified the Congregation of Occitania reformed by Michaelis (d. 1616) to which he added as a counterforce in Paris to recalcitrant San Jacques the observant Annunciation Priory in the Faubourg St. Honoré. The Chapter of 1628, held in Toulouse, center of Michaelis' movement, magnificently celebrated the translation of St. Thomas Aquinas' relics and the martyrs of the Philippines. Secchi, returning to Rome, was refused entrance to Avignon because he had come through plague-stricken territory. Awaiting admission he died, with a request his heart be buried at the Annunciation in Paris.

Nicholas Ridolfi, of a great Florentine family (and a penitent of a Savonarolian, St. Phillip Neri), Master of the Sacred Palace, was elected in 1629. At this time Urban VIII gave Chapters the right to change the *Constitutions* without papal approval, so the Chapter standardized the terms of provincials for four years and of priors for three. Ridolfi established a fund for the Master by confiscating all private funds in the provinces through special collectors. This money he used lavishly to aid poorer houses, novitiates, publications, and for building and ornamenting churches. He visited North Italy and France as far as Brittany and as a new method of reform founded a General Novitiate in Paris for all France. He made the mistake, however, of placing it for thirty years in charge of Jean-Baptiste Carré (c. 1593-1653), who aimed to use his novices to form a new Congregation based on his own notions of reform. Although a noted spiritual director, Carré believed God wanted him to be a spy for Cardinal Richelieu, to whom he had taken a secret oath of obedience. Ridolfi also permitted Antoine Le Quieu to form a Blessed Sacrament Congregation of still stricter observance until Le Quieu tried to become "discalced" (like St. Teresa of Avila's Carmelites). Le Quieu desisted from this innovation only when ordered by the General Chapter and the Pope. Michaelis' Congregation of St. Louis itself was torn between the Parisians and the Gascons and sought to protect itself from the conventuals by appealing to royal intervention, inclining thus to Gallicanism.

Ridolfi accumulated many enemies. Vincent Maculano, made Vicar by Urban VIII, later a cardinal, was alienated because Ridolfi rebuked him for exceeding his authority when Ridolfi was in Flanders and Germany, and was ambitious for his own nephew to succeed to the Mastership. Thomas Cattoni and other friars of Southern Italy were infuriated because Ridolfi's collectors had squelched their profitable cattle business. Ridolfi was also disliked by Richelieu, who was working to ally France with the Protestants against Spain and Austria, while the Master worked for peace between Catholic Spain and France. But Ridolfi's most dangerous enemies were the greedy Barberini family, including Pope Urban VIII and his cardinal nephews. Originally favorable to Ridolfi, the Barberinis were angered by his opposition to their dynastic schemes to marry one of their clan to the heiress Olympia Aldobrandini. Urban decided to have Ridolfi deposed by the Chapter at Genoa in 1642, and seized the opportunity from an appeal made to him by Fr. Hyacinth Lupi, who claimed Ridolfi had unjustly and scandalously struck and excommunicated him in choir, to conduct an investigation of his administration.

Pending judgment, Ridolfi was imprisoned at San Sisto Vecchio (whose restoration he had recently financed with profits made from chocolate, then much in vogue, from the missions). Urban appointed Michel Mazarin (brother of the French Cardinal Jules Mazarin, Richelieu's successor), also ambitious to be Master, to preside over the Chapter, but he so infuriated the Spanish and Austrian delegates that they withdrew and protested by electing a provisional Master. Pope

St. Rose
of Lima

Urban was thus forced to take responsibility himself for deposing Ridolfi. He offered to make him a bishop, but Ridolfi refused.

Hence, while continuing to protest the deposition of Ridolfi and demanding his rehabilitation, the Chapter of 1644 elected a brilliant theologian, Thomas Turco, and did little else except make regulations for the dress of young ladies being educated in Dominican convents, allowing them rings and earrings but no other finery. Turco made extensive visitations in Italy, Spain, France, and Belgium. He finally removed Carré from the General Novitiate in Paris and made it directly dependent on the Master. He tried to pacify the Congregation of St. Louis by assigning all the southern convents to the Toulouse Province under observant provincials and giving the conventuals a vicar. He also made the Gallican Congregation into the Province of France. The next Pope, Innocent X, was an Aldobrandini much influenced by his sister-in-law, the same Olympia, the affair of whose marriage had so angered the Barberinis. Hence he instituted a commission of cardinals to re-examine Ridolfi's case, which rehabilitated him. At Turco's death in 1649, Ridolfi missed being re-elected himself by dying ten days before the Chapter.

Jean-Baptiste de Marini, a Genoan patrician, one of three brothers all curial officials in the Order, was elected in 1650, probably because of his loyalty to Ridolfi. He ruled for twenty years, yet after his election, held only one Chapter, and (because papal policy forbade it) made no visitations but governed by letter. The 1650 Chapter made liturgical regulations, especially of the time of the night Office and tried without much success to check the habit of recourse to secular authority to settle conflicts in the Order. Urban VIII decreed the suppression of small convents, especially common in Italy, and Donna Olympia collected large sums for dispensation from this law. De Marini tried to check the growing war of polemic writings between Dominicans and Jesuits, and was much occupied with problems of the Order in France. He temporarily established a Congregation of Aquitania for the conventuals of the reformed Province of Toulouse until in 1663 they were united to the Province of Occitania.

In the reformed Province of Toulouse a description of their life shows that they never ate meat, kept the long Lent from September 14th, observed silence, had meditation twice a day, emphasized the assiduous study of St. Thomas, observed common life and the *Constitutions* "to the finger tips." St. Maximin tried to separate from the Order and become an independent abbey but was held within the Province of Toulouse. Renewed efforts to reform San Jacques and to prevent the Novitate General from becoming independent, as well as the conversion of the Congregation of St. Louis into a Province were all effected only by appeals to the secular power of Louis XIV. Meanwhile the controversy over Jansenism was calmed only briefly by Clement IX from 1667-69, when it broke out again even more bitterly. De Marini, grown old and feeble, spent much time in the country at San Pastore in the Sabine Hills, renowned for his hospitality and tender care for the rural poor. His term also saw the foundation of the reformed Congregation of Bl. James Salomoni in Northern Italy by Fr. Basil Spica, in addition to the existing Congregation of Our Lady of Santé in Naples.

De Marini died in 1669, hoping the distinguished theologian Passerini, his Procurator General, would succeed him, but instead the Chapter of 1670 elected the Aragon Provincial, Juan Tomás de Rocaberti, probably because at that time the Order flourished in Spain and in its Empire were more than half of all Dominicans. Rocaberti was a learned scholar who wrote many works, especially on papal infallibility, but he was also a Spanish grandee very deferential to the secular powers. For example, he readily yielded to Louis XIV by overriding the elective rights of the nuns of Poissy to institute an aristocratic prioress whom the King favored. He was also troubled in France with the affair of Noël Alexander and Gallicanism but left this problem to his successors. Rocaberti made few visitations and held no Chapters. He housed the persecuted Irish friars in San Sisto Vecchio and San Clemente in Rome, and greatly assisted the English Dominican refugees, including Phillip Howard who became a cardinal. He shared the interest in Dominican history, increasing at this time, and promoted the saints of the Order, especially St. Albert the Great. Made Archbishop of Valentia in 1677, he left the Order a big debt from the embezzlement by one of his agents, which he refused to make good on the grounds he had not personally incurred it.

Antonio de Monroy, was a Spanish missionary who was the delegate to the Chapter of 1677 for Mexico. He was an aristocrat, but modest in manner and unworldly. At this Chapter Innocent XI required the new Master to swear to (1) have a chapter every three years; (2) visit all European provinces; (3) restrict the number of Masters of Theology; (4) have the Acts of the Chapter signed by the Cardinal Protector before publication. Unfortunately the Popes themselves kept making it impossible to meet these obligations. Innocent also decreed that no convent failing to observe common life could receive novices, but failed to make this effective by also insisting that these novices once trained could be sent only to observant houses. This Chapter also prepared a revision of the *Constitutions*, and forbade the use any longer of the terms "observant" and "conventual." Most important, it decreed that the Order, which had too long emphasized university and special preaching at the expense of popular preaching should return to the example of St. Dominic, but it added that professors in the studium should not neglect their students in order to go preaching themselves. Monroy encouraged the Rosary Confraternities and worked to keep them under Dominican control. A former missionary, he was always favorable to the missions, especially those of the Philippines. It was during his term that Innocent XI condemned Laxism and the Probabilism Controversy became intense. In 1685 Monroy was made Archbishop of Compostella and he fulfilled the office with distinction.

Antonin Cloche, whose term was to last for 34 years (1686-1720), was from a rich French family and had entered Dominican life in the reformed Province of Toulouse. He always led a very ascetic life, and had served as companion of Rocaberti and Monroy, proving a good mediator in the many difficulties with the French King. In his first letter he insisted on common life and uniformity throughout the order especially as regards the habit. He stressed the need for popular preaching such as that performed by Le Quieu's Blessed Sacrament Congregation. He also urged the study of Greek and Hebrew and the Scriptures. Repeatedly prevented from visitation by the political situation, he produced new editions of the *Constitutions*, and also those for the Sisters and Third Order, and other official guides. After the Chapter of 1686 none were held until 1694, so that governance in the Order became as absolute a monarchy as that of the contemporary Louis XIV. During his term the Jansenist movement continued and Gallicanism took still deeper hold in the French Order. These struggles largely occupied Cloche's attention, although he encouraged studies and spiritual writing which flourished in this period. Missionary activity during this period was very great, and Cloche was deeply involved in the controversy over the Chinese Rites. Cloche, in the style of the day, for all his great personal asceticism, lived as a "grande seigneur," spending much time at the country house of San Pastore where he constantly was host to ecclesiastical dignitaries. He died at 92 in Rome and with him the baroque age of the Order.

Study

The Dominicans at Spanish universities continued to dominate the Order's intellectual life during most of this century, although the Friars of Italy and the Low countries were active also, and in the last half of the century France began to move into leadership. The controversies on grace were renewed when two secular theologians at the University of Louvain, Baius and then Jansenius, promoted an interpretation of St. Augustine's teaching on this subject that seemed Calvinistic. The great foes of Calvinism, the Jesuits, attacked this vigorously, using as one of their theological weapons the theology of grace of Molina, which in the previous century had led to the Congregation on Grace, in which Thomas de Lemos (d. 1629) and Diego Alvarez (d. 1635) had upheld the Thomistic case and continued to do so. Nor was this debate terminated as late as Giuseppe M. Paltinieri's (d. 1702) *The Molinist Vine Devastated* against Theophile Raynaud, S.J., (1683) or Antonin Reginald's (d. 1676) major work *The Council of Trent on Efficacious Grace* (Antwerp, 1706).

The Dominicans were caught in the middle of this controversy. As Thomists they opposed the pseudo-Augustinianism of the Jansenists because it conceived grace as determining rather than freeing human choice, but they also could not accept Molinism because it seemed to undermine the total dependence of the creature on the Creator. They were constantly embarrassed by attempts of Jansenists to claim Thomistic support for their position, and by Jesuit attempts to bolster Molinism by picturing its Dominican opponents as crypto-Jansenists.

As Jansenism spread to France and became the ideology of a militant middle-class, partly working for reform of both church and state in opposition to the corrupt aristocracy and royalty, the Dominicans had difficulty in keeping clear of this partisanship. When the French monarchy managed to get the Pope's support against the Jansenists, they became even more radically Gallican than was the king himself, and many of the French Dominicans tended to share these nationalistic sentiments. Yet the great majority of Dominicans remained true defenders of two positions typical of its whole history: (1) the sovereignty of God as source of all being, truth, and freedom; (2) the authority of the Petrine office as center of unity for the Church and its faith.

The controversy over Probablism had been initiated by a Dominican Bartolomé de Medina (d. 1598), a student of Vitoria at Salamanca. The theology of Christian life of St. Thomas Aquinas and indeed of the whole Catholic tradition before 1300 was *teleological*, i.e., it judged the morality of human actions primarily not in terms of conformity to God's will expressed in law, but in terms of participation in God's wisdom discerning whether these actions are suitable means to achieve the God-given goals of human life, individual and communal. But in the fourteenth century the dominance of Nominalism in the universities led to a marked shift in the directions of a legalistic moral theory which judged morality primarily in terms of the conformity of human actions to the *obligating will* of the sovereign—a reflection no doubt of the rising power of centralized absolute monarchies in Europe at that time.

Consequently, the Jesuits, who were much engaged in promoting frequent confession as a means of raising the moral standards of the laity, published very detailed manuals of moral theology, based on a legalistic approach to morality, to guide confessors. Yet they wanted to make this type of conscience-formation practical for the laity who had to live in the real world. Hence, the manualists were concerned to point out, among the welter of theological opinions about the morality of actions in concrete, puzzling situations, those which the laity would find most practicable as guides for decision. Thus they developed the system called Probabilism according to which one might in good conscience follow a more lenient yet probable opinion even if it was not the most probable.

Although originally proposed (in moderate form) by a Dominican, the Dominican moralists came to oppose it bitterly, because from the viewpoint of a teleological morality like that of Aquinas, the choice of the most probable way to reach a goal (even if more difficult) is always more reasonable than any other (Probabiliorism). This brought down on their heads the Jesuit accusation that they were favoring the Jansenists, who because of their pessimistic view of fallen human nature, had opted for Tutiorism (Rigorism), according to which one is held when in doubt always to follow the "safer opinion," i.e., the one that goes against one's corrupt inclination to take the easier way. Dominicans, however, denied that the Fall has totally obliterated the fundamentally good inclinations of our nature and pointed out that what is more difficult is not always the better means to a goal, since virtue makes good action easier.

In the end, the Popes, while favoring Probabiliorism, contented themselves with condemning numerous tenuously probable opinions (Laxism) found in some manuals (not in the main by Jesuits), and left a moderate Probabilism as common practice in the Church until this century, when a shift away from a legalistic to a more teleological moral theology seems to be taking place, although it survives in the form of a new system called Proportionalism (cf. Chapter 9).

Numerous commentaries on the whole or parts of Aquinas' *Summa Theologiae* were written, including the important ones by Serafino Capponi a Porrecta (d. 1614) and Giovanni Paulo Nazaris, (d. 1645) of Bologna, who had taught at Prague, been ambassador to Spain and also written against the Hussites and Calvinists. What characterizes the century, however, is a shift to "defenses" of St. Thomas (such as those of Giovanni Dominico Montagniuolo, 1609-10, and Baltazar de Navarette, 1634) and text books, chiefly of two types: lengthy "courses" in theology or philosophy, and brief manuals designed to prepare students for ordination as priests. Of the "courses," the most important are the *Cursus Philosophicus* and *Cursus Theologicus* of Jean Poinsot (John of St. Thomas, d. 1644). A Belgian by birth, educated at Coimbra and Louvain, Poinsot taught at Alcala, and was confessor to Philip IV, refusing any of the other offices offered him. With Capreolus, Cajetan, Vitoria, and Báñez, he is considered a leader of the Thomistic school. What characterizes his and other "courses" of this time is that, like Vitoria's *Reflections*, they are not commentaries but original works made up of a series of treatises dealing especially with questions disputed among the authors of the day. While this made such works highly relevant in their own time, it has the disadvantage today of failing to show clearly how Aquinas built up his world view step-by-step from experience. Instead we are presented with defenses of certain characteristic Thomistic theses, with some original developments, such as Poinsot's important anticipation of semiotics.

This also marks the works labeled "defenses of St. Thomas," such as the *Thomistic Shield* in 16 volumes of Jean Baptiste Gonet (1669), a professor at the University of Bordeaux, and proponent of Probabilism but also sometimes accused of inclining toward Molinism and as plagiarizing from an earlier work of the Spanish Cardinal Pedro de Godoy, O.P. (d. 1677).

Especially original was the nine-volume *Theology of Mind and Heart* of Vincent de Contenson (d. 1674), who taught in Toulouse, Albi, Paris, and then became a distinguished preacher until he died at only 33 after suffering from chronic asthma. While adhering to scholastic Thomism, he writes in a homiletic manner, with much use of quotations from the Fathers, and the constant aim to move as well as instruct. An example and summary of his aims is a "Dissertation On the Teaching and Preaching of Christ" in which in a "First Speculation" (theological exposition) he argues that Christ was the model of true preachers in his public teaching because: (1) He observed the order of charity (De Contenson quotes from John Chrysostom and Ezekiel 34); (2) He was not deterred by opposition (from Aquinas); (3) He showed love to the neglected (from Gregory the Great); (4) He spoke with simplicity so all could understand and profit (from Seneca, Peter Chrysologus, Augustine). On this last point, de Contenson denounces the abuses of Baroque preaching:

> Such preachers do not proclaim the glory of God, nor serve the salvation of their hearers, nor awaken the consciences of sinners, but obtain nothing but popularity. They stir up nothing but the glory of empty wind, the applause of their hearers. They are not concerned about what they can offer in a holy, useful, apostolic way, but how they can fret their theme with more curious wit, artifice, and flowery figures, with empty facts, emptier conceits, and most empty words, so that they may chatter rather than be of help, gain admiration rather than teach, flatter rather than arouse repentance, and foul the chaste eloquence of the Gospel with meretricious babble.

He follows each theological exposition with a "Reflection" or meditation, in this case urging preachers to aim always at instructing and moving their hearers to a more Christian life (Vincent of Lerins, Hosea).

In moral theology and canon law the outstanding authors of this time were Vincent Baron (d. 1674) who after a distinguished career in teaching, administration, and especially as a preacher, retired to the General Novitiate in Paris to live a rigorous life according to the reform of Sebastian Michaelis and devoted himself to extensive writings, at the request of the Pope, against the Probabilists and Laxists and against Calvinism; and Petro Maria Passerini (d. 1677), whose most famous work was a classic *Treatise on the States of Life* (1665). There were numerous able canonists such as Vincenzo-Maria Fontana (d. 1675) whose edition of the Order's *Constitutions* is fundamental for the study of its historical development up to his time.

This century produced many polemical and apologetic writings. Outstanding was the 12-volume work of the Sicilian, Dominico Gravina (d. 1643), which dealt with the whole history of Christian heresies. He wrote many other works, including *A Touchstone to Tell True from False Revelations*. A Pole, Bernardus Paxillus (d. 1630), defended the *filioque* against the Orthodox, but most of these writers were concerned with Protestantism.

The Order at this time was rather barren in Bible scholars. The most distinguished was Thomas Malvenda (d. 1628), a friend and aide of the great historian Baronius, who produced a new, critical Latin version of the Scriptures. He was commissioned by the Master of the Order to revise the Dominican Missal and Breviary, and was an early critic of the rosary legend. It was also a time of extensive historical studies in which a truly critical method was beginning to prevail.

The most important Dominican historian was the Polish Abraham Bozovius (d. 1637) who continued the great Church history of Baronius from 1198 to 1571; and the French Jacques Quétif (d. 1698) who began the pioneering bibliographical and biographical work for a religious order, *Writers of the Dominican Order* and Stephen Thomas Souëges (d. 1698), whose *Dominican Year* in French is a more hagiographical but comprehensive work in 12 volumes. Much of the historical work of this time was done by missionaries anxious to record their labors and the customs of new peoples. As for patrology and the history of liturgy, certainly the outstanding Dominicans were Jacques Goar (d. 1653), expert in Greek who before teaching in Rome had been a missionary in the island of Chios, who translated many Greek authorities, but whose greatest work was a collection of Greek rites, and François Combefis (d. 1679), who edited many of the works of the Eastern Fathers, notably those of St. Basil.

Philosophical commentaries on Aristotle and defenses of Thomism continued, but these began to be replaced by philosophy manuals. The most important of these was that of Antoine Goudin (d. 1691), who taught at the General Novitiate in Paris and then at St. Jacques and published a four-volume text (Lyons 1671), used for many years. Although the published editions do not reveal it, Goudin sought a compromise with Molinism, as we know from correspondence from his friend, the famous Oratorian, Richard Simon, the founder of modern historical-critical Bible scholarship, who was of the same mind. That this deviation was never published seems to have been due to the censorship of Massoulié. Seraphino Piccinardi (d. 1695), noted for his excellent Latin style, taught at Padua and wrote a *Dogmatic Christian and Aristotelian Philosophy* in 3 volumes (1671), which attempted to refute the atomism of Campanella, Descartes, Von Helmot, and Gassendi, and a seven-volume defense of Thomism.

The most original Dominican philosopher of this time was the astonishing Tommaso Campanella (1568-1639). We have noted in the last chapter in the cases of Fra Francesco Colonna and Giordano Bruno that there were Renaissance anti-scholastic currents of thought even among Dominicans, and such tendencies surfaced again in Campanella. Born in Calabria in 1568, he entered the Order at fifteen and became a true polymath (although also a dabbler in astrology and magic) but in 1599 was arrested and tortured by the Spanish government on charges of heresy and conspiracy to found a communistic republic and imprisoned at Naples for 27 years. On his release he was again brought before the Inquisition but released, and lived for a time at the Minerva in Rome. On the advice of Urban VIII (to whom he was acting as astrologer), to avoid further charges, he fled to France under the protection of

Richelieu and Louis XIII (also interested in his astrological services) where he died at Annunciation Priory in 1639. He had been friends with three Popes and many distinguished philosophers.

Campanella was author of some 80 works, including many poems, developed an eclectic anti-Aristotelian philosophy in which a Platonic epistemology and metaphysics based on the certitude of innate knowledge was combined in natural philosophy with an empiricist system of matter and energy in absolute space and time derived from (a non-Dominican) Bernardino Telesio. Campanella anticipated Descartes in turning to St. Augustine to find a way out of scepticism through the certitude of self-consciousness. His ethics argued that self-preservation is the fundamental human goal, although this can be achieved only by eternal union with God, while in politics he attacked Machiavelli and in *The City of the Sun* (1623) he proposed a utopian republic governed by philosophers, while in *The Messiah's Monarchy* (1633) he advocated the universal monarchy of the Pope both in the spiritual and temporal realms. Perhaps his most significant work was his *Defense of Galileo*, in which he argues for Galileo's orthodoxy, while admitting that his heliocentrism had undermined Campanella's own philosophy.

This century was the time when modern science began its rise, but few Dominicans (except Campanella) seemed in their preoccupation with grace, predestination and Probabilism, to grasp what this might mean for Thomism, but curiously a considerable number were noted as medical doctors and authors, and as mathematicians.

The higher level of education for women at this time made possible a considerable amount of writing by nuns, chronicles, biographies, poetry, and spiritual works. Two of these women are especially notable: Hipólita de Jesús, (de Rocaberti, d. 1624) of Barcelona, a relative of Master Rocaberti who wrote her biography, and whose mystical writings in Spanish were published in 13 volumes; and Juliana Morell (1653) also of Barcelona, whose life was written by Gabriella de Vallay (d. 1662). Juliana was a prodigy whose father had her instructed from an early age in Latin, Greek, and Hebrew, philosophy and music, and used to exhibit her from the age of 12 in public performances dressed in a blue silk, highly ornamented gown. When he was himself accused of murder he fled to Lyons and then Avignon where these performances continued, until Juliana, disgusted with being a freak fled to the Dominican nuns in that city. Among her works are a translation of St. Vincent Ferrer's *The Spiritual Life* with a commentary and of the *Rule of St. Augustine* with a commentary; *Spiritual Exercises*; a history of the reform of her monastery with lives of some of the nuns; and poems in Latin and French. In this context we should not forget Girolamo Ercolani (d. 1660) who besides commenting on the gospels and epistles for the year, wrote a huge work, beautifully illustrated with engravings, of royal women reputed for sanctity, and another work, also in eight volumes, on women who were holy hermits.

Prayer

In this age there were a remarkable number of Dominicans reputed for sanctity; among the Dominican women of Spain one author has listed 28 who are "venerable," including eight Tertiaries, and 13 of these were stigmatics. The many martyrs in the missions will be mentioned later. Three others have also been canonized: St. Rose of Lima (d. 1617); St. Martin de Porres (d. 1639); St. Juan Masias (d. 1645); all living in Lima Peru. St. Rose (known especially through the life by Leonard Hansen, O.P., d. 1685), followed the model of St. Catherine of Siena, remaining a Tertiary at her family home, living a life of penance and expiation and prayer in a hermitage constructed in the garden, and of care of the poor. Her early death at 31, the terrible severity of her asceticism and the sweetness of her personality (like the name miraculously given her at baptism) has made her a very popular saint throughout Latin America. She left no complete writings, but some notes explaining an embroidery panel on which she sewed slips of paper and symbolic hearts to indicate the *Mystic Stairway* and the *Mercies* of her spiritual experiences, including some of her spiritual advice to the physician of Lima, Dr. Castillo, who was her confidant. Martin de Porres, who was a Black with some Indian blood, was a lay brother noted for his service of the poor, especially as an amateur physician, and Juan Masias was another lay brother, an immigrant from Spain, who followed the same path of service. All three knew and supported each other in giving a Christian witness in the great new and disorderly city of Lima.

There were numerous Sisters of the Third Order, whether living at home like St. Rose or in a regular convent who achieved sanctity, such as Agatha of the Cross (d. 1621) in Toledo, teacher to the royal princesses, and engaged in many works of charity, although suffering the stigmata; Catherine Paluzzi (d. 1645) who founded a Third Order monastery in Rome; Marie of Lumague (d. 1657) who founded the Daughters of Providence for the care of the poor, one of the first such institutes that were to become common in the nineteenth century, who is reputed to have raised dead children to life; Jeanne of St. Martha (d. 1678), who after an unhappy marriage to a brutal alcoholic, became a Tertiary, then a lay sister and cook to nuns of Toulouse; Georgette Verrier (d. 1681) also an unhappily married working woman, finally allowed to live in a convent but not as a member, who suffered spiritual darkness for ten years; Louise Marie of St. Catherine (d. 1687) who died at seven (!), but was a Tertiary; Marie de Combe (d. 1692) of Leiden, converted from Calvinism, also unhappily married, who founded a home for delinquent girls under the patronage of the Good Shepherd; Magdalen Orsini (d. 1685) a widow who founded an observant convent in Rome; Anne Jesus Basset (d. 1689) an English woman in exile in Belgium; and Francesca Vacchini (d. 1689), a remarkable penitent like St. Rose, who died at 20.

Among the friars there were also many noted for holiness such as, Diego of Yanguas (d. 1606), one of St. Teresa of Avila's advisers and a defender of the natives of the Philippines, and Dominic of St.Thomas (d. 1676), the son of Ibrahim, heir to the Ottoman Empire of the Turks, who had been kidnapped by his mother to save him from the cruelty of his father, but had been captured by the Knights of St. John of Jerusalem and raised as a Christian by the Dominicans in Malta, but as a priest died at 35 while caring for those stricken by the plague.

Among the writers on spiritual questions were many hagio-

graphers and panegyricists and a vast literature for both religious and laity on mental prayer and the duties of a Christian
life, most of which is in a style suited to that age but not ours.
They include a good deal of writing on the preparation for a
Christian death, and the patient endurance of sickness and
mental depression not uncommon in that age of pomp and
glory. There were also many works on special devotions:
countless ones on the rosary and on retreats, the latter made
popular by the Jesuits.

The most important development of this period in spirituality was the writing of a *Mystical Theology* based on St.
Thomas by Thomas de Vallgornera (d. 1662), (although an
Italian Dominican Pietro Paolo Philippio (d. 1648) had previously edited with emendations and commentaries a work of
similar title by the famous Franciscan Observant Henry Herp
(d. 1478) of Eckhartian tendency, which had been put on the
Index). To this should be added the remarkable treatise of
John of St. Thomas *On the Gifts of the Holy Ghost*. Together
these two works formulate the classical Dominican spirituality.
A Master of the Order, Thomas de Rocaberti, in 1669 also
published a treatise on this subject.

The most original writers of the time, however, were Ignazio
del Nente (d. 1648) who, under the influences of the writings of
Henry Suso, greatly developed the theology of devotion to the
Sacred Heart of Jesus, which in the latter part of the century
with St. John Eudes and St. Margaret Mary Alacoque was to
receive universal recognition in the Church; and Louis
Chardon (d. 1651) whose *The Cross of Jesus*, which presented
spirituality as an identification with the interior suffering of
Jesus' whole life in the shadow of the inevitable Cross. Chardon
also translated St. Catherine's *Dialogue* and Tauler's *Conferences* into French. Antoinin Massoulié (d. 1706), at Rome and
again at Paris was a regular consultor to the Holy See on
theological questions, especially of Quietism and of Molinism,
of which he was a rigid opponent. His numerous works included *Meditations of St. Thomas on the Three Ways of
Prayer, On True Prayer against Quietism, On the Love of
God* in French, and in Italian *On the Virtue of Religion*.

Finally, Alexander Piny, a distinguished French philosopher
theologian (d. 1709) who had written a *Cursus Philosophicus*

in five volumes and works against Molinism, produced two spiritual classics *The Key of Pure Love*, (Lyons 1680) and *The Prayer of the Heart* (Paris, 1683). These French Dominicans thus made an important contribution to the French School of Spirituality of which one of the chief figures is the founder of the Sulpicians, Venerable Jean-Jacques Olier, himself a Dominican Tertiary, which through its seminary teaching so formed the Catholic clergy. This School emphasized identification with the inner life and intentions of Jesus and engaged in subtle discussions on the nature of "pure love." Piny teaches that pure love consists in the total submission of the will to the wise and loving will of God.

> What is the key which can open to us that precious treasure [of pure love]? That key, O souls who aspire to pure love, that key is none other than the *fiat*, "Let it be done," pronounced on every occasion of the Cross; it is the submission and acquiescence given to the Divine will in the occasions of suffering.... Whenever we say to God *fiat* to accept all He wills us to suffer, so often do we give proof of our pure love, a love which tends not to satisfy the one who loves, but the Beloved ... (Ch. 1).

Preaching

The Preachers of this century were especially distinguished by their great missionary work not only in the New World, but its extension into the Far East, which is marked by the extraordinary number of martyrs of this time, which it is sufficient to list. In the New World mission of Guadalupe six friars were martyred in 1604 and in Mexico, Sebastian Montagnol in 1616. In the Far East in Cambodia, Lopo Cardozo first stationed in Goa, martyred in 1605. In Japan St. Alphonse Navarette and companions (d. 1617) and William Courtet and his companions (d. 1637); the Tertiary Magdalena of Nagasaki (d. 1634); Sister Marina (d. 1634), a religious but mocked as a prostitute and then burnt; Juan Rueda of the Angels (d. 1621), a preacher of the rosary; the two Basques Domingo of Eriquicia and Hyacinth Esquivel in 1633; Thomas of St. Hyacinth, a Japanese, and the Sicilian Jordan of St. Stephen in 1634 and James of St. Mary, a Japanese priest educated in Manila, in 1635 in Nagasaki. In Formosa the Portuguese Francisco de Santo Domingo (d. 1633); and the Spaniard Luis Moro (d. 1636). In China St. Francis de Capillas (d. 1640), its protomartyr; the Tertiary Catherine Mieou (d. 1663); and Dominic Coronado who died in prison (1664).

Although not martyred, notable Dominicans working in China were Juan Baptista de Morales (d. 1664), who wrote a Chinese dictionary and grammar, a religious history of China, a biography of St. Dominic in Chinese, and works on the Chinese rites question. It was he who helped Gregory Lo (d. 1687), the first native priest to be ordained; and the native catechists and Tertiaries, the sailor Joachim Ko (d. 1649) and Catherine Sanzo (d. 1655).

But in the Old World there were also Dominican martyrs: in Ireland, Richard Barry and companions (d. 1647) under Cromwell; two nuns (d. 1653); the Tertiary Sir John Burke (d. 1610); many friars in Russia (d. c. 1649), where 21 large convents were destroyed by Cossacks; in Morocco Constantio Magni (d. 1624) who, while seeking to care for Christian slaves, died in prison; José Moran (d. 1643) who after apostatizing in Algeria, repented and witnessed the Faith; Alexander Baldrati a Lugo (d. 1645), killed on Chios by Turks; and Andrew Carga (d. 1697), an Italian, hanged from a ship's mast also by Turks, in Constantinople.

There were many writers on the missions. Thus Diego Collado (d. 1638), who worked in Rome in the Propaganda, wrote extensively on the missions, their history, and linguistic problems, and Baptista Verjuys (d. 1667) wrote a *Pastoral Handbook for Missionaries.*

The great missionary controversy on the Chinese rites began in this century. The Dominicans and Franciscans and the secular missionary priests, who worked chiefly with the Chinese peasants, regarded the prescribed Confucian rites as superstitious and idolatrous and therefore forbade them to their converts, while the Jesuits who had obtained a reputation with the Imperial court and upperclasses by their learning and their quick mastery of Chinese language and scholarship, took the view that these rites were purely formal and could be permitted as religously neutral. The issue was taken to Rome where the Curia was puzzled by such divergent reports and kept trying to obtain better information. Dominican missionaries produced many works in defense of their position beginning with Carlos-Clemens Gan in 1639 and at great length in a three-volume work, 1676-79, by Domingo Hernando de Navarette, of which the last two volumes were suppressed by the Spanish government and never published.

The European preaching of this time largely conformed to the Baroque ideals of somewhat theatrical oratory. As in past times some Dominican writers wrote works to assist preachers such as Tommaso Aloysio Francavilla, himself a noted preacher (d. 1694), who wrote *The Novice in the Pulpit* and other works for beginners; while Antoine Mazenod (d. 1689), developed methods of catechizing children and simple people by the use of diagrams and hymns, and Charles Roussel (d. 1648) based his preaching on the explanation of symbols. But some of the distinguished speakers of this time might be called "orators" rather than preachers, because they specialized in the delivery of elaborate panegyrics on state occasions or funerals of notables.

Yet in the more general work of preaching, each country produced its own notables. Among the French the most distinguished was Nicolaus Coeffeteau (d.1624), heard throughout France against the Calvinists, preacher ordinary to Henry IV, friend of the influential Cardinal Duperron, who was made bishop of Metz and Marseilles. He is recognized as one of the chief shapers of elegant French, maintaining clarity and moderation even in his polemics. He was especially a defender against the Calvinists of the Eucharist and papal authority, although he was a Gallican (but not a conciliarist) and denied papal infallibility as regards dogmatic facts. He did not favor the more extreme of the Dominican reformers in France. Thomas Le Paige (d. 1658) was said by Echard to be the greatest preacher of his time in France.

> "He had such dignity of speech, sonority of voice, gestures both vigorous and solemn, language elegant yet not obscure, not artificial, but so backed up with references to the Bible and the Fathers, especially St. Augustine whose many works

he knew completely by memory, that he could both persuade his hearers' minds and nourish their hearts and thus might through these impressions effect their conversion."

One of his works is the two-volume *The Contented Man: Weighty Opinions, Agreeable Repartees, and Wholesome Thoughts*. In the religiously divided Low Countries and Germany, the most noted preachers were chiefly engaged in polemics with Protestantism. Thus the eschatological tone of the preaching of Jacob Willart (d. 1682) is evident in the title of his work, *An Olive Branch Announcing the Wonderous Secrets of Divine Providence to be Accomplished in the Evening of this World*, while in Spain and Italy the preachers were more inclined to range over the traditional themes of Catholic piety and morals and to panegyrics.

This century did not lack Dominicans who preached through the arts. Some wrote poetry, such as the prolific Giovanni Battista Spadio (d. 1660) who wrote more than 11 volumes of poems, mainly panegyric odes; in Flemish, Christopher Van der Donck (d.1665), author of a biblical poem, *Judge of Hearts*, and Jordanus Van den Bempde (d. 1670), *Spouse of Blood*, etc. A good many wrote poetic dramas. Tragedies and other serious plays were written by Matteo Anna (d. 1641), saints' lives; Giovanni Battista de Franchis e Spinola (d. 1660 with a reputation of sanctity), *The Assumption* and saints' lives; Jean Baptiste Francken (d. 1660), *Tragedy of the Seven Macabbees*; Bernardino Faso (d. 1684), *Christmas Night; Death and Burial of St. Rosalia by an Angel*. Others wrote "tragicomedies," as Angelo Vincenzo Cerva (d. 1612), *Clorinda, William of Aquitaine*; Francisco Maldachini (d. 1644), *The Princess Coriana*; Simon Basin (d. 1671), *Extravagant Love*. A few tried their hand at epics, as Jordano Gargano (d. 1614), *The Parthian Woman*; in Portuguese, Francisco de Sa de Menses (of Jesus) (d. 1655), *The Conquest of Malaca*; Diego de Ojeda (d. 1615), *Life of Christ* in 12 books; and Stephan Pasquier (d. 1657), satiric epic on the French-Spanish war. In this age, rich in Baroque music, there were a number of Dominican composers or editors of music, such as Giovanni Nicolo Toscano (d. 1605); Dominico Campesio (d. 1629), and Adrian Cocquerel (d. 1647).

In the visual arts, undoubtedly the most notable painter was Juan Mayno (d. 1646), a pupil of El Greco and Titian, whose work belongs to the best period of Spanish painting. In the New World, in Quito, the Spanish-Indian Pedro Bedon (d. 1621), taught by a pupil of Michelangelo, was both a painter and stained-glass artist, while acting as Regent of Studies for his province and as a teacher of native languages. Priests, brothers, and sisters who were painters or sculptors in this century could be named, while Phillip Wicart of Ghent (d. 1694) was an artificer of bells and organs, and in the last part of the century, in Sicily and Spain, a lay brother, Fra Azarias, was a remarkable artist in glass. There were numerous Dominican architects and engineers, such as Antonio Brancuti (d. 1605); Lodovico di Bologna (fl. 1648); Cardinal Vincenzo Maculano, (d. 1667); and Gennaro Maria d'Afflitto (d.1673) of Naples, an expert on fortifications, or Thomas Maria Napoli (d. 1688), a writer on architecture.

Thus this century was marked by the large number of Dominicans, the diversity of their activities, their involvement in the Molinist, Probabilist, and Jansenist controversies, and their great missionary activity in the New World and Far East.

7

Survivors (1700s)

A New Rival to the Gospel

During the later 1600s the intellectual elites of Europe became increasingly disillusioned with Christianity and its religious wars between Catholics and Protestants on the Continent, and Anglicans and Puritans in England. The "Enlightenment" was essentially a search for an alternative to Christianity: first deism and then an agnostic or atheist secular humanism, bolstered by a co-option of modern science and technology, first developed in the 1600s under Christian auspices. Popular religion was at first unaffected, but as this Enlightenment spread from England to France, then to Germany, it attacked the religious orders with devastating ridicule. Gallicanism and German Febronianism, by removing the Church's counterforce to secular absolutism, cleared the way for the French Revolution in 1798 and the dictatorship and imperial wars of Napoleon Bonaparte up to 1815.

Moreover, this rival to Christianity fostered many values we all recognize today as genuine progress: democracy, emphasis on human rights, higher standards of living and health, the knowledge explosion—powerful pragmatic arguments that secular humanism had a greater claim to truth and effectiveness than the Gospel. The Church, ill-prepared for this unexpected challenge, could only denounce its outrages. The Dominican Order might have assimilated the Enlightenment as in the thirteenth century it assimilated pagan thought, but it was so caught up in the controversies on grace and Probabilism that it also was paralyzed by this "future shock."

In 1721 the long regime of Cloche was succeeded by the brief term of Augustino Pipia (1721-25), an Aragonese, and Master of the Sacred Palace. He constantly insisted that all correspondence with him be brief and precise and that all the brethren be undeviatingly Thomistic. In 1724, the Dominican Cardinal Orsini, became the fourth Pope from the Order, Benedict XIII, and during his six-year term showed himself its great friend, often coming to choir in its churches and even receiving the discipline with the other friars. He heaped privileges on the Order which were largely annulled by his successor. Perhaps his greatest favor was the bull *Demissas preces* which made clear that the Holy See's condemnation of Jansenism in no way applied to Thomism, as the Molinists had claimed. In 1724 he made Pipia a cardinal.

Pipia's successor was Tomas Ripoll, another Aragonese, and a contemplative, who had been the companion of both Cloche and Pipia. The elective Chapter received a letter from Benedict XIII insisting on attendance at choir, on the removal of all class distinction in the Order, and on strict Thomism. Benedict also restored the church of San Sisto Vecchio where St. Dominic had established his second community of nuns, and he tried to fuse the Congregations of Santé and St. Marc de Gavotis in the Kingdom of Naples and form a Province of Santé but his successor reversed this. Ripoll made no visitations. With his support, many of the important studies on the documents and history of the Order were completed and the Jansenist controversy brought to its end. In 1740 the great scholar Pope Benedict XIV, who had always been and continued to be a great friend of the Order and supporter of Thomism, was elected. Ripoll died in 1747.

Antonin Brémond, of the Province of Toulouse, a very lovable and popular friar but frail in health, was elected Master by acclamation in 1748. He had been a missionary for five years in Martinique, then under Ripoll an editor of the Order's documents, and had written a *Useful Manual for the Christian*

Life for the children of the English King James II, exiled in Rome. His health prevented much accomplishment and he died in 1752. One of the consolations of his term had been to see the revival of the Order in German lands.

The Spaniard Juan Tomás Boxadors had been a diplomat at the court of Emperor Charles VI. He had been a man of the world, well-informed, a connoisseur of the arts, when in 1755 he received news of his brother's death in the great Lisbon earthquake, renounced his ambitions and entered the Order. But after teaching theology for some years, he was chosen as a companion of Master Brémond, and then elected his successor in 1756. The elective Chapter had as always commissioned him to promote Thomism and the rosary and Boxadors did so faithfully. Through four years he painstakingly visitated the Spanish Provinces, enduring many discomforts of travel.

In the meantime the propaganda of the Enlightenment was beginning to have its effect, and to the young religious life began to appear obsolescent. By 1758 the Provinces of France, Paris and St. Louis had only three novices, Toulouse only one. In 1765, 28 Benedictines of the Congregation of St. Maur petitioned Louis XVI to absolve them of their vows and this led to the appointment of a royal commission to reform the religious orders. This commission was dominated by the Archbishop of Toulouse, one Loménie de Brienne, who was strongly influenced by the Enlightenment. No man less than 21, or woman less than 18 could be admitted as a novice, no religious house could have less than nine members, and each Order must rewrite its constitutions for royal approval. The same trend spread in the Empire under Joseph II and in Tuscany where all novitiates were closed. In 1773 Clement XIV was forced by nominally Catholic kings to suppress the Society of Jesus. Until made cardinal in 1776 Boxadors absolutely but helplessly resisted these attacks on the Order.

The elective Chapter of 1777 still had delegates from 30 provinces but was the first in twenty years. Pius VI, following the precedent of Benedict XIII and XIV, opened the Chapter in person. It chose one of Boxadors' officials, Baltasar de Quiñones of the Province of Spain, who, like Master Ridolfi, had a reputation for lavish generosity. The acts of this Chapter forbade public disputations that might anger secular authorities and were silent on the dire situation of the Order under secular attacks. They called for a Chapter in 1780, but in fact none was to meet until 1835! In the next years France was in the turmoil that led to the Revolution in 1789. Then the Constituent Assembly forced the clergy to swear primary allegiance to state authority, and by 1792 made clerical celibacy optional, forbade the religious habit, and began to depose and frequently to execute clergy who refused the loyalty oath.

In 1790 there were still at least 1,200 professed Friar Preachers in the seven provinces of France (an average of seven clerics and one lay brother per convent). As a result of the long struggle for reform within the Order, the friars' observance of their *Constitutions* was generally true to its essentials and in many houses quite strict, although their numbers had sharply declined and their average age was rapidly increasing. Most of the other orders were also relatively sound. Yet the First Republic suppressed them all, pensioning those who wished to be freed of their vows, while sending those who would not leave to government residences not of their choosing nor under their control. For example, in the Bordeaux convent (average in observance but larger than average) of the 25 choir religious, 13 wanted to remain, 6 wanted to leave, 4 abstained, 2 were absent; of the 7 lay brothers 1 stayed, 2 left, 4 abstained.

The last convent to survive in France was the Paris General Novitiate, finally closed in 1793. Many friars suffered imprisonment, death, or deportation. Others fled to Germany, England, and Spain but found their best reception in Italy.

On the eve of the Revolution there had been 45 Dominicans provinces, 30,000 to 40,000 friars in 1,200 houses, and 200 monasteries of nuns. After 1765 the governments of Vienna, Naples, and Madrid more and more interferred with any recourse to the Master of the Order. All religious houses in France, Belgium, Germany and many in Italy were suppressed from about 1789 to 1850. In Russia, Lithuania, and Poland this also occurred after 1842. The Portuguese and Spanish Provinces were separated from the Master's jurisdiction from 1802 to 1872. Only nine Provinces continued without interruption. At the end of the 1700s, the Master of the Order, Quiñones, as far as is known, remained strangely indifferent to these disasters. Exiled by Pius VI to La Quercia and then returning to Spain in 1798, he died at Florence.

Mother Mary Poussepin

Study

Right up to the French Revolution the chief theological issues which occupied Dominicans were still the debates with the Jesuits over the doctrine of grace in dogmatic theology and of Probabilism in moral theology. These issues were confused by the fact that on both issues the Jansenists also opposed the Jesuits in the name of authentic Thomism. Moreover, the all too patriotic French Dominicans were driven by their Gallicanism into resenting the efforts of the popes to suppress Jansenism and to resist the secular attacks on the Jesuits. Typical was the case of one of the greatest Dominican scholars of the age, Noël (Natalis) Alexander (d. 1724), who taught at Paris, was Regent of Studies for his own and other provinces, Provincial of the Province of France, tutor of the son of the great Minister Colbert. He was an enormously erudite controversialist who battled John Launoi of the Paris faculty, the man who denied that Aquinas was the author of the *Summa Theologiae*, and wrote learned polemic works on the Sacrament of Penance, simony, clerical celibacy, the authority of the Vulgate, Molinism, Probabilism, and the question of the Chinese rites.

Alexander also produced a large *Moral and Dogmatic Theology* according to the order of the *Catechism of Trent* and a literal and moral commentary on the New Testament. But his greatest work was his vast *Church History* which was put on the Index (along with some shorter works) by Innocent XI because of its Gallicanism (although an annotated edition by another Dominican, Roncaglia, was later permitted to be published by Benedict XIII and Benedict XIV) and he was forbidden to teach by Master Monroy in spite of the intercession of the French king on his behalf. In 1714 he became an "appellant" against the condemnation of the Jansenists, not because he favored them, but because he thought the decree condemned Thomism in favor of the Jesuit views on grace. He became blind, and shortly before his death submitted to papal authority, much to the relief of most Dominicans.

The two most distinguished dogmatic theologians of this century (although they also dealt with moral questions) were Gotti and Billuart. Ludovico Vincenzo Gotti (d. 1742), was an Italian who became cardinal and patriarch of Jerusalem. He wrote a five-volume *Scholastic-Dogmatic Theology*, works on celibacy and papal authority, an immense 12-volume *Applogetics* and many other apologetic works. He also wrote a study on the definability of the Immaculate Conception, advising against any further papal action. His treatise, *On the True Church*, was translated into Latin and annotated by Thomas Covi in 1752.

Charles René Billuart (d. 1757), a Belgian, was almost made a Cardinal. He had taught philosophy at Douay, theology at Revin, been regent of studies, prior several terms, provincial twice, and was a noted preacher especially on devotion to the Eucharist. His major work was a 19-volume commentary on the whole of the *Summa Theologiae*. His work was not especially original, depending in considerable measure on Gotti, and in its historical information on Noël Alexander, but it provided a comprehensive and up-dated statement of Thomism which was for a long time the standard interpretation. He wrote other works on the Eucharist and the question of grace. He was involved in the discussion over the spiritual works of the distinguished saintly and humanistic French Archbishop Fénelon, for a time suspected of Quietism.

More specifically on the great problem of grace Jacques-Hyacinthe Serry (d. 1738), a noted French preacher, besides many sermons, lectures on the Trinity, Christology, ecclesiology, papal authority, and defenses of St. Catherine of Siena and Melchior Cano, produced a *History of the Commission on Grace*, heavily biased on the Dominican side but unsurpassed in thoroughness and documentation. He was defended against Jesuit protests by Melchior-Thomas de L'Hermite (d. 1730). Many others defended the Thomistic view, such as Cardinal Tommaso M. Ferrari (d. 1716) who actively opposed the Jansenist Quesnel, and supported the Augustinian Cardinal Henry Noris in his notable study of the history of Pelagianism, a work much resented by the probabilists; and Gregorio Gelleri (d. 1729), Master of the Sacred Palace who wrote eight volumes to defend the papal decree *Unigenitus* condemning Jansenism. Norbert d'Elbecque (d. 1714), who published Noël Alexander's moral theology and wrote to refute the theory of "philosophic sin," was also thought to favor Jansenism, although he taught in Rome. On the other hand Vincent Rigal (d. 1722), Regent of St. Jacques in Paris, was repeatedly rebuked by Master Cloche for pertinaciously favoring Molinistic opinions; Sebastian Kippenburg (d. 1733) opposed the views of Lemos, the great defender of the Thomist position; while Antonio Dionysio Simon D'Albizzi (d. 1738) also of St. Jacques so harshly attacked the Molinists that the King's Jesuit confessor had him imprisoned (he later became an "appellant" against *Unigenitus*).

Some have charged a Dominican professor in Vienna, Pietro M. Gazzaniga (d. 1799), of falling into Calvinism in his attacks on Molinism. Finally, Giorgio Francisco Albertini (d. 1809), author of works on marriage and on original sin, seems to have yielded a good deal to Molinism. It is evident that Dominicans felt themselves very much on the defensive on this question in an age when deistic tendencies were beginning to make the Thomistic doctrine of the total dependence of human freedom on the *concursus* of God a distasteful doctrine.

Not all Dominican writing in dogmatic theology, however, was on the grace controversy. Ambrosio Peretti (d. 1712) of

Prague wrote on happiness, as well as on logic; Giuseppe M. Tabaglio (d. 1714) on the Mystical Body; Jean des Holias (d. 1715) on Purgatory, etc. Unusual undertakings were a historical and critical study (in 12 volumes!) of the principal signs by which humans, angels, devils, and God communicate with each other, by Alphonse Costadau (d. 1725), and another by the Belgian Matthias Dolman (d. 1728) to prove against Protestant attacks on the memory of St. Dominic and St. Pius V that the Pope is infallible in solemn canonizations.

Easily first among Dominican moralists of the time was the redoubtable Daniel Concina (d. 1756) who studied at a Jesuit college in Goritz, Austria, and then entered a strict observant Dominican congregation in Venice. He taught philosophy and preached extensively in North Italy, striving to revive the simplicity and austerity of the life of early Christianity. He wrote a work to refute the idea of the Bollandists that St. Dominic derived his ideal of poverty from St. Francis and attacked the claim of Raphael de Pornasio, O.P., (d. 1465) that modern Dominicans practice the same poverty as that of the first days of the Order, and in another work attacked the use of private accounts by religious, producing, of course, a vigorous controversy.

Concina's most important role, however, was played in the Probabilist controversy. The condemnation of certain Laxist moral opinions by Alexander VII (1665, 1666) and by Innocent XI (1667) had by no means ended Laxism which was even more congenial to the Enlightenment than to the Baroque Age. Benedict XIV was particularly concerned about this relaxation of morals and favored Concina's approach as when in his encyclical of 1741 he adopted Concina's view on the Lenten fast. But it was the Dominican's *History of Probabilism and Rigorism* (1743) which aroused great opposition from the Jesuits because it seemed to identify Probabilism as the root of modern Laxism. They were even more disturbed by his great 12-volume *Christian Dogmatic-Moral Theology* (1749-55) and its two-volume compendium, which were widely used as texts free of Probabilism. Benedict XIV rejected Jesuit efforts to have this work condemned and Concina declared he had no intention to attack the Society. While Concina's opinions on some topics inclined to severity, he was not a Rigorist but a

Probabiliorist who, in keeping with the teleological rather than legalist moral theory of Aquinas, sought to inculcate the use of the most effective means to attain the ultimate end of union with God through charity. With papal support he worked to maintain the spiritual values of the Christian life in the face of the indulgence of hedonism promoted by the Enlightenment *philosophes.* In beginning his treatment of charity, he writes:

> It is necessary for me to warn you, my Reader, lest I should incur many criticisms, that I will write about love at more length than younger writers are accustomed to do. For they accuse me of using the style of a preacher, padding my folios with too many words, figures of speech, and exhortations. But I will not tarry over these criticisms and I am astonished at their ignorance of the true method of teaching Christian theology. For the ethics of morals should not only illumine the mind but conquer the will and subdue the passions. Therefore if this is to be well constructed it is necessary to follow the right path to this end, a path that appears to the new casuists just the one that is sterile and thorny, but which the older Fathers left us as a theology fertile, flowery and most apt to excite the will.

An important supporter of Concina's views was Giuseppe V. Patuzzi (d. 1769) who produced an eight-volume *Ethica Christiana* and two works refuting the Aequiprobabilism of St. Alphonsus Ligouri and a defense of Aquinas against the old charge of favoring tyrannicide. Patuzzi, like Dante, wrote a work on the future state of the impious in which he detailed the degree of punishment awaiting each type of sinner or infidel. He did not seem aware that this mode of moralizing exposed Christian morality to the ridicule of Enlightenment satirist. Rather, what was needed was a revision of moral theology to free it from late medieval legalism and to revive the emphasis on true virtue of Aquinas and the other high scholastics. Fulgenzio Cuniliati (d. 1759), besides a complete moral theology and many saints lives, wrote an interesting application of moral theology to preaching, *The Catechist in the Pulpit*, and Dionysio Remedelli (d. 1765) performed an important service to moral theology by editing the great work of St. Antoninus of Florence.

Others dealt with special topics in moral theology, for example, Giovanni-Maria Muti (d. 1727) wrote against dueling and Machiavellianism; Joseph Roux (1748) on the duty to give alms to relieve a famine in France; Albert Oswaldt (d. 1711) and Edmund Burke (d. 1739) on the sorrow required for forgiveness of sin, etc. Although canon law played a great part in the moral theology of this time not many noted Dominican canonists can be mentioned.

It was the century when Richard Simon (d. 1712) opened the way to historico-critical study of the Bible, but Dominicans played little part in this new movement. The not very distinguished names that can be mentioned in this field are: Vincenzo M. Ferri (d. 1714) on *Matthew*; Giuseppe M. dalla Torre (d. 1719), introduction to the Bible; Emmanuel da Encarnacao (d. 1720) on *Matthew*; Lorenzo-Filippo Virgulti (d. 1735), a Hebraist engaged in polemics with the rabbis; Nicolo Agostino Chignoli (d. 1767) on *Daniel*; Vincenzo Penzi (d. 1773) on the authority of Scripture in theology; Dominicus Czerny (d. 1780) a text of hermeneutics; F.H. Arizarra (d. 1783) on the origin and antiquity of Hebrew writing; Giovanni Domenico Stratico (d. 1799) on the pastoral use of Scriptures; and Gabriel Fabricy (d. 1800) on the reliability of the Hebrew text of the Bible.

The Dominican achievement in patrology and liturgy was considerably better due primarily to the brilliant work of Michel Le Quien (d. 1733) whose *Oriens Christianus* on the Eastern Churches and his edition of the works of St. John Damascene were among the major scholarly works of the period. He also defended the Hebrew text of the Scriptures against the Septuagint; wrote on the nullity of Anglican ordinations, and produced numerous other works. Giordano Polisicchio (d. 1744) proved the correspondence of Jesus and Abgar of Edessa to be spurious and probably Arian.

Le Quien was a leader among the Parisian Dominicans in "appealing" against *Unigenitus* because they thought it denigrated the authority of Aquinas. Bernard M. De Rubeis (d. 1775), who while in Paris was a friend of Le Quien, Echard and other scholars, wrote numerous historical studies on the early Church, but his main work, still of importance, was his historical notes on Aquinas' *Summa Theologiae*. Vincenzo M. Fassini (d. 1787), an excellent writer but a violent polemicist, was a friend of De Rubeis and edited the life and studies of Concina (getting himself into trouble with the censors for arguing that the Jesuits had invented the "myth" of Jansenism). He wrote on Eucharistic practices of the Eastern Churches, on early Christian names, on the apostolic origin of Gospels, on the canonicity of the Apocalypse, and on Josephus.

Many Dominicans at this time engaged in historical writing, some of which has already been mentioned, such as the *Church History* of Noël Alexander and *The History of the Congregation on Grace* of Serry. The other most notable achievements was the completion (to 1700) of the *Writers of the Order of Preachers* started by Jacques Quétif (d. 1698) and completed to 1700 by the indefatigable Jacques Echard (d. 1724). About this work a sarcastic modern author wrote:

> These Friar Preachers who have destroyed the books of others, have written many themselves which have almost all been preserved; and they even have had the good fortune that the history which they have left of their Brothers who have written, is a masterpiece of literary history. Of course, it is true that it has been written at a time when they could no longer burn anyone!

Echard like Le Quien was a leader of the Paris "appellants."

Also of capital importance are the *Bullarium O.P.* and *Annales O.P.*, edited by Antonin Brémond (d. 1755) (assisted by Hermano Benedicto Christianopoli, Francisco M. Polidori and Vincenzo M. Badetto), collecting fundamental documents of the Order, and the *Illustrious Men of the Dominican Order* by Antonin Tournon (d. 1775) who also produced a 14-volume *General History of America* and apologetic works. Of more general interest was the great *Church History* of Cardinal Giuseppe Agostino Orsi (d. 1776) against Fleury's Gallican-tainted history. In 21 volumes Orsi got only to the seventh century but it was continued to 1529 in 42 volumes by Filippo Becchetti O.P. Orsi strongly defended papal infallibility. libility.

Ignace-Hyacinthe Amat de Graveson (1733) also wrote an

eight-volume *Church History*, a Bible history, a life of Christ, a work on the Messiahship of Jesus and interesting letters on theological method. He was influential in persuading the Jansenistic and Gallican Cardinal Archbishop Noailles finally to submit in the affair of the *Unigenitus*. Tommaso M. Mamachi (d. 1792), from the island of Chios, a friend of Benedict XIV and of Cardinal Orsi, wrote a pioneering work on Christian antiquities, defended the power of the Pope over councils, and worked with Remedelli on the edition of the works of St. Antoninus and on the *Annales O.P.* He had a controversy with the great collector of conciliar documents, Mansi on the dates of St. Athanasius and on what he regarded as his Laxist moral opinions. There were Dominican antiquaries such as Francisco Orlandi (d. 1733) who wrote an ecclesiastical geography and a work on feet-washing and forms of altars, Joseph M. Verdova (d. 1744), an expert collector of antique Roman coins; and Giuseppe Allegranza (d. 1785) an archaeologist, student of ancient tombs and inscriptions.

Many wrote on the missions, to mention only the Bolivian half-Indian Alonso de Zamora (d. 1717) on New Granada, and Francisco Serrano (d. 1748) on the Dominicans, many of them martyrs in China. The eighteenth century was avid for travelogues, and Dominican missionaries such as the Frenchman Godefrid Loyer (d. 1714), in his *Relation of a Voyage to the Kingdoms of Issyny, the Gold Coast, and Guinea in Africa*, were happy to oblige.

The liveliest writer in this genre was Jean-Baptiste Labat (d. 1738) who wrote an account of his missionary experience in the West Indies, especially Martinique, the frankness of which so offended its government as to prevent his ever returning. Subsequently, he wrote of his voyages in Italy and Spain, and then (with considerable imagination) voyages in Africa and the Near East based on the accounts of others. Finally, he wrote further on his memories of the West Indies. These works were literary and popular successes because of his vivid, humorous, and very personal style, quite different from that used by most of his confreres in their immense theological tomes.

There were innumerable writers of saints lives, such as those by Michael Navarro y Soria (d. 1739) and José de Natividad

(d. 1753). Many of these were uncritical, such as the efforts of Jean-Dominique Gavoty, (d. 1714) and Benedictus Behm (d. 1715) to defend the legends about Mary Magdalene; but there were also efforts to define standards of historical criticism as by Jacinto Segura (d. 1752). And there were studies of local interest, such as Augustin Michael (d. 1714) on the Christians of Mozambique; Pedro Monteyro (d. 1735), counselor of the King and Dauphin of Portugal, who left many documentary studies; and J.B.M. Contareni (d. 1752) and Giuseppe H. Triverio (d. 1754) on Italian topics.

In all these efforts, primarily theological in character, the underlying philosophy remained firmly Thomistic, yet sadly there was still no extensive effort to meet the challenge of the new science and philosophy since Descartes. The most successful statement of Thomistic philosophy was the *Summa Philosophica* (1777 in six volumes) of Salvatore M. Roselli (d. 1785). This work which had several editions is generally sound Thomism but shows some influence from a widely used work by Joseph Valla (d. 1790), General of the Theatines, which was moderately traditionalist and influenced by Descartes' and Malebranche's doctrine of innate ideas, and with Jansenistic tendencies. On the other hand, this work still rejects the Copernican-Galilean revolution in science as condemned by the Church!

Many wrote on logic (it seemed a safe subject), such as Augustinus Adler (d. 1711) and Pedro de Candamo (d. 1717); or grammar, Giacomo-Maria Rossi (d. 1727). Others wrote complete manuals: Giacinto-Rosa Cameroni (d. 1710), *Philosophy of Aristotle Purged from Errors*; Paulus-Maria Cauvinus (d. 1716); Antoninus Perenger, (d. 1717); Juan Villalva (d. 1722). Some, however, directly attacked the new science principally as mechanistic and atomistic, as Henrico Saccardi (d. 1716); Giovanni Domenico Siri (d. 1737) in his *General Aristotelico-Thomistic Philosophy* against Descartes and Gassendi (1719); and Giovanni Domenico Agnani (d. 1746) *Philosophy New Yet Old* (*Neo-Palea*). Nicolo M. Gennaro (d. 1714) also engaged a Franciscan in a controversy on atomism and Alberto M. Mannoliti (d. c. 1736) left a lengthy refutation of this error unpublished; but others such as

Vitus Kahl (d. 1735) serenely continued to comment on the works of Aristotle.

What is surprising is that a considerable number of Dominicans of this as in the previous century wrote or at least taught mathematical and engineering subjects, such as Gundisalvo Steffani (d. 1721); Tommaso Pius Maffei (d. 1717), an astronomer at Padua who was a Copernican and wrote on solar and lunar cycles and on the mechanics of Galileo and Descartes, and who, no doubt because of his eminence, had no difficulty with the censors of the Order; Philip Serrano (d. 1718) a lay brother who was an expert mathematician but did not publish; José Francisco (d. 1723), Juan Syra y Ferrer (d. 1730); and Benedetto M. Del Castrone (d. 1748) who wrote extensively on mathematics, geography, and navigation. But the most distinguished scientist and inventor in the Order at this time was Joseph Galien (d. 1762). Although accused of Jansenistic tendencies in his theological writings, he also vigorously opposed the Jansenist denial of the integrity of pure human nature apart from grace. He taught physics and meteorology at the University of Avignon, and became famous for his proposal (which he labeled an "Amusement") for aerial navigation to take troops to Africa. This proposal was based on previous discussion by two Jesuit scientists; but it probably influenced the Brothers Montgolfier who made the first hot-air balloon ascension in 1782.

The most important new development in Dominican studies in this century, however, was the attention given to apologetics in the face of the rising deism, agnosticism, and atheism of the Enlightenment. Early in France Ignace Piconne (d. 1713) was writing against "infidelity." In Belgium Francis Van Ranst (d. 1727) wrote works titled, *Truth is in the Middle*, and *History of Heretics*, and in England Ambrose Burgis (d. 1747), son of an Anglican minister, at Louvain a work on the Early Church and an *Introduction to the Catholic Faith*, but most of the apologetic works came in the latter part of the century. M.A. Bonetto (d. 1770) wrote on the existence of God; Pierre Thomas La Berthonie (1774), a defense of the Christian religion against unbelievers, Jews, and Spinozists; the Dominican historian already mentioned Antonin Touran (d. 1775), a comparison between the unbelief of ancient Israel and modern infidelity; Tommaso M. Cerboni (d. 1776), an important *On Revealed Theology*; Tommaso M. Soldati (d. 1782), on the role of the state in supporting or undermining religion; Edward Anthony Hatton (d. 1783), on the effects of the Reformation in England; Antonio Valsecchi (d. 1791), on the sources of impiety and the truth of Catholicism; and Ulrich Reiss (d. 1795), on true and false miracles.

Two Dominicans were especially important in this field. One was Casto Innocentio Ansaldi (d. 1779), who, like many of his time, found scholastic method distasteful, fled from his religious superiors for many years, then returned to the Order to write erudite and original apologetic works. Among these are studies in Egyptian, early Jewish, and Roman religion, on the notion of "primitive revelation," on the historicity of Herod's massacre of the Innocents (against Scaliger), and several studies on the historicity of the Christian traditions about the early martyrs.

The other, Charles Louis Richard (d. 1794), is called by Daniel-Rops the most distinguished apologist of the eighteenth century because of his *Universal Dictionary of the Sacred Sciences* (six folio volumes of almost 5,000 pages, completed 1765) written to counteract the famous *Encyclopédie* of Voltaire, the Bible of the Enlightenment. He also produced *A General Dictionary of the Theological Sciences* (*Bibliothèque Sacrée*, 1822, in 29 volumes, the basis of many later works) and 79 polemical works, plus four volumes of sermons characterized by one critic as "simple, natural, intelligible to all; it instructs, touches and convinces." In 1778, he fled the Revolutionary Assembly of Paris to Brussels, but could not keep quiet when he found that the University of Louvain had become Josephist, and fled again to Lille and Mons where he wrote *The Parallel*, comparing the execution of King Louis XVI by the French to the killing of the Messiah by the Jews. Hence when the Republican armies in 1794 entered Mons they arrested this octogenarian prophet. He refused a defender, admitted he had written *The Parallel* and declared he would sign it with his blood. To his condemnation he answered *Deo Gratias*, and in prison sang the *Te Deum*. Before his execution he divided what little he possessed with his barber and the jailers, saying, "Charity should be strong as death and zeal unyielding as hell."

Finally, in this time there were not a few Dominicans engaged in the patient work of the bibliographer, compiler, and editor. Some, such as Jacques Echard, have already been mentioned but other examples are the Bohemian Reginald Braun (d. 1742), editor of works of Vincent Ferrer, Henry Suso, etc.; Alfonso Manrique (d. 1711) who published an encyclopedic *School of Princes and Knights on Geography, Rhetoric, Economics, Politics, Logic, and Physics*, an annual cycle of Dominican saints' lives, and a compendium of moral theology; Thomas M. Alfani (d. 1742), founder of a Neapolitan academy of scholars; and Giuseppe B. Audiffredi (d. 1794), a bibliographer.

Prayer

Although religious observance was essentially sound in most parts of the Order at the time of the Revolution, it had markedly receded from its height during the reforms of the seventeenth century. Thus by 1686 strict observance was declining throughout the French provinces as regards midnight office. By 1697 habits and tonsure were relaxing and private life was beginning again. The General Chapter in 1706 pointed out that the former model Province of St. Louis was slipping. By 1710 vocations were diminishing, and houses were reluctant to send novices to the General Novitiate. Friars had private accounts, and superiors had special dishes. Often the Divine Office was not said when the organ had to be used. Fewer people came to church because sermons were less frequent. By 1758 the General Novitiate in Paris had such poor food that it was decided to send the novices elsewhere, but this was not actually done until 1773. Elections became quarrels and many were disaffected by the results. In 1778 the Archbishop of Paris protested to Master Quiñones against the election of a certain Dominican as provincial saying the friars were "worldly and dissipated." As the historian Abbé Roy remarks:

> Their elegance and an entirely worldly manner distinguished them. Was it the air of the most dissipated street of Paris

which had changed them? If so, what would St. Dominic have said if he saw them with curled and powdered hair, trimmed and coifed like the little Lords of the World?

In such an atmosphere it is no wonder that prayer did not flourish in this century. Yet it was not lacking in sanctity, as is obvious from the history of the many martyrs in the missions. But there were also many contemplatives, especially among the women of the Order. Only a few of these, however, are known through their own writings. Thus Ottavia Arditi (d. 1739) left spiritual meditations and letters; Gertrude Salandri (d. 1748) a spiritual autobiography, as did Columba Scagilone (d. 1753) along with letters; and Deodata del Divino Amore (d. 1754), a number of works that have not been published.

Others left no writings but are known to us through biographies of their directors or others, of whom perhaps the most notable is Maria Rosa Giannini (d. 1741) of the Dominican laity, who attained the mystical marriage fifteen years before her death, and who spent her life caring for the poor of Naples. Other women with a reputation for sanctity were: Claudia De Angelis (d. 1715); Frialetta R. Fialetti (d. 1717), directed by the learned moralist Patuzzi; Benoite Rencurel (d. 1718), of the Dominican laity from a very poor family, a stigmatic who lived in a hermitage near the shrine of Our Lady of Laus; Maria della Volonta di Dio (d. 1722); Maria Caterina Rosetti (d. 1754); Domenica Prati (d. 1804); Columba Wifl (d. 1783); Columba Weigl (d. 1783); Paule Graessle (d. 1793). In Spain some seven stigmatized nuns of this period have been listed. In the lives of some of these women it is especially noted as in the case of Cecilia Mayer (d. 1749) that they offered themselves in prayer and penance for the survival of the Church under the Enlightenment onslaught.

The canonized saint of the Order (other than the martyrs) of this period is St. Louis Grignon de Montfort (d. 1716), significantly perhaps not of the First but the Third Order. Born in Brittany, he had a long struggle to be ordained, and then began a remarkable mission of preaching to the rural poor of France who under the Ancient Regime had become very much neglected. He especially preached the rosary, and in order that he might do so effectively joined the Dominican

Tertiaries, but founded his own institutes, the De Montfort Fathers and the Daughters of Wisdom. He especially worked against the spirit of Jansenism, which in spite of its reforming intentions made the access of the simple poor to Jesus seem too difficult. Consequently, he wrote two spiritual classics, *True Devotion to the Blessed Virgin* and *The Book of the Eternal Wisdom*. These should be read together to see how much De Montfort is in the tradition of Henry Suso. To consecrate oneself to Mary is to build one's spiritual life on total trust in Jesus, the Eternal Wisdom.

Blessed Francis de Posadas (d. 1713), a child of war refugees, was in Spain, as what De Montfort was in France, a great preacher who commonly preached six times a day, and left five volumes of posthumous works, chiefly sermons. He was also remarkable as a confessor, seemingly gifted with the ability to read the secrets of souls. The Blessed Pope Benedict XIII (Pietro Francesco Orsini, d. 1730) was for many years as priest and bishop a man of upmost pastoral dedication. As Pope he continued this attitude, and spent as much time as he could living the Dominican life with his brothers. His reign, however, suffered greatly from his trust in a friend, who as a powerful cardinal proved as corrupt as Benedict was a saint. Benedict's mother and sisters joined him in the Dominican family as Tertiaries.

As ever there were many writers on the rosary during this century, such as Louis Meijere (d. 1729), whose works on the rosary and on the Holy Name were frequently republished; and Giovanni T. Bianchi (d. 1748), who produced no less than 12 volumes on the Perpetual Rosary! In spite of the critical researches of Echard, some still defended the rosary legend, such as Tommaso Vincenzo Moniglia (1767), of the Casanatensian Library, who had at one time been persuaded to leave the Order for a life in London, but had returned—an example of the absentee clergy not uncommon at this time. There were many other Marian works like that of De Montfort. Thus Pedro Sanchez (d. 1719) wrote on Mary at the Cross; Sante Pascucci (d. 1728) and Serafino Montorio (d. 1729) on her feasts; Giacinto M. Anti (d. 1732) on her life; Matthaeus De Brie (d. 1738) on her name and a *Rosa Mystica*; Piero G. Caravadossi (d. 1746) on her maternity.

Otherwise the spiritual writing of this period is not out-standing. Jean Francois Billecoq (d. 1711), associated with Alexander Piny mentioned in the last chapter, wrote on similar topics. Francois Chauchemer (d. 1713) published thirty years of sermons, many delivered during his term as Preacher Royal and a two-volume *On the Advantages of a Christian Death.* He was cautious about mystical experiences and was involved in the cases of Fénelon and of the Spanish Franciscan Maria of Agreda, but he used the mystical writings of Louis Chardon. Similar caution was shown by Domenico Ricci (d. 1712) who wrote against Quietism and Cardinal Thomas-Maria Ferrari (d. 1716) who criticized Fenelon's *Maxims.* But Thomas Du Jardin (d. 1733) of Louvain, an opponent of Jansenism, de-fended the Dominican mystical tradition of Tauler and Suso.

The style of many of these works was aimed at a refined and "sentimental" audience. The Pole Nicolaus Oborski (d. 1716) wrote *Familiar Instructions on the Practice of True Devotion* and *The Ways of God.* Gaspar-Charles de la Feuille (d. c. 1724) wrote *Familiar Instructions for Ladies, Theology of Heart and Spirit* in 11 volumes, and *Reflections of a Penitent Soul for Every Day of the Year*, a bit melancholy but not Jansenist in tone. Other authors were more traditional such as Andreas Roth (d. 1735) on God as Alpha and Omega; Hyacinthus Reisner (d. 1743) on the soul and the fall; Peeter van Muyssen (d. 1744) on the seven gifts of the Holy Spirit; Seraphino Brienza (d. 1752), who had a great reputation as an exorcist, wrote an interesting work on Thomistic spiritual direction, making use also of the tradition of Tauler and Suso; and there were composers of prayers and hymns such as Raymund Bruns (d. 1780).

Some followed the Jesuit method by producing "spiritual exercises": Francois Mespolié (d. 1727), a famous preacher; Cesare Samminiati (d. 1729); P.M. Lauro (d. 1763); Salvatore Arcieri (d. 1788). Others dealt chiefly with various states of the life, such as Dominique Vautrin (d. 1713), *Rule of Life for Soldiers*; Stephan De Foucher de Salles (d. 1718), *The Perfect Lay Person*; Giuseppe Aldrisi (d. 1730), *A Model of Religious Life*; Gundisalvo Carattini (d. 1734), *Claustral Life*; Domenico M. Pascucci (d. 1746), *Spiritual Exercises for the Clergy.* Others were devoted to special devotions: Giovanni Battista

Mazzoleni (d. 1712), devotion to the Holy Cross; Domenico
M. Celli (d. 1730) to Holy Communion; José Garcia Fulla (d.
1749) to the Sacred Heart. Some wrote on purgatory as
Dominic Bullaughan (d. 1746) on pilgrimage to the purgatory
of St. Patrick and Giacomo Boni (d. 1747). Many others such
as Seraphino Thomas Miguel (d. 1722), Emmanuel Guilherme
(d. 1730), Domineco Ponsi (d. 1740) and Louis Robyn (d.
1743) wrote saints' lives.

Preaching

Eighteenth-century preaching ranged from the remnants of
Baroque eloquence to the beginnings of a new simplicity and
naturalness just as its art and literature moved through the
Rococo to Romanticism. Examples of the more Baroque style
are Jacques-Hyacinthe Fejacq (d. 1715), a renowned preacher
often called on as a panegyricist for the French royal family;
Michael Nanca (d. 1714), an Italian panegyricist; the Swiss
Leonard Leo (d. 1715), whose published sermons are titled
Sweet Honey from the Lion's Mouth; the Polish orator
Cyprian Sapecki (d. 1724); and Vincenzo M. Sasseti (d. 1729)
who left two volumes of sermons in a turgid style in which
biblical events are described as if they were works of sculpture.
Preaching on the rosary was common everywhere, but what
is notable at this time is the prominence of preachers in many
of the more peripheral provinces of the Order. Thus in Ireland
and England we note Ambrose O'Connor, (d. 1711), Provincial
of Ireland, imprisoned for four years; Dominic Williams (d.
1739), English bishop; and Bl. Arthur MacGeoghan (d. 1713)
martyr—among these were Peter O'Higgins, hanged, drawn
and quartered; John O'Mannin who lived after having his
back broken and returned to preach;—and Bishop Edmund
Burke (de Burgo) (d. 1776) author of a history of Irish Dominicans. Thomas Buccelini (d. 1718) was an Italian who preached
in German and refounded the Hungarian Province. In Poland
we have Johannes-Thomas Bogdanowicz (d. 1718) whose
preaching took on an apocalyptic tone; Dominic Frydrycho-
wicz (d. 1718), a prolific writer; and Johannes-Evangelista
Gawlowicz (d. 1720), a renowed orator, as well as Bonaventure

Awedyk (d. 1743), an Armenian preaching in Poland; and in Bohemia Cajetan Burger (d. 1740), whose orations were often expositions of symbolic images, and Leopold Erbeni (d. 1743). In Spain, France, and Italy a host of preachers published sermons and some wrote works on the art of preaching as Alberto Maria Pontierei (d. 1738), *Christian Eloquence for Beginners*, and André Le Fee (d. 1717), a very famous preacher (and also a promoter of a patent medicine), *The Ideal of Preachers, Their Dignity, Duties, and the Abuses of Their Ministry, with the Uses Their Hearers Should Make of God's Word*.

No great preacher through the arts can be named for this period, yet in the rococo age when the arts were becoming ever more secularized there were still friars engaged in art, music, and literature. There were composers, such as the Portuguese Domingo Núñez Pereira (d. 1729) and Joao Chrysostomo a Cruce (d. 1743), author of an *Art of Music*: and the Frenchman Gabriel Deslondes (d. 1733). Thomas-Maria Napoli (d. 1724) was an important Neapolitan architect who specialized in fortresses. But the chief activity was in poetry, none of it very distinguished, but plentiful. Thus a Belgian Gregorie de Lewincque (d. 1711) wrote a Latin ode with the bombastic title *Louis XIV Triumphant, Happy, Pious*. More modestly Giovanni Baptista Pichi (d. 1715) composed *Sacred Poems*; Thomas Gay (d. 1717) *Elegies*. Also in elgiac verse was Isidore López' (d. 1732) *The Passion*. Giacinto-Maria Anti (d. 1732) wrote *Sacred Sonnets;* Phillip Joly (d. 1734), poems in the Burgundian dialect; and Lucas a Sancta Catherina (d. 1740) and Francois Dominique Rouvière (d. 1743), various poems. Another poet, Louis Robyn (d. 1743) incurred the wrath of Master Ripoll for engaging in a publicized discussion with Jesuits that seemed to cast some doubt on the accepted account of St. Dominic's life and work. Some others tried other literary forms such as Vincenzo M. Dinelli (d. 1754) who carried on the Probabilist controversy in satirical poems; Thomas Leopoldus Gaianzell (d. 1716) and Joseph Maria Ferrarini (d. 1744) devised epigrams; and Thomas Spinelli (d. 1748) wrote a critical work, *The Mustard Seed of Letters*.

During this time of general Christian decline in Europe the missions, although very active, also began to suffer. In the

New World the Latin American missions continued to progress, although at the end of the century the Enlightenment began to spread to these regions and eventually to place the governments of the new nations as they won their independence from Spain under anti-clerical ideologies. Mention should be made of Bartolomé Navarro a S. Antonio (d. 1710), the Mexican Provincial, an author of theological treatises and many sermons, who set a high standard of religious observance, and Augustino de Quintana (d. 1734) who produced catechetical works in the native languages.

In the Far East the missions in the Philippines flourished. Notable were the linguist Juan de Yñiguez, (d. 1720) and the preacher reputed for holiness, José a Sanctissimo Rosario (d. 1742). The missions in Vietnam (Tonkin) were initiated by Juan de Santa-Cruz (d. 1721), who left many letters and other works describing missionary problems, as also did Francisco Gil de Federich (d. 1745).

Among the martyrs of Vietnam were Bl. Bishop Pedro Sanz and Companions (d. 1747-48) of Tonkin (now Vietnam). The bishop was beheaded, the other four priests and a catechist were tortured, imprisoned, and finally strangled.

The Spanish Provinces continued to send missionaries to China and Japan with at first great success. But soon the great problem of the Chinese rites brought a severe reversal to these missions. The Jesuit missionaries under the remarkable Matteo Ricci had penetrated into the court circles of the Chinese Empire by skillfully combining Western and Eastern culture and had advocated a form of "missionary adaptation" which permitted their many converts to conform to the Confucian rites as civil rather than religious ceremonies. The missions of the Franciscan and Dominican friars and of the French secular missionary priests, however, were to the peasant classes, and these missionaries regarded such adaptations as a compromise with the rank superstition and idolatry of the people. The endless series of protests and explanations to Rome, begun in the previous century, continued, e.g., in the works of Pedro Muñoz (d. 1730), Francisco González a S. Petro (d. 1730); and Hernando Eusebio Oscot y Colombres (d. 1743). After long and serious discussion these adaptations were condemned by the learned Benedict XIV. Subsequent experience and reflection have led the Church to a much broader view of such adaptation and seem to have justified the Jesuit position, but the difficulty of the question even today cannot be underestimated. In any case, these condemnations were received by the Chinese as an insult to their culture and resulted in a severe persecution from which the missions still have not recovered.

The most hopeful outcome of the age, however, was the beginning in the Order of a new active role for the communities of Third Order Sisters who until this time had been simply less strictly cloistered versions of the Second Order contemplative nuns. St. Catherine of Siena had provided a model for a Dominican woman engaged in active apostolate in the world, and this model had been followed by many Tertiaries as individuals, as we have seen, but not by communities. A wonderful example of this during the Revolutionary period was Catherine Jarrige (1754-1836), a peasant woman who organized an underground refuge and escape network for priests during the Terror, and who then spent the rest of her long life in the care of the poor with whom she lived as a Tertiary.

But the real originator of a new model of Dominican women's community was Marie Poussepin (d. 1744). From a working-class family, raised by her mother who was the treasurer of a charitable confraternity founded by a disciple of St. Vincent de Paul (founder of the Sisters of Charity as one of the first active women's communities). Marie ran her father's business after her parents' death and cared for her brothers until they could take it over. Then she met François Mespolié (already mentioned as a spiritual writer and preacher) and became a Tertiary. At this time Louis XIV was organizing a system of schools and hospitals, and Marie seized the opportunity to start the Sisters of Charity of the Presentation of Tours. The community was eventually recognized by the bishop of Chartres in 1728 with 20 houses in six dioceses. The community, although dispersed in secular garb by the Revolution, survived and revived, but did not receive recognition as part of the Dominican family, as Marie had always desired, until 1897.

It was also at this dark hour of the Order's history that Dominic Edward Fenwick founded the first Dominican community in the United States in 1805.

8

The Age of Compromise (1800s)

Revival and Expansion

The 1800s began with the Napoleonic conquests, their collapse and the reaction we think of as the Victorian Age and the "Victorian Compromise" between Christianity and the Enlightenment, which only covered over the steady advance of the new culture of secular humanism with its faith in inevitable progress through science and technology. This meant also increasing urbanization and the rise of industrial capitalism and rivalry for colonial empires. England and a unified Germany became the chief powers, while the United States (united after its great Civil War) began to enter into the competition. This new non-Christian culture was internally polarized between a materialistic scientism and a subjective idealist romanticism. This strain generated still more radical revolutionary movements, including that of Marxism.

The Dominican Order seemed to be dying. When Quiñones departed for Spain he left two vicars in Rome; Pius-Joseph Gaddi and Angelico Fanelli. Gaddi, an Italian of stately bearing, fearing Quiñones might die in Spain and perhaps ambitious to be Master himself, obtained from Pius VI authority as vicar general until an elective Chapter. But his authority was resisted as unconstitutional for six years by the provincial of Spain, Joseph Muñoz. Muñoz was backed by the King of

Spain who ordered a congress of the Provinces of Spain, Betica, Aragon and the Philippines to settle the matter. Through the efforts of another Spaniard, Joachim de Téran, former companion of Quiñones, this failed, but Téran, deviously intriguing to get the Mastership for himself, induced the king to request Pius VII to appoint a separate Master over the Spanish provinces, then the largest and healthiest part of the Order. Thus for the first time in its history (except for the time of the Great Western Schism) the Order was divided.

The Pope by the bull *Inter graviores* in 1804 limited the Master's term to six years only and provided that if he were not Spanish, then the Spanish provinces could elect a Vicar resident in Spain, yet approved by the Master and consulting with him on graver matters. As Master the Pope appointed not Téran but Gaddi and as Vicar in Spain one Joseph Díaz, but Díaz promptly yielded to the Spanish King's demand that Gaddi's authority be ignored in Spain. The Spanish Dominicans took an active part in the heroic but futile resistance to Napoleon's invasion of their country. Napoleon made a concordat with Piux VII, but the religious orders for a time remained suppressed. When Napoleon exiled Pius from Rome, Gaddi also was deported, first to Paris, then to Auxerre for 18 months, then to Milan for a year, and finally, still under surveillance, to his native Forli. On the fall of Napoleon in 1814 Pius returned to Rome, where Gaddi was accused to him of swearing fidelity to the secular government at Auvergne, but when Gaddi was able to clear himself the Pope appointed him Vicar General of the non-Spanish part of the Order, and Raymond Guerrero as Spanish Vicar. Guerrero, against the desires of the Spanish King, petitioned the Pope to unite the Order under one Master, but Gaddi died in 1819.

There followed those whom Mortier calls "the Masters of the Desolation." Since the state of Europe made an elective Chapter impossible from 1819 to 1825, the popes named a succession of Vicars for both parts of the Order until Leo XII finally appointed Joachim Briz as Master in 1825, the only Master to live in Spain for his six-year term, but his New World Provinces were isolated from him by their nations' wars of independence. Many friars in Spain failed to return to their convents, or did so only under the coercion of the King, and over 400 Brothers and Sisters had died between 1808 and 1815. In 1832 Briz became bishop of Segovia. Since the Roman Vicar, Thomas Ancaranai, died at the same time, Briz agreed to restore the unity of the Order under Ferdinand Jabalot, who however died in two years. The Pope next appointed Maurice Olivieri who resigned in two years because the Pope wanted to limit his powers by a council, and the Pope appointed Hyacinth Cipolletti.

Meanwhile in Spain the King, urged by anti-religious factions, instituted a Commission of Reform. Soon mobs began burning convents and massacring religious until in 1837 the Cortes suppressed all religious orders and forbade the wearing of the habit. The 200 convents of Spain were gone, leaving only the novitiate for the missions of the Philippines and China founded in 1830. Thus, except for Ocaña, in 1838 in France, Portugal, and Spain the Order was extinct.

In Holland the only Dominicans were parish priests without the habit or community. Only a few were left in Germany. The Province of Austria-Hungary had only 40 friars; Bohemia, 43. In Poland, Russia and Lithuania political troubles had almost or entirely annihilated the Order. A scattered few friars were in England and Ireland and a certain number of Irish were in exile in Rome, Louvain and Lisbon. In Italy a number of houses were recovering but the situation was still chaotic. In the New World the Spanish-speaking provinces also were undergoing the devastations brought by the struggles for independence from Spain. Yet in 1807 an American from Maryland, Edward Fenwick, educated by exiled English Dominicans in Belgium and later first Bishop of Cincinnati, founded St. Joseph Province in the United States, at St. Rose, Kentucky, and Joseph Sadoc Alemany, later first Bishop of San Francisco, founded communities in California in 1849 (made Holy Name province in 1912).

At the Chapter of 1838 were only the provincials of the eight Italian provinces, of Ireland and England, the Vicar General of Malta, and the delegate from the United States and they elected Angelo Ancaranai, brother of the Thomas Ancaranai who had been Vicar General. The great event of his Mastership was the reestablishment of the Order in France by Henri Lacordaire who had been a secular priest, a noted orator at Notre Dame, and a supporter of De Lamennais the influential journalist who advocated a Romantic, democratic Catholicism consistent with the ideals of the Revolution. Lacordaire broke with De Lamennais when the latter refused correction by Gregory XVI. Lacordaire then decided that the best way to work for renewal of Christianity in France was to become a Dominican; so he entered the Order and founded a first community at Nancy in 1843.

The Chapter of 1844 elected as Master, Vincent Ajello, who resided in Naples and because of ill health gave little leadership. Pius IX at the end of Ajello's term in 1850 took matters in hand and, after inquiring carefully about the charges of "liberalism" which some had brought against Lacordaire and his friend Vincent Jandel, appointed the 40-year old Jandel as Vicar General and in 1855 made him Master, but he was regularly elected in 1862 when a twelve-year term replaced the six years set by *Inter Graviores*. Jandel was sometimes in conflict with Lacordaire, because Jandel, in the manner of Romantic Catholicism which looked back to the Middle Ages as the Age of Faith tended to emphasize monastic observance, while Lacordaire, although himself much attached to this Romantic ideal, nevertheless, insisted on the subordination of observance to the preaching mission. It was Jandel, however, who had Dominic's talent for organization, and he adopted Bl. Raymond's method of reform by establishing houses of observance in each province, beginning with Santa Sabina in Rome. Jandel himself tirelessly visited Italy, France, England, Germany, Bohemia, Hungary and Poland and the other provinces through visitators. He consolidated and reorganized what remained of the ruined provinces, and shortly before his death in 1872 reunited the Provinces of Spain, whose status had till then remained confused, to the Order.

Yet the decline in membership continued so that from 4,562 in 1844 it fell to 3,474 in 1876, the lowest since the thirteenth century. To offset this, however, during this period there was an amazing growth of congregations of Third Order Dominican religious women with active apostolates of charity, care of the sick, and education, something never anticipated by its founder. For example, in the United States at the turn of the century there were about 5,000 Sisters in rapidly growing

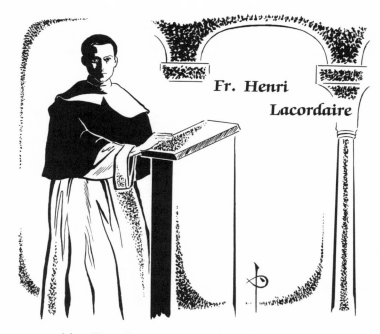

Fr. Henri
Lacordaire

communities. Thus Jandel, after 22 years of leadership, left an almost extinct Order well-organized, and vigorous.

Yet the situation in Europe made an elective Chapter impossible, so that for seven years it was administered by the Vicar General, Joseph M. Sanvito, until in 1879 Joseph M. Larroca, then acting as visitator in Manila, was elected by mail, the first Master elected by all the provinces since the devastation. He continued visitations of the whole Order, and the Chapter of Louvain in 1885 furthered devotion to the rosary and established the Ecole Biblique in Jerusalem and the theology faculty at the University of Fribourg in Switzerland. Perhaps the most important event for the Order was Leo XIII's encyclical *Aeterni Patris* in 1879 making the Christian philosophy and theology expounded by the medieval scholastics, and especially that of St. Thomas Aquinas, the basis of all philosophical and theological education in Catholic schools.

Larocca died in 1891 after a long illness and an Austrian, Andreas Frühwirth, was elected. He re-established the regular meeting of General Chapters, promoted special convocations throughout the Order, issued encyclical letters on preaching and other topics, published new editions of the liturgical books and instituted the Leonine Commission for a critical edition of the works of Aquinas and the *Analecta* of the Order, and constantly promoted common life, before being made Archbishop in 1904 and Cardinal in 1914, serving the Holy See in many diplomatic missions, but always helpful to his Order.

Study

It is obvious that until Lacordaire's restoration of the Order in 1839 and the actual re-establishment of the Province of France in 1850 there is little to record about studies in an Order seemingly on its ways to extinction. There were a few writers such as Francis D.J. de Kinder (d. 1816), at Louvain, who wrote on apologetics; Domenico M. Pellegrini (d. 1820), a canonist who wrote on the history of matrimony; Ludovico V. Cassito (d. 1823) who produced a widely used manual of dogmatic theology and a book on Dominican liturgy. Thus Filippo Anfossi (d. 1825) wrote against Scipio Ricci, Bishop of Pistoia (a Josephist), on divorce, reason and faith, and indulgences; Thomas Lewis (d. 1827) an Englishman in Belgium who wrote on the principles of the Catholic faith and on the divinity of Christ; José Vidal (d. 1826) wrote on pastoral theology; Juan Antonio Díaz Merino (d. 1844), Bishop of Minorca known for his care of the poor and defense of the rights of the Church produced a collection of Spanish church documents; and Cardinal Francisco Gaude (d. 1860) was a defender of the temporal rights of the papacy, who in 1854 also wrote on the definition of the Immaculate Conception. Moreover, Dominicans still held the ancient office of the Pope's theologian, the Master of the Sacred Palace.

The intellectual condition of the Order in these years is illustrated by the fact that when the newly converted John Henry Newman inquired about the Order he was told that it was "a noble ideal, now dead" and when he tried to find someone in Italy to guide him in the study of Aquinas he could find no one. The history of how Thomism came to be revived has been much researched. The General Chapter of

1748 recalled the older ordinances on the study of Aquinas, and in 1757 Master Boxadors insisted on their observance. In the Chapter of 1777 his letter was again promulgated, and Salvatore Roselli published his philosophy manual discussed in the last chapter. But the effective movement in the Church was not instituted by Dominicans but by a Canon Vincenzo Buzzetti (1777-1824) who had been a disciple of Locke but was led by a Spanish Jesuit, Baltasar Masdew (1741-1820), to read Roselli's and Goudin's manuals. Buzzetti began enthusiastically to teach Thomism as he had thus come to know it at the Vincentian Collegio Alberoni in Piacenza and wrote a manual of his own, too much influenced by the Leibnitzian idealism of Christian Wolff but essentially Thomistic.

As students Buzzetti had the brothers Serafino and Dominico Sordi and a Giuseppe Pecci, all of whom became Jesuits. Giuseppe Pecci drew his brother Gioachinno into this circle from which came the Jesuits, Luigi Tapparelli d'Azeglio, Matteo Liberatore, Carlo M. Curci, and Giuseppe Cornoldi, and finally a diocesan priest, Gaetano Sanseverino. Their writings, still lacking depth and historical sophistication and rather too polemically anti-modern, nevertheless, showed Thomism to be a viable alternative as against the positivistic and idealistic philosophies of the day. Gioachinno Pecci became Leo XIII and made Thomism the official basis of Catholic education by his encyclical *Aeterni Patris* in 1879.

In the meantime the professors of the Order's chief intellectual center, the College of St. Thomas at the Minerva in Rome (closed from 1810-15 by the French), in an effort to modernize had been following the Wolffianism and Eclecticism of the Austrian Jesuit, Sigismund von Storchenau, and then that of Jaime Balmes. Alberto Guglielmotti (d. 1873) was moderator of the College from 1840, assisted by Mariano Spada who became Master of the Sacred Palace and Filippo M. Guidi, who as Cardinal of Bologna played an important role at Vatican I in 1870. Guglielmotti's enthusiasm was for naval history and he produced a 10-volume *History of the Pontifical Navy*. The Peccis founded the Accademia Tomistica in 1846 and many Dominican students attended its classes, until the General Chapter of 1838 again ordered the revival of Thomism and the *Summa Theologiae* began to be used at the College of St. Thomas once more.

Jandel started a Thomist chair at the Casanatense Library in 1850 with Giacinto De Ferrari and Girolamo Gigli as first professors, then Guidi and Vincenzo Nardini (d. 1913) were added. Nardini, who took over the physics department, started an observatory and opposed mechanism in the philosophy of science. Other important professors were Mariano Spada, Narciso Puig (d. 1865), Paolo Carbo, Francisco Xarrie (d. 1866), Gaetano Lo-Cicero, an inventor, Gian Battista Embriaco, and especially Tommaso Zigliara who with Nardini founded the Academia Romano di San Tommaso in 1870. In 1873 the Dominicans were expelled by the government from the Minerva and had to move the school to various locations and then restricted their faculty to theology, adding philosophy in 1892 and canon law in 1896. Nardini had left for Ecuador but when the president Garcia Moreno was assassinated, went on to Peru to found a province, an observatory and an Institute of Physics at the Dominican college there in 1892.

Tommaso Zigliara (d. 1893) was a Corsican who studied at Rome, taught at Viterbo and the Collegium Divi Thomae and became regent of studies in 1873. Leo XIII, who before his election as Pope had been Zigliara's friend, in 1879 made him a cardinal. Zigliara became involved in the controversy over the saintly and liberal Rosmini-Serbati who had attempted a reconciliation of Thomism and idealism. Zigliara also helped prepare the great encyclicals *Aeterni Patris* and *Rerum novarum* and strongly opposed traditionalism and ontologism in favor of the moderate realism of Aquinas. His chief works were a *Summa Philosophica* in two volumes, which had 19 editions and a *Propadeutica theologica* with five editions, and an important essay, *Intellectual light and ontologism*, against an idealistic interpretation of Aquinas. These works, especially the first, became the basis of the Thomistic revival, at least as far as Dominicans were concerned. It was based largely on Goudin and Roselli rather than directly on Aquinas' commentaries on Aristotle, but it was written in elegant Latin.

The Thomistic movement took on a more international character after 1891 when Leo XIII established an Institute of Philosophy at the University of Louvain under the leadership of Cardinal Mercier (not a Dominican), a psychologist of note. Moreover, with the Pope's support the Jesuits and other

Orders made Thomism the basis of their own theological and educational work. The other chief Dominican figure of this revival in the Order was Zephirino González y Díaz Tuñón (d. 1894), who reflected the fact that Thomism had remained a living tradition in the Spanish provinces even at their lowest ebb and especially around the world at the University of Manila where he taught for some years. He was made Bishop of Córdoba and then Archbishop of Toledo and Primate of Spain and finally Cardinal by Leo XIII, as well as a member of the Royal Senate by the King of Spain. He wrote an *Elements of Philosophy* (1868, 1877) and a six-volume *History of Philosophy* (1885), two volumes of *Religious Studies* and *The Bible and Science* (1891). Like Mercier at Louvain, Gonzales was concerned that the Thomistic movement should be progressive, open to dialogue with modern philosophy and science.

In 1882 Leo XIII initiated and in 1894 entrusted to the Order the production of a critical edition of all the works of Aquinas (the *Leonine Edition*) which is still in progress over a hundred years later. Begun by Zigliara, Frati, Lyttleton, and Mackey, and then Clement Suermondt, its method was at first faulty but from the fifth volume of the *Summa Theologiae* and with the *Summa Contra Gentiles* improved and after interruptions is now of the highest standard. The growing understanding of the text of Aquinas assisted Zigliara and Alberto Lepidi (d. 1925), Master of the Sacred Palace to oppose efforts to interpret Aquinas in an ontologistic and Cartesian sense.

Dominicans also began important journals. The French began *L'Année Dominicaine* in 1859 and the *La Revue des Sciences Philosophiques et Théologiques* in 1907, the *Revue de la Jeunesse* 1909 and the *Revue Thomiste* (editor Thomas Coconnier) in 1908. The *Analecta* of the Order with important historical documents and studies was founded in 1893. The most important step, however, was the foundation of the École Biblique with its *Revue Biblique* in 1898 in Jerusalem which placed Dominicans at the heart of the great development of biblical studies then taking place in the Church, soon to result in the Modernist crisis. Thus with amazing rapidity the Order, from its intellectual decline at the beginning of the century, had by the end taken its place at the frontlines of the modern scholarly battle.

Among the notables not already mentioned of this century were in biblical study: Francis Link (1812) who wrote a history of the Jews and was in correspondence with Protestant scholars; Giuseppe Montaldi (d. 1816) author of a dictionary of Hebrew and Aramaic (d. 1784); and Pietro Dandini (d. 1841), an apologist. In history were Augustinus Kratzer (d. 1811) on the history of liturgy; Bishop Filippo Angelo Becchetti (d. 1814), who continued Orsi's church history to 1587 and was for awhile in difficulty with papal authority; Benedetto Maurus Olivieri (d. 1835) author of a history of the Church in the eighteenth century; Francisco Rivaz y Madrazo (d. 1884), of an often published textbook of Church history; Emmanuel Ceslaus Bayonne (d. 1885) historian of the Monastery of Nagres and a life of Savonarola; Antoninus Danzas (d. 1888) antiquarian of things Dominican; Tommaso Michele Salzano (d. 1890) Archbishop of Edessa, author of many seminary textbooks including a Church history (four editions) and one in canon law. He also wrote on poverty, on the Immaculate Conception, and an essay on *True and False Progress.*

By far the most important historian, however, was the famous Joseph Denifle (d. 1905) born in the Tyrol, a student of the Jesuits at Graz, and then as a Dominican a student at Rome and St. Maximin. As a professor he always emphasized the study of sources and his own research was directed especially to the German mystics, then little known. His reputation in Austria as a preacher was great. In 1880 Master Larroca called him as Assistant and to work on the Leonine, and the Pope made him sub-archivist of Vatican. He wrote on the rise of the medieval universities, and a great work on the Chartularium of the University of Paris commissioned by the French government, then on the desolation of the Church in France by the Hundred Years War. With Franz Ehrle he founded the *Archiv für Literatur und Kirche des Mittelalters.* Posthumously published was the *Quellenbelege* of documents on German mysticism, a mosaic of whose writings, especially Tauler he had published in 1873. From 1899 he devoted himself to research for his *Luther and Lutheranism*, a refutation of misrepresentations of the medieval Catholic teaching on faith, grace, and good works. This work, with its exploration of sources, is now recognized to be a caricature of Luther but reaction to it was an enormous stimulus to Lutheran studies. Denifle's researches were undoubtedly a major factor in the recovery of a historical understanding of the Middle Ages.

Thus, although all this century had a meager harvest of scholarship, it ended by a return to the sources of the Dominican tradition that was to bear great fruit in the twentieth century.

Prayer

This revival by Denifle of the Northern Dominican tradition of spirituality was probably the greatest gift of the century to the Order's prayer. The other was the emphasis placed by Jandel on a return to strict observance of the Dominican liturgy in all its details. Yet this return was not as yet backed up by profound historical understanding of liturgical development, nor even as yet by the enthusiasm of the romantic "liturgical movement" that began with the great reviver of the Benedictines, Dom Guéranger.

Yet there were many examples of sanctity among the founders of the numerous active congregations of women and among the friars both scholars and missionaries who are mentioned elsewhere in this chapter, and the reviving Order had a wide influence; as, for example, on Placidus Busher (d. 1851), a Neapolitan priest of great holiness who became a member of the Third Order. Moreover the revival itself had its source in the prayers of contemplatives such as Mother Dominic Clara Moes (d. 1895). We learn from her lengthy autobiography that from an early age she received revelations that she was to pray and suffer for a revival of an Order whose name she did not know. Under a Redemptorist director at Limpertsberg she became a stigmatic and founded a community which after many years she discovered should be affiliated to the Preachers, for whose renewal she had unknowingly been praying. Yet the Dominican Provincial agreed to this only after careful examination of the mystic.

Among the writers not mentioned elsewhere in this chapter were Joseph-Gonzalve Barthier (d. 1911) who wrote an important two-volume work on *Christian and Religious Perfection according to St. Thomas and St. François de Sales* and Thomas Faucillon (d. 1901) who was twice Provincial of France and founder of the first Dominican convents in Canada. A noted retreat master, he wrote on St. Mary Magdalene and other works of spirituality of a traditional but solid character.

Preaching

If this record of spirituality for the nineteenth century seems meager, it is amply filled out by the record of preaching and works of charity. The most remarkable preacher of the century was undoubtedly the reviver of the Order Jean Baptiste Henri Lacordaire (1802-61), of a well-to-do family and whose brother was a noted zoologist. Lacordaire as a young man was a follower of Rousseau and remained after his conversion even to his death, as he said, "a repentant sinner, but an unrepentant liberal" i.e., a believer in the ideals of "equality, liberty, and fraternity" of the Revolution, values not very popular among most Catholics who were monarchists. As a lawyer he was deeply interested in politics. As a priest, trained at St. Sulpice and ordained in 1827, he became discouraged with the situation in France and almost accepted the invitation of Bishop Du Bois of New York to come to the United States as his vicar-general; but he met the brilliant liberal priest Lamennais and after the Revolution of 1830 worked with him in publishing the newspaper, *The Future*, fighting for the rights of religious education until it was condemned by Gregory XVI for its identification of Christianity with democracy. He was supported and encouraged to greater moderation by a friend, Madame Sophie-Jeanne Swetchine (1782-1857), a Russian convert from Orthodoxy whose salon included Joseph de Maistre, Count Montalembert, Frédéric Alfred de Fallioux and Alexis de Tocqueville.

In 1834 he began preaching conferences at Collège Stanislas where he was regularly heard by Chateaubriand and Victor Hugo. After his lectures were subject to censorship because of his association with Lamennais, in 1835 he was invited by Archbishop of Paris to be Lenten preacher at Notre Dame where he attracted crowds of 6,000. These famous conferences lasted for ten years but were twice interrupted, the second time by his entry (he first thought of being a Jesuit) in 1839 to the Dominican novitiate and in 1840 his return to France in the habit (not seen there for fifty years). He wrote a life of St. Dominic, and went back to Rome with ten novices. In 1843 he founded a community at Nancy. In 1845 his sermons on the divinity of Jesus Christ were rated by Montalembert as the "greatest triumph of modern Christian oratory." After the Revolution of 1848 (which he greeted from the pulpit with joy) he was elected as Deputy from Marseilles taking seat on the Extreme Left, but soon resigned as the Assembly degenerated. He gave up preaching in Paris when Napoleon III came to power. From 1854 his health declined and he retired to Sorèze Military Academy where in 1860 he wrote against Napoleon III's interference with the States of Church. He was elected to the French Academy and spoke on his predecessor De Tocqueville. In 1861 he resigned as Provincial and soon died, leaving nine volumes of writings.

Lacordaire introduced a new manner of preaching, closely reasoned, but impassioned, which made use of current ideas but reinterpreted them in a Christian sense, and especially dwelt on the human attractiveness of Jesus and the Church. A sample is the following, making use of one of the basic themes of the French Revolution, "fraternity":

> Since human reason, under different colors, has begun to combat and enfeeble Christian doctrine in the world, what advance has *fraternity* made? Its name is in every mouth, it is the basis of systems and of desires; we hear nothing spoken of but the spirit of association and community; everywhere the hand of fellowship is held out: and, nevertheless, a profound sigh, an unanimous complaint denounce to the whole earth the coldness of hearts. When I hearken to the man who bears the burden of military service, to the magistrate devoted to the functions of justice, to the professor revealing to the soul of the young man the secret of his vocation, to the politician studying closely the mainsprings of life; when, in fine, I hearken to the voice of society issuing from every pore, but one word strikes upon

my ear—egotism. Humanity is cold and void.... The resurrection will come, Christians, and will come through us. As the world, which desires not humility, which desires not chastity, which desires not the apostleship, desires *fraternity*; as it must desire it, and ever exercises its ingenuity to practice it, there is common ground whereon we may meet the world. Let us profit by it. Between the world and us, the question is who will spread abroad more of real love, who will give more while receiving less. In this conflict, no one can accuse us. Let us fling ourselves into it with generous hearts; we have received so much love that it costs us little to give it. Let us win over our brethren with benefits; and as coldness increases daily in the world, let warmth increase daily in us, to be communicated to the world.

I have already described the character and work of Alexander Vincent Jandel (d. 1872), but among Lacordaire's other companions was Hyacinthe Besson (d. 1861), a talented painter, who attempted to apply some of the ideals and style of the "Nazarenes," artists who wished to recapture pre-Raphaelite religious art. Rohault de Fleury a noted medievalist and expert on Gothic architecture also became a Tertiary. Jandel and Lacordaire both worked for the building of Sacre-Coeur on Montmarte in Paris as a national shrine of Catholicism. Throughout the century other Dominicans occupied Lacordaire's pulpit in Notre Dame, notably Montsabré, Joseph Ollivier, Thomas Étourneau, and the most famous preacher of all was Henri Didon (d. 1900). These all published sermons, particularly Jacques-Marie Monsabré (1827-1907), ordained 1851, then a Dominican in 1855 at Paris until he was elected prior at Le Havre in 1881. Monsabré made his name as a preacher at Lyons in the Lent of 1857 and the same year he started conferences for youth at Paris. He preached at Notre Dame for Advent in 1869 and then for Lent in 1872. In 1873 he began a systematic exposition of the Creed which took until 1890! These conferences fill 18 volumes and he published other volumes of sermons and meditations on the rosary, two volumes of sermons on prayer, nine volumes of Easter retreats. His *Ore and Dross in the Devout Life* is more psychological and experiential.

The Dominican renewal touched many in France. Thus Charles Desgenettes (d.1860) priest of Our Lady of Victory, a church ruined by Revolution, heard the voice of the Immaculate Heart of Mary telling him to found a confraternity at the church. He met Lacordaire and in old age became a Tertiary who rejoiced to see the Dominicans fulfill the revelation made to him. Jean Joseph Lataste (d. 1869) rehabilitated women prisoners and offered his life for the declaration of St. Joseph as Patron of the Universal Church. He founded the Dominican Sisters of Bethany in 1866, and also the Congregation of Bethany (de Venlo) in 1914, as well as the secular institute of the Mission of Our Lady of Bethany, and the Fraternities and Foyers Lataste. The Revolution of 1870 also resulted in the martyrdom of Luigi Raffaele Captier and 12 companions in Paris (Martyrs of Arcueil College) by the Commune in 1871. Captier, a priest of the First Order, was one of the first four recruits for Lacordaire's Congregation of Third Order teaching priests. His companions were four other priests of the Congregation, a clerical student, a secular priest, four lay teachers, and twelve other employees, martyred without a trial.

Among the French women Dominicans we have already mentioned the Revolutionary heroine Catherine Jarrige (d. 1836). Others founded active congregations such as Thérèse Dominique Farré (d. 1894). Her father to whom she was much attached was a manual worker and she became breadwinner of her family at the age of 12. From the age of twenty-two she experienced interior graces and in 1860 founded the Dominican Sisters for the Care of the Sick (Bourg) which was soon affiliated to the Order of Preachers. She made only two foundations, then in the upheavals of 1870 offered herself for the Church and then lived for 24 years in sickness. She left a Spiritual Directory for her Congregation edited with her other works by A.M. Meynard, O.P. Her spirituality was *laisser faire Dieu*, but in an active not a quietist sense.

Mother Thérèse (Vincent Ferrer) Chupin (d.1896) was born in Brittany. For 12 years she cared for women prisoners of St. Lazare in Paris. Some of the ex-prisoners insisted she found a community for them, and their first Mass was said by Père Bourard, one of the martyrs of the Commune. Pius IX had them affiliated as Dominican Tertiaries in 1854, although Thérèse did not much like the Sister of Langres sent to discipline the community in Dominican ways. The novelist Alexander Dumas befriended her and her work.

But undoubtedly the most remarkable of these women was Marie-Pauline Jaricot (1799-1862) of Lyons. Converted 1816 after the death of her mother and a serious illness, she vowed chastity and worked for sometime for the poor in hospitals. In 1817 she wrote her autobiography and started a group "Réparatrices of the Heart of Jesus." In 1820 her interest in the missions led her to join the newly founded Society for the Propagation of Faith and began her system of getting persons to subscribe a penny a week for the missions, which proved an enormous success. In 1823 she wrote *Infinite Love in the Divine Eucharist*. Following the Jubilee of 1825 she founded the Living Rosary, a devotion affiliated to the Order in 1836. Her circulars emphasized the value of communal prayer and the diffusion of good books. In 1830 Pauline founded "Daughters of Mary" for reparative adoration. An insurrection of workers in 1831 led her to found a "Bank of Heaven" but this undertaking failed and left her in poverty the rest of her life, begging to pay her debts. Her work for the Gospel was one of the fundamental forces for the Church's expansion in the nineteenth century.

The Order had returned to England in the 1700s but had painful struggles to recover, assisted, however, by the Oxford Movement back to Catholicism of the Anglicans. Typical was Bertrand Wilberforce (d. 1904), a grandson of the famous abolitionist William Wilberforce. Bertrand became a Catholic, along with his father, and after his ordination became a Dominican in 1864. He was prior of St. Dominic's in London 1872-5, and in 1877-78 chaplain to the Dominic nuns at Stone. From 1878 he served as a preacher and a notable spiritual director. He wrote works on the Japanese missions, a life of St. Luis Beltrán, a memoir of the nuns of Stone and a very popular work on mental prayer.

The Dominican women were re-established at Stone by the courageous Mother Margaret Hallahan (1803-1868), an Irish woman born in London who went to serve in a doctor's family in Belgium where she became a Dominican Tertiary in 1835 and founded a Third Order Congregation in 1845 which, though she was often ill, she administered with great care. She was a friend of the chronicler of Vatican I, Bishop Ullathorne, and of Cardinal Newman. Margaret's successor was an Oxford convert Mother Frances Raphael Drane (d. 1893). Her father was the manager of an East India mercantile house. She became a Catholic in 1850 and the next year a Tertiary. Guided by Lacordaire's companion, Père Besson, in Rome she entered Margaret Hallahan's community. She was prioress from 1861 and provincial from 1881. During her term she founded a community in Australia. She was an excellent writer and produced 19 works, including novels, and an outstanding life of St. Catherine of Siena. Her own life was written by Bertrand Wilberforce.

The Order, in spite of persecution, did not die in Spain, as is illustrated by the martyrdom in Vietnam of Saints Bishop Ignatius Delgado and Bishop Dominic Henares, along with Joseph Fernández, Augustine Schoeffler (a Tertiary) and 21 native members of the Rosary Confraternity in 1838, Bishops José Díaz Sanjurjo and Melchior García Sampedro (d. 1857-8) and 23 companions, and Jerome Hermosilla and Valentine Berrio-Ochoa and Companions (d. 1861). In Spain itself Bl. Francis Coll of the Aragon Province (1812-1875) born of a wool-carder's family was ordained as a Dominican in 1836, but because of the suppression of the Order in Spain spent almost all his life as a Dominican without a community, yet wearing the habit and tirelessly carrying on itinerant preaching. He founded the Congregation of the Annunciation of Sisters in Europe, America and Africa. In his old age he became blind but rejoiced in the restoration of the Order. Dominic Canubio (d. 1864) Bishop of Segovia, a Dominican at 14, who experienced the same Revolutionary troubles as a student, first taught and then as a bishop was famous for his personal charity. He celebrated the declaration of the Immaculate Conception and was present at Jandel's election. The record of other struggling provinces remains to be studied, but I would mention Jacques Zebedes Falkowski, (d. 1836) in Poland who wrote 12 volumes of sermons, works on the Rosary, etc., and also restored 50 church organs.

It was, however, in the United States that at the darkest

hour of the Order's history new provinces and congregations stemming from Italy, Spain, England, Germany had their birth. The father of all United States Dominicans, however, was Bishop Edward Dominic Fenwick (1768-1832). Born in the originally Catholic colony of Maryland, after an early education at home he was sent to the English Holy Cross College, Bornheim, Belgium, where he was professed as a Dominican in 1790 and ordained in 1793. When the English fled the French Revolutionary invasion, they left him in charge but he was briefly imprisoned and then joined the English Dominicans at Carshalton near London and was given permission to return to Maryland with three of his English confreres to found a college on his family estates.

But Bishop John Carroll, a member of the suppressed Jesuits who had recently founded a college at Georgetown, encouraged Fenwick to sell his estate and move across the mountains to Kentucky, as he did in 1806. By 1812 he had built St. Rose Church, a Priory and a College of St. Thomas Aquinas and initiated a community of Third Order Sisters at St. Catherine's headed by Mother Angela Sansbury (d. 1839). He then traveled as a missionary through Kentucky and Ohio where after 1816 he concentrated his work at St. Joseph's, Somerset, where he and Nicholas D. Young opened the first Catholic church of Ohio. As an itinerant preacher he gained the title of "Apostle of Ohio" and he was consecrated first Bishop of Cincinnati in 1822 by Benedict Flaget. In 1823 he went to Rome to obtain more priests and in 1828 established a Province of St. Joseph's. He built a cathedral, St. Francis' Seminary and Athenaeum and published the first diocesan paper. By 1832 his diocese had 22 churches and 24 priests, Fenwick died of cholera while on visitation at Wooster, Ohio, and was buried at St. Joseph's. Humble, always conscious of the brevity of his education, and tireless in his ministry he fully realized St. Dominic's ideal.

Among the men who struggled for the survival of St. Joseph's Province which had only 32 priests in 1865 and barely 100 at the turn of the century, notable was Matthew Anthony O'Brien (1804-1871). Born in Ireland, he studied and taught at St. Mary's College, Marion County, Kentucky, then entered the Dominicans at St. Rose. Ordained in 1839 by the Dominican Bishop Richard P. Miles of Nashville, he became novice master at Somerset and in 1850 Provincial over no more than 20 missionary priests scattered throughout Kentucky, Ohio, Tennessee, and Wisconsin. He opened St. Joseph's College in Somerset, and preached parish missions from the Great Lakes to the Gulf of Mexico and east to the Alleghenies. As prior of St. Rose 1854-7 he reopened the College of St. Thomas and then resumed missionary preaching except for two years as pastor of St. Peter's in London, Ontario.

In the Northwest Territories the founder of the Order was an Italian, Samuel Augustine Mazzuchelli (d. 1864). Born in Milan 1806 of wealthy parents, he entered the Order in Rome in 1822 and, still only a sub-deacon, sailed to America after meeting Fenwick in 1828. He studied at St. Joseph's and was ordained in Cincinnati in 1830. He then went as a missionary to the Indians on Mackinac Island and in 1833 to the Winnebagos at Portage, Wisconsin, translating a prayer book into their dialect. Then in Galena, Illinois, and Dubuque, Iowa, he built the first churches in 1835, and became Vicar-General to the first bishop, Loras, in 1839.

Mazzuchelli built 20 churches and designed the Old Market House and courthouses in Galena, and also for Madison and Dodgeville and in part the old state capital in Iowa City. In failing health in 1843 he returned to Milan and published his *Memoirs*. Appointed a missionary apostolic in 1844 he was authorized by the Pope to establish a new province of the Order on the upper Mississippi and he founded a novitate, built several small churches and opened the Sinsinawa Mound College for boys in 1846. When in 1859 his collaborators deserted him he turned this property over to St. Joseph's. Meanwhile he directed the Congregation of Sisters he had founded at Sinsinawa in 1847, moving them to Benton, Wisconsin in 1852. As pastor at Benton, he died after ministering to the sick during an epidemic.

His extraordinary mind, zeal and vision are best seen in his *Memoirs* (really an account of the missions) of which the following gives an idea:

> The reader should not imagine that the intelligence of the American Indian is less fitted than his own to comprehend the truths of our holy religion. Such an entirely erroneous

supposition would lead to the absurd belief that the Indian is incapable of becoming a perfect Christian who lives by faith. Unlike human teachings, Christ's doctrine is intelligible to all without distinction. Otherwise, how could the Messiah have commanded his Apostles to teach all nations? ... Among the Indians one had to be satisfied to find shelter in a lodge of mats and sleep as he could, wrapped in a blanket without a bed.... Sometimes during his many years of life on the missions, the circumstances of some families or the priest's lack of money obliged him to sit at table with persons not only poor, but the coarsest, roughest, wildest of men; and what was still more repugnant to human pride, often to eat the plainest food given as charity. One who is not of ignoble birth and who knows that his education and ecclesiastical profession deserve some consideration is strongly tempted on such occasions to consider the humiliation too great. But then faith makes him think of Jesus in the company and at the table of sinners. The vow of poverty that the religious has taken extinguishes in the depths of his heart the most secret movements of pride and makes him reflect that, to eat what is given in charity, is most fitting for one who professes to be poor like his Divine Master.... "Do not go from house to house. Eat what is set before you" (Lk 10:8).

I am convinced that most of our Indian wars are the natural and unavoidable consequences of the misconduct of the whites. Most of our Indian treaties are badly planned by individuals, unfairly ratified and shamefully executed. Individuals make their fortunes at the expense of justice, government is deceived and the Indians abused. The President and the members of Congress judge from what they have read in statements, but the Indians, a little wiser than we are, judge from facts only."

The most remarkable head of Mazzuchelli's foundation of Sisters was Mother Emily Power (1844-1909). Her family came to St. Louis and her widowed mother moved to a farm near Sinsinawa where she entered Mazzuchelli's academy at 13 and became a Sister at 17 in Benton. In 1867 she was made Mother

General and moved the community back to Sinsinawa and continued in office until her death, building an apostolate of education at all levels that extended to 20 states, Europe, and South America. She was one of the first superiors to send her sisters to secular schools and The Catholic University of America. Nor did she neglect the social apostolate for laborers in Minnesota, Montana and the Chicago stock yards.

Other communities had European origins. Thus two choir nuns Augustina Neuhieral (d. 1877) and Josepha Witzlhofer with two lay sisters Francisca Retter and Jacobina Rieder from the thirteenth-century monastery of the Holy Cross in Regensburg at the invitation of Abbot Wimmer, founder of the abbey of Latrobe, Pennsylvania, were sent by Mother Benedicta Bauer to New York in 1853. They settled first in Brooklyn, then, Williamsburg, and finally Amityville, New York and began conducting schools. From this grew a great tree of similar congregations of Newburgh, New York (1869); Caldwell, New Jersey (1881); Mission San José, California (1888); Tacoma, Washington (1888); Blauvelt, New York (1890); Grand Rapids, Michigan (1896); Great Bend, Kansas (1902); Adrian, Michigan (1923); and Edmonds, Washington (1923). Racine, Wisconsin (1862) was also founded separately from Regensburg. The same process of vast expansion of Third Order Sisters was going on throughout the world in this century. Thus nine congregations in Ireland, New Zealand, Africa, the United States, etc., sprang from the Irish monastery-in-exile of Cabra, Spain; six from St. Catherine's in Kentucky, four from Albi in France, and many were founded independently. In each case there were remarkable and holy women founders and leaders. Some 34 such congregations were added to the Order in this century and began greatly to surpass in numbers the friars and nuns.

Another notable preacher of this time was the Irishman Tom Burke (d. 1883) who entered the Order in Italy and was sent as novice master by Jandel to England at 21 when not yet ordained. Back to San Clemente in Rome, he became famous as a preacher. In Ireland at Daniel O'Connell's funeral he preached to 50,000. He was a theologian at Vatican I. Averaging at least two sermons a day, he preached for years in Europe and came to America, preaching through Kentucky,

Ohio, and New York, and other eastern cities for a year and a half, although always in poor health. "I can only compare myself to Ned Burke's dog during the famine; they had to support his back at the wall to enable him to bark." He died at 54 after preaching in England for the starving children of Ireland.

Joseph Sadoc Alemany (1814-1888) was no less remarkable than Mazzuchelli. A Catalonian from a family of seven, all of whom became priests or religious, he was ordained in Viterbo in 1837 with the intention of going to China, but instead went with Bishop Miles of Nashville to America. He learned English at Somerset and then collected funds in Cuba, taught at the Nashville Seminary, was pastor in Memphis, became a United States citizen, novice master at Somerset, and then Provincial. But on a trip to Rome Pius IX made him bishop of Monterey, California, where he had been preceded by a Franciscan. He built three churches in San Francisco and two others in his diocese from which the Franciscans had been expelled 50 years before. At Vatican I and Baltimore III he made a strong impression and headed a commission to prepare the famous Baltimore catechism. In 1884 he returned to Spain and died three years later at Valencia. His original companion to California was Francisco Sadoc Vilarrasa (d. 1888) who founded the Dominican Holy Name Province on the West Coast. Vilarrasa was also a Catalonian who had served as Novice Master at Viterbo under Lacordaire and Jandel. In America he was novice master at Somerset and attended the General Chapter of Naples in 1849. He went with Alemany to California, taking Sister Mary Goemare, a young novice, to begin a Third Order community in 1850. He started the novitiate at Monterey with six Catalonian novices whom he taught strict observance, then he transferred the novitiate to Benicia. He went to St. Dominic's in San Francisco in 1873 as Dominican superior until his death in 1888 and did not live to see the actual establishment of the Province in 1912.

Thus at the end of the century, the Order, almost dead at the beginning, was flourishing in many countries, and not least in the United States. Other than its renewal, the most striking feature was the proliferation of active Third Order women's congregations, some 34 of them, throughout the world.

9

Ecumenists (1900s)

Community

The 1900s have seen the full dominance of secular humanism and a vast expansion of science and technology, so that for the first time in human history, humanity has the power to control its environment, produce an economic abundance, and establish global communication. But it has also seen two vast World Wars and the possibility of the end of human life by nuclear war, especially between the rival empires of the United States and Communist Russia, or by environmental pollution. As the century draws to a close there is much talk that our age is "post-modern," that is, that there is as much disillusionment with secular humanism as there was with Christianity at the end of the 1600s.

In 1962-65 the Catholic Church, which was no longer dominated by the European bishops, held the great Second Vatican Council, which called for a reunion of all Christians, dialogue between all religions, and a positive attitude toward science and technology and democratic political forms. The Church must herself readjust her institutions to meet these ideals. Dominicans, along with others played an important role theologically in this Council, just as at Florence, Trent and Vatican I.

In the aftermath of the Council, there has been a great adjustment of the religious Orders themselves. The ahistorical ideal of renewal through "return to the primitive observance" has given way to that of "return to the spirit of the Founder" which was to meet the new situation of his or her times. Liberation theology has called, to a sense, that the Kingdom of God must come on earth as it is in heaven. So profound has this shift been that in all religious communities, and in almost all countries, there has been an exodus from priestly and religious life on a scale comparable only to that before the French Revolution. The Dominican Friars have fallen from 10,000 members to 7,000 in this century, and the decline of vocations to the active Sisters' congregations has been even more severe. The Dominican self-image has been especially damaged by the dethronement of Thomism in a Church that accepts a theological pluralism. Yet there are many signs of renewed Dominican vitality.

In spite of many political troubles in France, leading for a time to actual suppression of religious orders, the French Provinces have been perhaps the most creative during this century. The Chapter of 1904 elected, as the successor of Andreas Frühwirth, Hyacinth M.Cormier, then Procurator General and formerly three times provincial of Toulouse. True to the tradition of observance of that Province his emphasis was primarily on spiritual matters both in the Order and in his influence on the sisters and others through writing and spiritual direction. He wrote a letter on religious life to Americans, and encyclical letters on freedom, on the study of Scriptures (in view of the Modernist crisis), on vocations, novices and students, for whom he promulgated a new Scheme of Studies (1907). His most important encyclical on community made the shrewd comment that "some live *outside* community, some merely *in* it, some *off* it, and, happily, some *for* it." But he also made visitations of Italy and central Europe, and sent visitators to other provinces, including the Latin American ones which were not in very good condition as regards the common life, while in 1910 the Mexican Dominicans had been suppressed by the government, as the French had been in 1903. The Provinces of Bohemia-Austro-Hungary and Sicily were restored, the restoration of that of Portugal initiated, and that of

Canada founded (1911). Cormier also founded the Angelicum in Rome and reorganized the Curia there.

The elective chapter at Viterbo in 1904 enforced mental prayer in common and urged stricter observance of common life. That of Viterbo in 1907 re-emphasized Thomism and weekly recitation of the Office of the Dead (initiated in 1551). That of Rome in 1910 insisted on a convent of strict observance in every province, improvements of the liturgy, the habit and tonsure, and condemned Modernism. That of Venlo, Holland, in 1913 required better preparation in preaching, urged perpetual abstinence from meat, and promoted community recreation. It also called for suitable textbooks to implement the new Scheme of Studies. Cormier resigned in 1916 shortly before his death in the same year, and has been proposed for beatification. His stress on traditional observances in the Jandelian tradition and of disciplined study of St. Thomas continued to dominate the first half of this century and had considerable success.

While World War I raged, a Hollander, Louis Theissling, was elected in 1916, a man who under Frühwirth had visitated the Slavic provinces and who proved an energetic Master especially concerned about the missions and studies. He regularized the General Chapters to every four years, repeatedly visited all parts of the Order, made required studies more uniform (he approved the founding of Providence College, Rhode Island, and the studium in Washington, D.C.). He reformed the liturgy in 1923 and worked to unite more closely the Third Order regular and secular to the First Order with a new Rule in 1923. Theissling visitated New York, Cuba, Canada, Japan, Taiwan, China, Vietnam, Manila, South and Central America (suffering from a disastrous earthquake in Guatemala) and Spain (an 18-month absence from Rome 1917-18). His health broken by his labors by 1924, he died the next year.

In 1926 a doctor of civil law and former provincial of the Philippines, Bonaventura García de Paredes was elected, but he resigned in 1929 and was killed by Communists in the Spanish Civil War. During his term the Historical Institute of the Order was initiated.

He was succeeded by a Frenchman, Martin Gillet, noted

as a writer on moral and spiritual topics. During his term, World War II made advance difficult. Over one hundred Dominicans were killed in the war, some in the resistance to Nazism, others by the Communists in Spain. After the war the Communists suppressed the Order in Hungary and Bohemia. Gillet visited Mexico, Canada, the United States, Philippines, Vietnam and Japan and parts of Europe. He saw the suppression of the flourishing Chinese missions in 1946 by the Communists. In Rome, Gillet moved the Angelicum to its present quarters and moved his offices to Santa Sabina where he located the Leonine, Historical and Liturgical (founded in 1934) and other Commissions. Because of the war his term of office was extended by the Pope. He gave much attention to his fine but conservative encyclicals on Thomism, preaching, Dominican spirituality, the rosary, etc., and to the revival of the school for novice and student masters initiated by Cormier, and a new Scheme of Studies in 1935. Perhaps the most important event of his term was the final approval of the first great revision of the *Constitutions* (1932) to conform to Canon Law, an undertaking begun under Theissling but which proved very difficult to finish. On completion of his office he was made archbishop by Pius XII.

Gillet's successor in 1946 was a Spaniard and noted canonist, Emmanuel Suárez, who labored to restore the Latin America Provinces, suffering from few vocations, large properties obtained in colonial times to administer, and severe anti-clericalism, especially in Mexico. In 1953 he (and subsequent Masters) had to deal with the controversy created by the priest-worker movement in France and the "new theology," as well as with a threat by the Holy See to change the system of electing local superiors in the Order. He approved new provinces for Australia-New Zealand, 1950, Brazil, 1952, and Switzerland, 1953. Everywhere after the war, the Order was growing rapidly. Suárez was killed in an automobile accident.

A giant Irishman, Michael Browne, long Master of the Sacred Palace, and theological conservative, was elected in 1955 and made cardinal in 1962. By the end of his term after the restoration of the Provinces of Belgium, Mexico, and Portugal the Order consisted of 39 provinces. Browne was succeeded by a Spaniard, Aniceto Fernández.

Fr. Yves Congar

Fernández (d. 1981) studied at Salamanca, received his Licence in Physical Science at the Central University of Madrid 1926 and taught the physical sciences and cosmology at the Angelicum, 1950-58, and then was Provincial of Spain until elected Master of the Order in 1962. During his term the Provinces of Vietnam (1967) and of the Philippines (1971) were created, and Vicariates of Central Africa (1963) and of South Africa (1968). He obtained the elevation of the Angelicum to the status of the Roman University of St. Thomas Aquinas, attended Vatican II, and rejoiced in the declaration of St. Catherine of Siena as a Doctor of the Church (1970).

Fernández, conservative by temperament, was faced with the vast changes initiated by Vatican II and the subsequent exodus of many priests from the Order, but with great equanimity carried through the radical revision of the *Constitutions* effected in the two months Chapter of 1968 in River Forest, Illinois, after ample consultation of all the Provinces. The Third Order Rule had already been revised in 1964 and the women members of the Order began a long process, not yet completed, of revising their own congregational constitutions. This exodus was not peculiar to the Order but general throughout the Church. The number of Dominican friars in 1876 had been 3,474; in 1910, 4,472; in 1949, 7,661; in 1963, 10,150; but by 1984 it was only 7,112 (1,000 in the U.S.A.) and in most provinces the number of novices was small. By 1975 more than 700 priests had been laicized.

Vincent de Couesnongle, (elected in 1974 for 9 not 12 years) a Breton, who had been Fernández's Assistant for the Intellectual Apostolate, proved to be an inspiring leader, tireless in visitation of all the provinces, seeking to encourage them in a difficult time of change and a startling decline of vocations with a vision of future opportunities. He too was constant in his visitations of the Order and especially successful in promoting the missions which as vicariates began to move toward a native membership and a fuller place in the Order, as was evident from the General Chapter in Quezon City, the Philippines, in 1977. He also gave much attention to trying to restore studies in the Order, much confused by the decline of Thomism and the abandonment of provincial houses of study for study in universities throughout the Order. This culminated in the approval of new Schemes of Study for each Province and in a new policy of "permanent formation" for all members of the Order, i.e., life-long patterns of education, and implementation of the ancient "conventual lector" to have charge of studies in each house. Moreover, a new thrust toward the preaching of social justice in the spirit of Bartolomé de las Casas was strongly encouraged. With de Couesnongle's example, the new spirit of "collegiality" initiated by Vatican II began to flourish in harmony with the primitive ideal of fraternity.

The Chapter of 1983 marked a new epoch in the Order, in that for the first time the mission Vicariates were directly represented, with the result that the non-Europeans outvoted the Europeans, and it first elected Albert Nolan from South Africa. Nolan asked to be excused because of his involvement in the struggle for Black liberation in his country, and in his place was elected the Provincial of Ireland, Damian A. Byrne, whose priestly life had also been mainly in the missions of Latin America and with whom the Baroque image of the

Master as primarily a courtly Roman official has been completely liquidated. The Chapter at Walberburg, Germany, in 1983 marked out the future by setting as priorities for the mission of the Order: (1) preaching in a de-christianized world; (2) evangelization of non-Christians; (3) social justice; (4) use of social means of communication for spreading the Gospel.

Study

Leo XIII had given the Order the special mission of leadership in remolding Catholic education on the basis of Thomism, which it carried out to the eve of Vatican II in 1962 with notable success but with many struggles. The first problem was to recover the real teaching of Aquinas, purifying it from distorting traditions, one-sidedness, and lack of historical perspective. The strong Jesuit tradition of Thomism, stemming from St. Ignatius himself and the role played by the Society in the renewal of Thomism by Leo was strongly colored by the interpretation of their own great master Francisco Suárez (d. 1617), who had attempted to reconcile the Aristotelianism of Thomas with the Platonism of Scotus. Against this interpretation authors like Antoninus Dummermuth (d. 1918) and Norbert Del Prado (d. 1918) showed that at the heart of Thomistic metaphysics was the "real distinction" of essence and existence and the *analogia entis* rejected by Scotus and Suarez. This battle culminated in Pius X's approval of the *Twenty-Four Theses* by which Edouard Hugon (d. 1929), a tireless traveler and retreat preacher, counseler to Pius X, Benedict XV and Pius XI, defined authentic Thomism. Others such as the anti-Modernist Thomas Pègues (d. 1936) in his 21-volume commentary on the *Summa Theologiae* in catechetical form were content to popularize Thomism.

This recovery was greatly assisted by the growth of historical studies initiated by Denifle and carried on in this period by Pierre Mandonnet (d. 1936) and later by Chenu (b. 1895) and Congar (b. 1904) and the layman Étienne Gilson and the Pontifical Institute of Toronto of which he was the director. These studies made it clear that Aquinas' work was not so much part of a "medieval synthesis" as a radical turning point in the history of Christian thought from Platonic essentialism to Aristotelian epistemology and yet it surpassed Aristotle's metaphysics in its understanding of God as Creator and Existence Itself. Yet the efforts of Chenu and Congar to insist on the study of Aquinas in historical context were at first censored by Rome as modernistic in tendency.

Meanwhile, difficulties were arising from a quite different source. Leo XIII to promote Thomism had founded the Higher Institute of Philosophy at Louvain in 1889 under Desiré Mercier, later cardinal (not a Dominican), hoping to bring the thought of Aquinas into more vital contact with modern science. But with time and especially under the leadership of Joseph Maréchal, S.J., P. Rousselot, S.J., and Ambroise Gardeil, O.P., an effort was made to discover in Aquinas an element transcending experience or an *a priori* in human cognition, and to reconcile it with the philosophy of Immanuel Kant, thus moving Thomism toward idealism. Out of this came what is now called Transcendental Thomism as in the work of Karl Rahner, S.J., and in another version of Dominic M. De Petter, O.P., (b. 1905) and his disciple Edward Schillebeeckx, O.P., (b. 1914). There were also tendencies (which became suspect of Modernism) to modify scholastic thought in the direction of a Philosophy of Action such as that of Le Roy and Blondel, thus weakening Thomistic intellectualism.

The most prominent opponents of these tendencies were the laymen Etienne Gilson, already mentioned, and Jacques Maritain, but supporting them was the redoubtable Dominican Reginald Garrigou-Lagrange (d. 1964), (as interested as Maréchal in the nature of Christian mysticism) who stoutly maintained the interpretation of Aquinas of the pre-Cartesian commentators. The Spaniard Santiago Ramírez (d. 1967), a profound commentator of Aquinas, and the Canadian University of Laval under the former Dominican novice Charles De Koninck (d. 1965), although critics of Maritain and Gilson, were also advocates of an "original Thomism." This sometimes led to an intransigency as in the opposition of Garrigou-Lagrange to the brilliant, Philippine-born Francisco Marín-Sola (d. 1932) who attempted to revive the Grace Controversy from a new angle and to develop the notion of development of doctrine.

A third problem arose from the growing interest in the pre-scholastic thought of St. Augustine and the Church Fathers, east and west, as among the Jesuits of Fourviére, such as Daniélou and Du Lubac, the ex-Jesuit Urs von Balthasar, and the pupil of the phenomenologist Husserl, Dietrich von Hildebrand. Yves Congar and other Dominicans attempted to enter this fray by their own interest in patrology. Finally, there was the rise of the new evolutionary philosophy of Teilhard de Chardin, with Scotistic overtones, which challenged all these thinkers to a more direct contact with the modern scientific world-view.

This philosophical ferment reflected a still deeper theological disturbance that had arisen early in the century about the historical-critical interpretation of the Bible and which depended also on an application of Cardinal Newman's theory of doctrinal development to the whole of theology, a disturbance that is called Modernism. Pope Pius X, a pastoral Pope, saw in this "the synthesis of all heresies" because it meant that the continuity of the faith through history was merely one of symbols whose meanings essentially shifted with the times. His efforts to shut off this modernistic tendency succeeded for a time, but could not eliminate the necessity in the Church of facing the problem of historicity.

As far as Bible studies were concerned, a sounder direction was opened by Marie-Joseph Lagrange (d. 1938). After teaching history and philosophy at Salamanca and Toulouse, he was sent for a brief study in oriental languages in Vienna and then sent to open a Biblical Institute in Jerusalem, the first of its kind, which he led for 45 years, founding the *Revue Biblique* in 1892. In the year 1912 his works were forbidden in seminaries and he ceased teaching under suspicion of Modernism, but he returned to Jerusalem the next year, shifting his studies to the New Testament. He showed on a Thomistic basis related to the old problem of "physical premotion" (the Grace Controversy) that biblical inspiration is compatible with the proper use of the historical-critical method; a view anticipated by Leo XIII and fully developed later by Pius XII in *Divino afflante Spiritu* (1943) and adopted by Vatican II in its *Decree on Revelation*. His cause for beatification has been proposed.

A similar reconciliation for ecclesiological and sacramental development was achieved by Yves Congar and Edward Schillebeeckx and largely accepted by Vatican II. Although as a result of this ferment, which became acute during the underground days of World War II, Pius XII in his encyclical *Humani Generis* (1950) found it necessary to issue cautions, Vatican II found it possible to chart a more open and dialogic course, allowing for a truly historical approach to theology without, however, abandoning the recommendation that St. Thomas Aquinas continue to provide a secure guide to a balanced and metaphysically grounded theology. Many Dominicans were engaged in the conciliar work both as conservatives and progressives, along with Jesuits with whom they had long been in controversy and dialogue.

Since the council there has, of course, been a continuation of this intellectual ferment along with efforts of the papacy and episcopacy to moderate its more radical tendencies. The French provinces, which had played so large a part in all this, were hard struck by the swing toward Marxism and Liberation Theology from "the events of 1968" (the student movement in France). Speculative theology seemed remote from the pressing social issues in the Nuclear Era. Already in the 1950s Chenu, Congar and others had been involved in the priest-worker movement (of which more later), but now younger Dominicans wanted to abandon scholarship for social activitism, and with this came many defections and a famine of vocations. Only in the 1980s are there signs of returning stability. What happened in France was soon reflected in a variety of ways throughout the Order and led to the closing of houses of study in favor of university studies with a minimum of philosophical preparation and a strongly pastoral, rather than a scholarly orientation.

All this is recorded in the great variety of Dominican publications which characterize this century, such as *Revue des Sciences Philosophiques et Théologiques, La Vie Intellectuelle, Divus Thomas, Revue Thomiste, La Ciencia Tomista, The Thomist, Filosoficka Revue* (Prague 1928), as well as those devoted to spirituality, etc.

Among other theologians of the Vatican II period and after can be mentioned Cardinal Luigi Ciappi, formerly Master of the Sacred Palace, and Fabro Guardini in Italy; Benoît Lavaud (d. 1979), who prepared the way for the newer theology of marriage; Valentine Walgrave (d. 1979) on the development of doctrine; Jean-Hervé Nicholas, Humbert Bouëssé (d. 1975), and Albert J. Patfoort in Christology; Claude Geffré and Jean-Pierre Jossua, editors of *Concilium;* in Spain Marcelino Bandero Gonzalez; in the United States John Edward Sullivan (d. 1981) on Augustine and the theology of history, William Hill on the Trinity, and Thomas F. O'Meara on grace.

In moral theology which Dominicans have always stressed in view of preaching, at the beginning of the period the emphasis was on the production of manuals of which the outstanding were those of Dominic M. Prümmer (1931), Benedict H. Merkelbach (d. 1942), and Ludovico G. Fanfani (d. 1951), and in English that of Charles J. Callan and J.A. McHugh. These last two Americans for years taught at Maryknoll, New York and had great influence on that new missionary society.

New elements in these works were the incorporation of modern canon law, Merkelbach's efforts to develop a more Thomistic method based on the development of virtues, and Prümmer's special treatises on morality and sexual ethics and psychopathology. Pedro Lumbreras was an important commentator of the moral parts of the *Summa Theologiae* and Louis Binder (d. 1981) also wrote on special moral topics, and Franziskus Stratmann (d. 1971) became famous as an advocate of Christian pacifism in the face of totalitarian militarism. There were also important canonists such as Juan Ylla, Esteban Gómez, Ludovico Fanfani and Albert Blat. More recently writers such as Servais Pinckaers and C.J. Pinto de Oliveira have worked for a more thorough revision of moral theology based on a historical understanding of the effects of voluntarism in the late Middle Ages and on a return to a morality of character rather than of legality and casuistic decision, which promises well for the future of this discipline. This entails an opposition to the theory of Proportionalism advocated by some Jesuit theologians and others which seems to revive the least desirable aspects of Probabilism.

Vatican II theology is marked by its emphasis on historicity, and a great deal of Dominican energy in this century both before and after the council, has been historical, most of it, however, devoted to achieving a historical understanding of the Order's traditions. In this first place goes to the remarkable *History of the Masters General* of Antonin Mortier in eight volumes completed in 1920, the *Monumenta O.P.* begun in 1896, the *Analecta O.P.* begun in 1893, the *Archivum Fratrum Praedictorum* begun in 1931, the *Quellen und Forschungen* begun in 1907, and the dissertations of the Dominican Historical Institute begun in 1931. The most complete history of the Order is the *Compendium Historiae, O.P.* of Angelus Walz, 2nd ed. 1947. In English William A. Hinnebusch covered this history still more thoroughly up to 1500 in two volumes, 1973, and the whole in his *A Short History*, 1975. The bibliography of this book will show how industrious Dominicans have been on special topics and here it is sufficient to mention the important work on medieval history of Daniel Callus, Leonard Boyle, and James A. Weisheîpl; on the history of the German Provinces by Walz; of the Dutch by Stephen Axters; on England by Godfrey Anstruther; of the American by Victor O'Daniel and Reginald Coffey; on the Spanish and Latin American by Vargas, Getino, Beltrán de Heredia (d. 1973), etc., and the continuation of Quetif-Echard by Remy Coulon and its complete revision by Thomas Kaeppeli.

During this period there was great activity in apologetics and especially after Vatican II in ecumenism. In the early period the leading apologist had been Albert M. Weiss (d. 1925), followed by Étienne Hugueny, *Critique and Catholicism*, and Benedict Schwalm. Vincent De Groot (d. 1922) and, notably, Garrigou-Lagrange and Reginald Schultes (d. 1928) wrote important ecclesiologies from an apologetic point of view common at this period. Later interest turned more to comparative religion, as in the work of Jean de Menasce (d.1973). Born of an Egyptian-Jewish father, his mother French, he studied at Oxford where he knew T.S. Eliot, Graham Greene, and corresponded with Charles du Bos. He then studied philosophy with an interest in Bergson and Russell in Paris and met a militant Zionist related to Chaim Weizmann. He also came in Paris to know Stanislas Fumet, Jacques Maritain, and Olivier Lacombe. In existential despair he almost commited suicide but found his way to baptism in 1926 and entered the Order in 1930. He taught at the University of Fribourg in history of religions and missiology until 1948, studied ancient Iran in Paris where he taught before going to teach at Princeton until 1959. A stroke left him progressively paralyzed before he died in 1973. He was noted as a spiritual director and left many letters. Two of his works are *When Israel Loves* and *The Door of the Garden.* This universality of outlook more and more characterizes Dominican thought in our century.

In biblical studies the École Biblique made the biggest contribution including, besides Lagrange's work, the important archaeological work of Louis H. Vincent and F.M. Abel and of Roland de Vaux, one of the greatest authorities on Qumran and the Dead Sea Scrolls, and the *Jerusalem Bible*, as well as the *Revue Biblique.* This work continues with such scholars as Jerome Murphy-O'Connor, Emile Boismard, and Benedict Viviano. But there were others, chiefly outside Jerusalem, such as Marc Sales, Hugh Pope, P. Savignac, V. Zapletal, Bernard Allo, Francis Ceuppens, Alberto Colunga, Jacques Vosté (d. 1949), Serafin Zarb (d. 1976), Ceslaus Spicq, Lucas Grollenberg, *et al.*

In philosophy there were the metaphysical issues already mentioned and also such writers as Alberto Lepidi, Master of the Sacred Palace, on Kant and religion, M.D. Roland-Gosselin on epistemology; Alexander M. Horváth on the metaphysics of religions, Gallus M. Manser on Thomism as a total system, Dominic M. De Petter (d. 1971) on epistemology, and Mannes M. Mattijs (d. 1972) on anthropology. More original were Innocent Bochenski in symbolic logic and Marxism, Emmanuel Barbado (d. 1945) and Edward Robert Brennan (d. 1975) in psychology, Ambrose McNicholl (d. 1982) in esthetics, Leonard Lehu, Thomas Richard, Marcel Lachance (d. 1974), Ignatius Eschmann (d. 1968) in social philosophy, L.J. Lebret, Eberhardt Welty, and Arthur Utz in sociology and politics. The most pressing problem, the relation of science to modern philosophy was studied by Aniceto Fernández Alonso (d. 1981) before becoming Master of the Order, William H. Kane, Dominique Dubarle, William A. Wallace, James A. Weisheipl and Albert Moraczewski. Finally, André Gigon (d. 1977) and René-A. Gauthier made important historical contributions to the study of philosophical texts, as did

I. Bochenski. The Leonine Commission continues its patient labors on the critical edition of Aquinas' works.

It was during this time that in Rome the Angelicum first became Pontifical and the Roman University of St. Thomas Aquinas, in 1963. It quickly adopted the use of the vernacular, especially English after Vatican II and has a large Third World enrollment. The Order also provides the ecclesiastical faculty of the University of Fribourg in Switzerland, has a house at Louvain, administers the University of Manila, largest Catholic school of the Far East, and staffs the École Biblique in Jerusalem. After Vatican II many provincial houses of studies were closed or relocated at university centers, as the English had already done earlier at Oxford and Cambridge, thus returning to the original pattern. In the United States there are similar arrangements in Washington, St. Louis, and Oakland.

Prayer

Besides the movement toward stricter use of the so-called "monastic observances" promoted by Cormier, which continued up to World War II, the most significant events in the prayer life of the Order in this century were three: the liturgical movement culminating in the reforms of Vatican II, the changes in the *Constitutions* as regard observances, in 1968, and especially the renewal of the belief in the universal call to contemplation of all Christians.

As regards this last, the central figure was Juan Gonzáles Arintero (d. 1928) whose cause for beatification is progressing. He began his work as a Dominican as a teacher of biology at the College of Corias, then taught at Salamanca, and, from 1909-1912, apologetics at the Angelicum. On his return to Salamanca, he became a director to contemplative Dominican nuns and discovered the world of contemplative prayer. Later he returned to Salamanca, as an editor and a spiritual director. His studies led him to adopt the view of Canon Saudreau (against A. Farges and the traditional position of many Jesuits and Carmelites) that all Christians are called to mystical contemplation, and began to confirm this theory from Aquinas' doctrine of the gifts of the Holy Spirit and from the experiences of the saints. At the same time he continued his interest in the significance of the theory of evolution for theology (later to find a better known advocate in Teilhard de Chardin) in a series of works beginning in 1890. His major work applied this concept of evolution to the cosmos, biology, and the development of the Church and the spiritual life of the individual Christian (this last part translated in English as *The Mystical Evolution in the Development and Vitality of the Church*). He defended his basic position in many other works including (now in English) *Grades of Prayer* and *The Song of Songs*. With the assistance of a Passionist nun, Mother Mary Magdalen, he founded *La Vida Sobrenatural* which became the model of many other journals of spirituality, such as the French *La Vie Spirituel* and the American *Spirituality Today* (formerly *Cross and Crown*), now published by several provinces.

Arintero's position on mysticism was adopted by Reginald Garrigou-Lagrange, already mentioned. He had been a medical student, before becoming a Dominican and then studied under Ambroise Gardeil who was exploring the psychology of mysticism. Gardeil (d.1931) became a Dominican in 1878. He helped found the *Revue Thomiste* in 1893 and organized the French house of studies, Le Saulchoir, in Belgium, during the government expulsion of religious Orders. His chief work was the very original *The Structure of the Soul and the Mystical Experience* (1927) in which he attributed such experience to the gifts of the Holy Spirit given all Christians in baptism, and explained infused contemplation as produced not by the infusing of concepts but by affective connaturality of the soul to God. Emmanuel-Louis (Antonin) Lemmonyer (d. 1932) who founded, with A.M. Jacquin, the *Revue des sciences philosophiques et thé*ologiques (1907) and with M. Barge the *Revue de la Jeunesse* for young people (1909), succeeded Gardeil as Regent of the Saulchoir, and then served as an assistant to Master Gillet. Lemmonyer worked especially against the separation of moral theology from mystical and ascetical theology. Living in this milieu, Garrigou-Lagrange, who also knew Bergson, Levy-Bruhl and Maritain, was thus in touch with many currents of French thought. As a teacher he spent all but one year at the Angelicum, on vacations preaching in Italy, France, England, Holland, Canada, and South America, retiring in failing health to Santa Sabina in 1964. He became doctrinally somewhat fixed, but was always a perfect religious, a beggar for the poor, and a helpful spiritual director to many. His principal works on spirituality are *Christian Perfection* and the classic *The Three Ages of the Spiritual Life.* An interesting application of this same view is Barthélemy Froget's *The Gifts of the Holy Spirit in the Lives of Dominican Saints*, as well as Clement Thuente's *Come Holy Spirit*, and Gerald Vann's *The Divine Pity* and Hyacinth Petitot's biographical studies of the spirituality of particular saints.

One of the consequences of Arintero's view was to emphasize the need to make the treasures of the contemplative life available to the laity, Denys (Achille) Mezard (d. 1930) had tried to do this by collecting meditations from Aquinas for each day of the liturgical year, as well as others based on Hugh of St. Cher's biblical commentaries and St. Jane Chantal's writings. An outstanding apostle of spirituality for the laity was Antonin Gilbert (Dalmatius) Sertillanges (d. 1948) who entered the Order in Spain and was exiled from France in 1883. He taught in Corsica then at the Catholic Institute in Paris but his conferences there were interrupted by the later expulsion of religious in 1903. He published more than 700 books and articles. He was a friend of the philosopher Bergson and the scientist Claude Bernard on whom he wrote a book. His works were directed especially at French intellectuals (as his famous *The Intellectual Life*) and ranged from *Christian Politics* to *Prayer and Music* and were in a literary style that disturbed the scholastic minded. A sermon preached during World War I led to his exile in Jerusalem, Holland, and Belgium, but he returned to France in 1939 and continued his writing.

Humbert Clérissac (1864-1914) also spent much of his life abroad in England as a retreat master. He spoke to the Lutherans of Stockholm, helped Ernest Psichari return to the Church, and was the spiritual director of the novelist Léon Bloy and of Jacques Maritain. His works reflect the Modernist crisis but also are directed to the cultivated laity such as his classic *The Mystery of the Church* (1919). Later in the same tradition Jean-Pierre Maydieu (d. 1955), was a collaborator in *La Vie Intellectuelle* founded by M.-V. Bernadot in 1927, and after 1945 edited it. He served in the army in World War II, participated in the Resistance and was imprisoned. His works included *The Beatitudes, Christ and World*, and *A Catechism for Today*. He was noted for his ability to stimulate dialogue with the most diverse groups. Similarly, Pius Raymond Régamey was able to reach the laity on such topics as Christian poverty.

In England another Preacher with a gift for speaking to the laity about prayer was Bede Jarrett of whom more later, and among his successful disciples was Gerald Vann (d. 1963). After studies in the Angelicum, he read modern philosophy at Oxford and became interested in the psychology of Carl Jung. He taught and was headmaster at the Dominican school for boys at Laxton until 1952. In 1938 he had organized the Union of Prayer for Peace. From 1952 to his death, he wrote and lectured at Cambridge, Edinburgh, Newcastle, and in the United States. A shy but exceedingly witty man, in his *Morals Makyth Man, The Divine Pity, Eve and the Gryphon*, and *The Paradise Tree* as well as a work on marriage problems published pseudonymously, he tried to bring a more psychological and symbolic approach to morality and spirituality. Similarly, his confrere Thomas Gilby, along with his new translation of the *Summa* also applied Thomism to poetry and to logic in a delightful way.

The tradition of Arintero in Spain was carried on by men such as Ignacio González Menéndez-Reigada (d. 1951), who taught both morals and mysticism at Salamanca, writing on the gifts of the Spirit, as well as on international law and the problem of the just war (in the case of the Spanish Civil War) and Victorino Osende who wrote excellent practical guides to prayer.

This lay spirituality was exemplified in life and writing by such persons as the Tertiary Soledad Arroyo who wrote a *Key of Paradise* (1918), and Elizabeth Leseur (d. 1914), married to Felix Leseur, but without children. She had given up the faith but was led back to it by reading the agnostic Renan's *Life of Jesus* and as a Tertiary under the direction of Joseph Hébert led a life dedicated to God. After her death her atheist husband on reading her spiritual journal was himself converted and became the Dominican Albert Leseur (d. 1958), who wrote her biography. Other members of the Dominican Laity were the apostle of the Rosary, Bl. Bartolo Longo (d. 1926, beatified 1980) and Giorgio La Pira (d. 1977) who as mayor of Florence gave an example of a politician truly concerned with the poor. It was during this period that some six Secular Institutes were added to the Dominican family, such as *Caritas* founded by J.M. Perrin, a blind priest.

But the older devotion to the rosary dear to the laity as a means of contemplation did not disappear, as evidenced by some 30 periodicals published to promote it. E.M. Rossetti (d. 1974), Joseph Eyquem, and E. Limeck of Australia founded new rosary societies and experimented with new forms of it, more biblically based.

The spirituality of this century was also reflected in the increasing number of martyrs caught in the conflicts of our times such as the 107 Dominicans massacred in the Spanish Civil War including the former Master of the Order, Bonaventura García de Paredes, the German Tito Horten killed in a Nazi prison, and many members of the Family killed in the Congo, Peru and Central America even recently.

Finally, there have been many who have worked for the renewal of religious life, whether in official positions as cardinals, Paul Philippe and Jerome Hamer; or through a study of the Dominican spiritual tradition as Hieronymus Wilms, Paulino Alvarez, André Duval, and Raimundo Spiazzi, or by I. Taurizano and I. Colosio through their *Rivista di Ascetica e Mistica*.

Preaching

One of the marks of this century in the Order is the increasing specialization and professionalism required in the apostolate. Thus most young Dominicans today earn academic degrees not merely in philosophy or theology but in a diversity of fields, and we read of a Louis Kelly, who worked for 25 years exclusively with prisoners, and Henry Pire, who in 1958 won the Nobel Peace Prize for caring for war refugees, and a young member of the Dominican Laity (as the secular Tertiaries are now called) Peter George Frassati, who died of polio while a leader of Catholic Action for youth, and whose cause for beatification has been introduced. The variety of apostolates in the Order is immense.

Obviously this means that "preaching" is no longer only or even chiefly done in the pulpit or even by sermonizing but through a variety of media and on a diversity of occasions through which others may be reached. Yet direct preaching still remains important, whether in the liturgy or in retreats and small groups. Among the notable preachers in this older sense can be mentioned Casal Carmelli (d. 1904), a noted preacher in North Italy who ended his life paralyzed for eight years; the Croatian Angelus M. Miskov (d. 1922), a pioneer in women's education and a preacher of "missions"; Henry Ignatius Smith (d. 1957), who founded the Preachers' Institute at The Catholic University of America, and Walter Farrell (d. 1951), well known for his great influence on the teaching of theology in Catholic colleges in the United States; Vincent F. Kienberger (d. 1963), a preacher of the Eucharist and the spiritual welfare of priests; John McNicholas, Archbishop of Cincinnati (d. 1950); Henry Hage (d. 1917), founder of the Canadian Province, etc.

But if we are to pick out three leaders in this field in this time, I would select first, Albert Janvier, who for 23 years preached at Notre Dame, until 1924, and left a great collection of sermons, polished in style and like Lacordaire's, solid in substance and fitted to the needs of the time. Second would be Bede Jarrett, the English Provincial and medieval historian who brought the Dominicans back to Blackfriars at Oxford. Jarrett, who had a wonderful gift for friendship and a style that was modern, direct, informal, yet elegant, knew how to reach his audiences in Britain and America and set for Anglophiles a type of simple eloquence far different from the medieval scholastic sermon or the Renaissance and Baroque oratory. The third would be Vincent McNabb, an Irishman who rivaled the English in his eccentricity, who revived open-air controversial preaching in London (the Catholic Evidence Guild) and strode the London streets in his full habit.

Most of this direct preaching took place in parishes in our

charge, typical of the missionary or former missionary countries. In 1983 this meant some 438 parishes, which generally have a good reputation for preaching, although Paul VI in 1979 could still exclaim that "One says of the Dominicans that they are preachers. But it is rare to hear the preaching of a Dominican!"

Certainly one could not complain that Dominican Third Order Sisters were not evident, since their mission of education, hospital, social, and missionary work spread throughout the world. To exemplify this by an especially interesting example we have only to recall the life of Mother Alphonsa Lathrop (1851-1926), born Rose Hawthorne, the daughter of the great American (and Calvinist-Transcendentalist) Nathaniel Hawthorne. She lived in England and Italy as a child while her father was American Consul, but returned to Concord in 1860. Acquainted with all the luminaries of the Transcendentalists as a girl, she married George Parsons Lathrop, and lived in New York and then in Boston while he was assistant editor of the *Atlantic Monthly*, and she herself wrote poems and short stories for many publications, and a book of poems *Along the Shore*. After suffering the death of a son both became Catholics in 1891 and together wrote *A Story of Courage* about their conversion, but George sank into alcoholism and she was forced to separate from him. Her Paulist director told her of the neglected death of a young seamstress sent to Blackwell's Island to die of cancer.

Rose trained for three months at the New York Cancer Hospital and began work in a small building for cancer victims on the Lower East Side, supporting her project by writing articles and a memoir of her father. She consoled George in his last illness, in 1898; and in 1899, Clement Thuente, O.P., received her and her friend Alice Huber as Tertiaries. As Alphonsa and Mary Rose they took vows in 1900 and established the Dominican Congregation of St. Rose of Lima or Servants of Relief for Incurable Cancer, with a motherhouse and novitiate at Hawthorne, New York, and a magazine, *Christ's Poor*.

Rose Hawthorne's work typifies the many Congregations of active women which, as in the 1800s, continued to be founded in this twentieth century, at least 114 with about 40,000 members. There are also some 5,000 Second Order nuns. Yet the crisis of vocations has hit the women of the Order even more severely than the men and many of these congregations are rapidly aging. To meet this crisis, a marked shift from institutional missions to less formal and largely social ministries seems to be taking place, often with the necessary adoption of a style of life which suggests these Tertiaries in the future may be Dominican secular rather than religious institutes.

Among the Dominican Laity, besides those already mentioned were others such as Práxedes Fernández García, called the "Mother of Mine Workers" in Spain and Lucie Feliz-Fauré-Goyau (d. 1913), daughter of the President of the French Republic who, guided by the Dominican preacher Raymond Feuillette, sought to be a "servant of souls" in social work but especially in counseling unbelievers and in writing on the role of women and education of children. Among her works were books on Newman and Dante, *Toward Joy: Christianity and Feminine Culture.*

But this was also especially the time of the expansion of missionary activities, in spite of tragic setbacks in China and Vietnam. Not only did Dominicans continue missionary work in Europe, as in Scandanavia and Russia (through the ecumenical Istina Institute), but also to Islam, as in the work of the Cairo Institute under George C. Anawati, in Lebanon, and in the work of Joseph Kenny in Nigeria, and to the Jews at Isaiah House in Jerusalem. The purpose of such work is not proselytism but ecumenism. In addition, there was evangelization in over 88 countries in all the continents, especially in Africa, New Zealand, New Guinea, India, Pakistan, Japan, Taiwan, Vietnam, the Philippines and in Latin America.

Typical of this endeavor was Mary Joseph Rogers (d. 1955), who founded the Maryknoll Sisters of St. Dominic. Born in Boston in 1882, she studied at Smith College and taught biology there, then taught in the Boston public schools. While she was still at Smith, James F. Walsh helped her start a mission study club and when the Maryknoll Missionary Society was founded by Walsh and Price, she and some secretaries of the society formed their Third Order community in 1920. She was re-elected until she resigned in 1946, after also founding a cloistered branch of the community to pray for the missions. Maryknoll has become one of the greatest of missionary societies and prominent for its support of the movement toward Liberation Theology.

Perhaps the most significant advance in preaching was the increasing use of a variety of media, including fine arts. Here two events are especially notable. One was the efforts of French Dominicans, publishers of *Art Sacrée*, to once again enlist leading artists, so often today alienated from the Church, to take an interest in liturgical art. Pierre Marie-Alain Couturier (d. 1954), himself a talented painter induced such artists as Léger, Rouault, Matisse, Chagall, to contribute to the Chapel at Assy, Switzerland. Sister Jacques who had nursed Matisse at Nice interested him in the Dominican Sisters' Chapel of Rosary at Vence assisted by Br. L.B. Rayssiguier, clerical student and architect, and the architect A. Perret, which resulted in a masterpiece. Another notable event was the formation, chiefly under the leadership of Conrad Pepler of a group of artists, including the sculptor and calligrapher Eric Gill and the painter and critic David Jones to form a Dominican Laity community at Ditchling, in which the distributist social ideals of Hilaire Belloc and G.K. Chesterton in the English tradition of Christian socialism of William Morris were for a time successfully put into practice.

Numerous liturgical musicians such as P.J. Harrison, Bruno Hespers, Vincent Donovan, F.A. Ellington, Frank M. Quinn, and James Marchionda can be mentioned, and both painting (Couturier, the Argentinian William Butler, Angelo Zarlenga) and sculpture (Henry Flanagan of Ireland, Thomas McGlynn of the United States) were widely practiced. Others wrote on the arts such as Giacinto D'Urso, Alfonso D'Amato, Venturino Alce and Val McInnes, or were known for their excellent literary style such as Dalmatius Sertillanges or Ambroise M. Carré, elected to the French Academy.

An example of the possibilities of this approach was the remarkable work of Urban (Edward J.) Nagle in Christian theater. He taught at Providence College, edited a spiritual periodical and acted as a chaplain to Sisters, but he and Thomas F. Carey, founded the Blackfriars Guild, the Speech and Drama Department of The Catholic University of America, and the Catholic Theater Conference (1937). At

Catholic University he was succeeded by another successful drama director, Gilbert Hartke, O.P. From 1940-1951 Nagel was moderator for the Blackfriars Guild in New York City of the first of the "off-Broadway" theaters, for which he also wrote plays. His experiences were related in a witty book, *Behind the Masque*, 1951. He was also speaker on many radio and television programs. Since then pioneer radio and television are increasingly used by Dominicans to proclaim the Gospel.

10

The Future

Sometimes in the post-Vatican II crisis, as at many points in its long centuries, it has seemed as if St. Dominic's Order might have no future. The Church has been promised the future by its Lord, but religious orders come and go in the service of the Church. Yet, today, the need of an Order to preach the Gospel and to encourage and assist others in preaching it is still urgent. The survival of the Order of Preachers depends primarily on the generosity of young women and men in perceiving this need and responding to it. Our numbers have dwindled before the onslaught of social change but are still far greater than at other crisis points in our history, and the activity of the Order is global and intense.

Two ways seem open. One is to return to Jandel's romantic dream of a revival of the Order in all its original details of strict observance as a challenge to the spirit of the modern world. The adoption of the *Constitutions* of 1968, while returning to the spirit of the founder, as Vatican II had demanded, did not take that way. It is not likely we will go back to Office at midnight, woolen underwear, and flagellation. The ideal of "strict observance" to be logical must be consistent, and that would mean really living the thirteenth century in the twenty-first.

The other is to accept Lacordaire's principle against Jandel, that the essential thing in the Order is its mission, adjusted to the circumstances of the times, and its life must be adjusted to the demands of that mission. This is the way proposed by the new *Constitutions* and actually coming into effect almost everywhere in the Order. Yet, Lacordaire loved the Order's identifying traditions as much as Jandel did and modified them only reluctantly.

Since now it seems clear we are living in a post-modern era of global plurality, it is also obvious that these modifications must be more radical than Lacordaire could have foreseen. We must "preach the Gospel to *every* creature" "in season and out of season" as did its first preachers. This implies several things about our life.

First, it means that community life cannot usually be that of large houses living an unchanging monastic regime, but for that reason, must consist of smaller communities living a more intensely fraternal life in order to support and give identity to its members, even to those who must for a time live and work alone. As Cormier said, "Some Dominicans live out of community, some merely in it, some off it, and, happily, some for it." More of us must live for it and for each other in intense communication, exchange of ideas, cooperation. And there must be room for diversity of community life to fit local circumstances.

Second, it means that our study can no longer have the uniformity of the marvelous synthesis of St. Thomas Aquinas' thought, although his wisdom remains one of our precious resources. Rather our communities must be able to sustain the dialogue, often the difficult debate, of competing ideas, in a pluralistic world, if the Gospel is to be preserved and communicated integrally. There has to be a new asceticism of the mind, for nothing is more painful than to maintain charity alive in the midst of genuine argument about serious issues.

Third, our prayer has to remain contemplative and liturgical in a world of activity and change without isolating itself from that ever shifting stream of events. It must be liturgical, because our contemplation must be in and for the Church, not lost in mere individualistic psychological "experiences." To be this it must be supported by a serious asceticism of the body as well as of the mind. We must remain truly religious, authentically celibate, genuinely poor, intelligently obedient in a world of consumption, possession, selfishness. There can be no illusion that we can simply adopt the middle-class life of modern professionals and still be contemplatives. Our traditional forms of asceticism still have much to teach us, but they too must be intensifed not abandoned. For this the nuns of the Second Order must remain a constant source of inspiration, not isolated from the rest of the Family, but central to its life.

Finally, our work of preaching must not lose its definition in the multiplicity of the media we use and of the other good works by which it is supported. We must keep before us the words of St. Paul, "If I preach the Gospel, this is no reason for me to boast, for an obligation has been imposed on me, and woe to me if I do not preach it" (I Cor 9:16).

The active Sisters of the Order and the Dominican Laity share in this same obligation but they, in particular, need today to rethink, as Catherine did, what their opportunities are. In some ways more possibilities are open to them than to clerics, who are tied by the very nature of their office as priests to certain primary sacramental tasks. But it is even more difficult for them to find and express the Dominican identity in the world of which they are so much a part. They must decide with courage exactly what their relation is to the Dominican Family, and the friars must be open to supporting their decisions and cooperating in its fulfillment to meet the needs of the times.

I hope this sketch of what has been done in the past and this even briefer peering into the future will stir up in young hearts a sense of the call that Dominic heard and to which he responded heart and soul, "Come after me and I will make you fishers of men and women" (Mk 1:17).

The Future

Select Bibliography

For those wishing to do further research, very complete bibliographies will be found in: Angelus Walz, *Compendium Historiae Ordinis Praedicatorum*, rev. ed. (Rome: Pontificium Athenaeum "Angelicum," 1948) and William A. Hinnebusch, *The History of the Dominican Order* (to 1500), 2 vols. (Staten Island, NY: Alba House, 1965-1973). For the total history, besides these two works, see Daniel Antonin Mortier, *Histoire des Maitres Généraux*, 8 tom. (Paris: A. Picard et Fils, 1920) and William A. Hinnebusch, *The Dominicans: A Short History* (Staten Island, NY: Alba House, 1975). The 1968 revision of the *Book of Constitutions and Ordinations of the Order of Friars Preachers* in English translation (Rome: General Curia, 1984) is also fundamental. The most complete collection of short biographies in English is Mary Jean Dorcy, *Saint Dominic's Family: Lives and Legends* (Dubuque, IA: Priory Press, 1963). The following are works available in English which illustrate the various centuries. Secondary sources are indented and follow the primary source to which they are relevant.

1200s

M.-H. Vicaire, *St. Dominic and His Times* (New York: McGraw-Hill, 1964). The definitive biography.

Leonard Von Matt and M.H. Vicaire, *St. Dominic: A Pictorial Biography* (Chicago: Regenry, 1957).

Saint Dominic: Biographical Documents (Washington, D.C.: Thomist Press, 1964), Francis C. Lehner, ed. and trans. This is essentially a translation of M.-H. Vicaire, O.P., *Saint Dominique de Caleruega d'après les documents du XIIIe siecle* (Paris: Cerf, 1955) which, however, has more complete introduction and notes.

Early Dominicans: Selected Writings, Simon Tugwell, ed. and trans. (The Classics of Western Spirituality, New York: Paulist Press, 1982).

Jordan of Saxony, *On the Beginnings of the Order of Preachers*, Simon Tugwell, ed. and trans., *Dominican Sources* (Dublin: Parable, USA, and Springfield, IL: Templegate, 1982).

Aaron, Marguerite, *Saint Dominic's Successor* (Bl. Jordan of Saxony) (St. Louis: B. Herder, 1955).

Mechtild of Magdeburg, *The Revelations of Mechtild of Magdeburg or The Flowing Light of the Godhead*, trans. by Lucy Menzies (London: Longmans, Green and Co., 1953), not complete.

Tournon, Antonin, *The First Disciples of St. Dominic*, adapted and enlarged by Victor F. O'Daniel (Washington, DC, The Dominicana: Frederick Pustet, 1928).

Weisheipl, James A., *Friar Thomas D'Aquino*, (Garden City, NY: Doubleday, 1974). Contains ample bibliography and listing of English translations of the works.

1300s

St. Catherine of Siena, *The Dialogue*, translated and introduced by Suzanne Noffke. (The Classics of Western Spirituality, New York: Paulist, 1980).

_____ , *Prayers*, translated by Suzanne Noffke, (New York: Paulist Press, 1983).

Levasti, Arrigo, *My Servant Catherine* (London: Blackfriars, 1954).

Meister Eckhart: The Essential Sermons, Commentaries, Treatises and Defense, translated and introduced by Edmund Colledge and Bernard McGinn. (The Classics of Western Spirituality, New York: Paulist, 1981).

Richard Woods, *Eckhart's Way* (The Way of the

Christian Mystics, vol. 2, Wilmington, DE: Michael Glazier, 1986), with good bibliography.

Suso, Henry, *The Exemplar*, 2 vols. (Dubuque, IA: Priory Press, 1962).

Tauler, John, *Spiritual Conferences*, ed. and translated by Edmund Colledge (Rockford, IL: Tan Books, 1978).

1400s

Ferrer, St. Vincent, *A Christology* from the Sermons of St. Vincent Ferrer, O.P., selected and trans. by S.M.C. (London: Blackfriars, 1954).

Ghéon, Henry, *St. Vincent Ferrer* (New York: Sheed and Ward, 1954).

Jarrett, Bede, *S. Antonino and Medieval Economics* (St. Louis: B. Herder, 1914).

Pope-Hennessy, John, *Fra Angelico*, 2nd ed. (Ithaca, NY: Cornell University Press, 1974).

Savonarola, Girolamo, *The Compendium of Revelations* in *Apocalyptic Spirituality*, ed. and introduced by Bernard McGinn (The Classics of Western Spirituality, New York: Paulist, 1979) pp 192-276.

_____ , *The Triumph of the Cross*, ed. with an introduction by John Proctor (London: Sands and Co., 1901).

Ridolfi, Roberto, *The Life of Girolamo Savonarola*, translated by Cecil Grayson, (New York: Knopf, 1959).

Wilms, Jerome, *Lay Brother, Artist and Saint* (Bl. James of Ulm) trans. by Sister M. Fulgence (London: Blackfriars, 1957).

1500s

Brown, James Scott, *The Catholic Conception of Natural Law: Francis de Vitoria, Founder of the Modern Law of Nations*, etc. (Washington, DC: Georgetown University, 1934).

Cano, Melchior, *Victory Over Self*, translated by E.J. Schuster, *Cross and Crown*, 8 (1956): 1-21, 141-161, 340-359.

Casas, Bartolomé de las, *Bartolomé de las Casas: A Selection of His Writings*, ed. and translated by George Sanderlin (New York: Knopf, 1971).

> *Bartolomé de las Casas in History*, ed. by Juan Friede and Benjamin Keen (De Kalb: IL: Northern Illinois University, 1971).

St. Catherine de' Ricci, *Selected Letters*, ed., selected and introduced by Dominico Di Agresti, translated by Jennifer Petrie (Oxford: Dominican Sources in English, 1985).

1600s

Campanella, Thomas, *The Defense of Galileo*, ed. and translated by Grant McColley, *Smith College Studies in History* (Northampton, MA): 22 (3-4, April-July, 1937).

Chardon, Louis, *The Cross of Jesus*, 2 vols. (St. Louis: B. Herder, 1957).

Luis of Granada, *Summa of the Christian Life*, 3 vols. (St. Louis: Herder, 1954).

Morrell, Julienne, *A Treatise on the Spiritual Life*, a commentary and text of the work of St. Vincent Ferrer (Westminster, MD: Newman Press, 1951).

Oechslin, R.L., *Louis of Granada* (St. Louis: B. Herder, 1962).

Ridolfi, Nicholas, *A Short Method of Mental Prayer*, translated by Norbert Georges (New York: Bl. Martin Guild, 1952).

Sister Mary Alphonsus, O.SS.R., *St. Rose of Lima: Patroness of the Americas* (Rockford, IL: Tan Books, 1982).

1700s

Unfortunately, the best book on the "Desolation" has not been translated. It is:

Chapotin, M.-D., *Le dernier prieur du dernier couvent (1734-1806)* (Paris: Picard, 1893).

Flynn, L., *Billuart in His Summa Sancti Thomae* (London, Canada, 1938).

St. Louis-Marie Grignion de Montfort, *True Devotion to the Blessed Virgin*, trans. by Frederick William Faber (New York: P.J. Kenedy and Sons, 1909).

Rigault, Georges, *Bl. Louis-Marie Grignion de Montfort* (London: Burns Oates and Washbourne, 1932).

1800s

Burke, Thomas N., *Lectures and sermons* (New York: P.J. Kenedy, 1875).

Burton, Katherine, *Difficult Star: The Life of Pauline Jaricot* (New York: London: Longmans, Green and Co., 1947).

Devas, Raymund, *The Dominican Revival in the Nineteenth Century* (London: Longmans, Green and Co., 1913).

Drane, Augusta, *A Memoir of Mother Francis Raphael (Augusta Theodosia Drane) with Some of Her Spiritual Notes and Letters*, ed. by Bertrand Wilberforce, New ed. (London: Longmans, Green and Co., 1923).

Lacordaire, Henri, *Essay on the Re-Establishment in France of the Order of Preachers* (Dominican Sources in English, Dublin: Parable, 1983).

————, *Jesus Christ: Conferences Delivered at Notre Dame Cathedral* (New York: P. O'Shea Publisher, 1885).

————, *Thought and Teachings of Lacordaire,* (New York: Benziger, 1902).

Shephard, Lancelot C., *Lacordaire: A Biographical Essay* (New York: Macmillan, 1964).

McGloin, John Bernard, *California's First Archbishop: The*

Life of Joseph Sadoc Alemany, O.P., 1814-1888 (New York: Herder and Herder, 1966).

Sister Mary Hortense Kohler with help of Mary Fulgence Frantz, *Life and Works of Mother Benedicta Bauer* (Milwaukee: Bruce, 1937).

Mazzuchelli, Samuel, *Memoirs* (Chicago: Priory Press, 1967).

1900s

Arintero, Juan G., *The Mystical Evolution in the Development and Vitality of the Church*, 2 vols. (St. Louis: B. Herder, 1949).

_____ , Stages in Prayer (St. Louis: B. Herder, 1957).

_____ , with Mother Mary Magdalene, C.P., *Towards the Heights of Union with God* (Erlanger, NY: Passionist Monastery).

Burton, Katherine, *Sorrow Built a Bridge: A Daughter of Hawthorne* (New York: Longmans, Green and Co., 1937).

Congar, Yves, *Lay people in the Church*, rev. ed. (Westminster, MD: Newman, 1965).

_____ , *Tradition and Traditions* (New York: Macmillan, 1967).

Gardeil, Ambroise, *The Gifts of the Holy Ghost in Dominican Saints* (Milwaukee: Bruce, 1937).

Garrigou-Lagrange, Reginald, *Christian Perfection and Contemplation*, translated by Sister Timothea Doyle (St. Louis: B. Herder, 1939).

_____ , *The Three Ages of the Interior Life*, 2 vols., translated by Sister Timothea Doyle (St. Louis: B. Herder, 1948).

Gill, Eric, *Autobiography* (London: J. Cape, 1941).

_____ , *Social Justice and the Stations of the Cross* (London: James Clarke, 1939).

Jarrett, Bede, *An Anthology of Bede Jarrett*, ed. by Jordan Aumann (Dubuque, IA: Priory Press, 1961).

_____ , *Meditations for Layfolk* (London: Catholic Truth Society, 1946).

Wykeham-George, Kenneth and Matthew, Gervaise, *Bede Jarrett, O.P.* (Westminster, MD: Newman, 1952).

McNabb, Vincent, *A Father McNabb Reader*, ed. by Francis Nugent (New York: P. J. Kenedy and Sons, 1954).

_____ , *Old Principles and the New Order* (New York: Sheed and Ward, 1942).

Valentine, Ferdinand, *Father Vincent McNabb* (Westminster, MD: Newman).

Jean-Pierre Jossua, *Yves Congar: Theologian in the Service of God's People* (Chicago: Priory Press, 1968).

Schillebeeckx, Edward, *Christ, the Sacrament of Encounter with God* (New York: Sheed and Ward, 1963).

Sertillanges, Antonin S., *The Intellectual Life* (Westminster, MD: Newman, 1947).

_____ , *What Jesus Saw from the Cross* (London: Burns Oates and Washbourne, 1937).

Name Index

Names of persons not known to be members of the Dominican Family (some may have been Tertiaries) are indented. Masters of the Order are marked with an asterisk *.

Subject Index

Abbot, title of, 8
Acts of Canonization of St.
    Dominic, 6, 11–13
Afro-Americans, 140
Agnosticism, 167
Albigensians, 3–5, 10, 31, 62
"Alleluia" preaching, 43, 56,
    86
"Ancient Theology, The", 132
Anorexia nervosa, 82
Apocalyptic writing, 109 (see
    Prophesy)
Apologetics, Dominican writers
    on, 30, 37, 54–55, 115, 127,
    140, 156, 164–165, 172; post
    Enlightenment, 180–182,
    199–200, 202–203, 223–224,
    228
Apostolic life, 5–6, 16–17,
    22–23 (see *Preaching,*
    itinerant)
Archeology, 178
Architecture, 101, 166, 203
Aristotle and Aristotelianism,
    32–39, 55, 63, 97–99, 112,
    130, 157, 180, 218–219
Arts, Fine, Dominicans in, 99,
    111–112, 137–138, 165–166,
    187, 203; writers on, 224,
    232–233

Asceticism, of Albigensians, 4;
    Dominic's, 12–13; essential
    to Dominican spirituality,
    22–23, 42–43, 72–73, 86, 159;
    preaching as, 55; of nuns,
    62–63, 76–78, 159; of Ter-
    tiaries, 62–63, 79–81, 159; to-
    day's need for, 236–237 (see
    Observance)
Assassination of Henri III, 125
Atheism, 167
Augustinianism, 39, 128, 220
Augustinians, 133
Averroism, 35–36, 63, 97, 129
Avignon Obedience, 57, 59

"Babylonian Captivity" of
    papacy, 57, 80
Baianism, 128
Beatific vision, controversy on,
    32
Beguines and Beghards, 45–46,
    62; reform of, 109 (see also
    Tertiaries and *Sisters*)
Bible, Dominican writers on,
    31–32, 37, 52–53, 66, 87,
    126–127, 129, 156, 176–177,
    199, 224; use in sermons,
    50–51, 136; in theology, 37,
    127, 176; memorization of,